British Activist Authors Addressing Children of Colour

Bloomsbury Perspectives on Children's Literature

Bloomsbury Perspectives on Children's Literature seeks to expand the range and quality of research in children's literature through publishing innovative monographs by leading and rising scholars in the field. With an emphasis on cross and inter-disciplinary studies, this series takes literary approaches as a starting point, drawing on the particular capacity for children's literature to open out into other disciplines.

Series Editor
Dr Lisa Sainsbury, Director of the National Centre for Research in Children's Literature, Roehampton University, UK

Editorial Board
Professor M. O. Grenby (Newcastle University, UK), Dr Marah Gubar (University of Pittsburgh, USA), Dr Vanessa Joosen (Tilburg University, The Netherlands)

Titles in the Series
Adulthood in Children's Literature, Vanessa Joosen
The Courage to Imagine: The Child Hero in Children's Literature, Roni Natov
Ethics in British Children's Literature: Unexamined Life, Lisa Sainsbury
Fashioning Alice: The Career of Lewis Carroll's Icon, 1860–1901, Kiera Vaclavik
From Tongue to Text: A New Reading of Children's Poetry, Debbie Pullinger
Literature's Children: The Critical Child and the Art of Idealisation, Louise Joy
Rereading Childhood Books: A Poetics, Alison Waller
Irish Children's Literature and the Poetics of Memory, Rebecca Long
Metaphysics of Children's Literature, Lisa Sainsbury
British Children's Literature and Material Culture, Jane Suzanne Carroll
Space, Place and Children's Reading Development, Margaret Mackey

Forthcoming Titles
The Dark Matter of Children's "Fantastika" Literature, Chloé Germaine Buckley
British Children's Literature in Japanese Culture, Catherine Butler
Marketing Chinese Children's Books, Frances Weightman

British Activist Authors Addressing Children of Colour

Karen Sands-O'Connor

BLOOMSBURY ACADEMIC
LONDON • NEW YORK • OXFORD • NEW DELHI • SYDNEY

BLOOMSBURY ACADEMIC
Bloomsbury Publishing Plc
50 Bedford Square, London, WC1B 3DP, UK
1385 Broadway, New York, NY 10018, USA
29 Earlsfort Terrace, Dublin 2, Ireland

BLOOMSBURY, BLOOMSBURY ACADEMIC and the Diana logo are
trademarks of Bloomsbury Publishing Plc

First published in Great Britain 2022
Paperback edition published 2024

Copyright © Karen Sands-O'Connor, 2022

Karen Sands-O'Connor has asserted her right under the Copyright, Designs and
Patents Act, 1988, to be identified as Author of this work.

Cover design by Eleanor Rose
Cover image © Graeme Weston / Alamy Stock Photo

This work is published open access subject to a Creative Commons Attribution-
NonCommercial-NoDerivatives 4.0 International licence (CC BY-NC-ND 4.0,
https://creativecommons.org/licenses/by-nc-nd/4.0/). You may re-use, distribute, and
reproduce this work in any medium for non-commercial purposes, provided you give
attribution to the copyright holder and the publisher and provide a link to
the Creative Commons licence.

Bloomsbury Publishing Plc does not have any control over, or responsibility for, any
third-party websites referred to or in this book. All internet addresses given in this
book were correct at the time of going to press. The author and publisher regret any
inconvenience caused if addresses have changed or sites have ceased to exist, but
can accept no responsibility for any such changes.

A catalogue record for this book is available from the British Library.

Library of Congress Cataloging-in-Publication Data

Names: Sands-O'Connor, Karen, author.
Title: British activist authors addressing children of colour / Karen Sands-O'Connor.
Description: London; New York: Bloomsbury Academic, 2023. |
Series: Bloomsbury perspectives on children's literature |
Includes bibliographical references and index.
Identifiers: LCCN 2022010091 | ISBN 9781350196032 (hardback) |
ISBN 9781350196124 (paperback) | ISBN 9781350196049 (ebook) |
ISBN 9781350196056 (epub) | ISBN 9781350196063
Subjects: LCSH: Children's literature, English–History and criticism. |
English literature–White authors–History and criticism. | English
literature–20th century–History and criticism. |
English literature–21st century–History and criticism. |
Children, Black–Books and reading–Great Britain. | Children's literature,
English–Political aspects. | Children's rights in literature. | Race in literature. |
Publishers and publishing–Great Britain–History–20th century. |
Publishers and publishing–Great Britain–History–21st century. |
LCGFT: Literary criticism.
Classification: LCC PR990 .S265 2023 | DDC 820.9/9282089–dc23/eng/20220517
LC record available at https://lccn.loc.gov/2022010091

ISBN: HB: 978-1-3501-9603-2
PB: 978-1-3501-9612-4
ePDF: 978-1-3501-9604-9
eBook: 978-1-3501-9605-6

Series: Bloomsbury Perspectives on Children's Literature

Typeset by Newgen KnowledgeWorks Pvt. Ltd., Chennai, India

To find out more about our authors and books visit www.bloomsbury.com
and sign up for our newsletters.

For Gwen, who inspires me to fight

Contents

List of Figures	viii
Introduction: Get up, stand up – then sit down and read: Books, and rights, for readers of colour	1
1 Empire and activism: A pre-Windrush history of activist British children's authors and issues of race	17
2 Black, white, unite and fight: Children's books and activism across racial lines	53
3 To be young, British and Black: Writing for a new generation of British readers	91
4 'Good' Britishness: Black identity, white racism and children's publishing 1965–95	121
5 Hostile environments for history and publishing: Activists addressing children of colour 2012–21	151
Bibliography	175
Index	201

Figures

1 Lloyd creates a multiracial and inclusive Britain that emphasizes the belonging of Black Britons; note New Beacon Bookshop in the background   98
2 The first front cover of Naidoo's book is designed for a white audience taught to feel sympathy for distant Africans through charity appeals   146

Introduction
Get up, stand up – then sit down and read: Books, and rights, for readers of colour

I was astonished – a black man, writing his own story! I thought books were for white people. Maybe it would be worth learning my letters if only to be able to read Mr Equiano's book. Or perhaps, one day, to have the chance to tell my own story, to write it up and have folk read it.

Catherine Johnson, *Freedom* 97

Britishness, Blackness, bookishness

'Books are for white people.' It's an old idea, and historically, mostly a true one, at least in British publishing. Not only have most books, including children's books, been written for and about white people in Britain, the scholarly and critical histories of literature, including children's literature, have focused on these same books and their presumed-white audiences. While it is perhaps unsurprising that a book such as F. J. Harvey Darton's *Children's Books in England*, first published in 1932, discusses only white authors and only the very rare Black character, even more modern histories of British children's literature have been comfortable largely dismissing if not completely ignoring authors, characters – and readers – of colour. This continuing lack of attention to people of colour can be put down to two primary factors: the British Empire and population demographics.

Although Britain has been producing reading material for children for hundreds of years, the so-called Golden Age of British children's literature occurred during the late Victorian period and early twentieth century; it is during this time that many of the books considered 'classics', including

Andrew Lang's 'colour' fairy books (the first of which, *The Blue Fairy Book*, appeared in 1889), Stevenson's *A Child's Garden of Verses* (1885), Barrie's *Peter Pan* (play version 1904, novelized as *Peter and Wendy* in 1911), Kipling's *The Jungle Book* (1894) and *Just-So Stories* (1902), Nesbit's *Five Children and It* (1902) and Burnett's *The Secret Garden* (1911) were all first published (and none of these books has ever been out of print in Britain since). These books produced an idea of Britishness that continues to reproduce and reinforce ideas and values extolled in the British Empire, leading M. Daphne Kutzer to comment, 'where attitudes towards empire are concerned, they have continued to be conveyed in British children's books well into the 1980s. The longing for empire, or at least for national importance, is reflected in children's books both of the golden age and our age' (2000: 11). These attitudes about empire are, more specifically, attitudes that normalize the idea of whiteness. As Afua Hirsch puts in in *Brit(ish): On Race, Identity and Belonging*, the 'real power of British imperialism … was the mental regime, the intellectual brainwashing, inflicting upon Africans the belief that they were people who had no history, had achieved nothing' (2018: 82). It also suggested to white British people that their history was *the* history, so that even today, as Hirsch goes onto point out, 'White history is seen as "history", black history is seen as "black history" – a specialist subject for those who wish to opt out of the mainstream' (2018: 309). One of the lasting effects of the British Empire is its racial hierarchies; as Sadia Habib, in *Learning and Teaching British Values*, argues, 'Distinct minority groups, despite claims of equality, have historically been placed somewhere in a "hierarchy of Britishness" by political elites, which impacted how they "experienced" Britishness' (2018: 13). Britishness has historically been coded as white, just as British children's literature has historically been represented as being for, by and about white people. At best, this idea of the whiteness of British children's literature renders readers of colour invisible; at worst, it perpetuates racist ideas through valorizing classic, Golden Age children's books.

There have always been authors who have written against the status quo, and it is these authors I am interested in writing about in this book because much of their output has been ignored by standard histories of children's literature. Some of these writers can be considered activists – people who advocate vigorously for social or political change – and some are more radical, in that they want to overthrow or entirely bypass the systems and institutions in place. I distinguish between activists and radicals based on Moskalenko and McCauley's definition, 'readiness to engage in legal and non-violent political action (activism)' (2009: 240) or 'readiness to engage in illegal and violent political action (radicalism)' (2009: 240). Klar and Kasser define activism as

> The behaviour of advocating some political cause (for instance, protecting the environment, human rights issues, opposing abortion, or preventing wars) via any of a large array of possible means, ranging, for example, from institutionalized acts such as starting a petition to unconventional acts such as civil disobedience. (Moskalenko and McCauley, 2009: 757)

It is not possible to advocate in a vacuum – an activist has to use their voice in some way. Panaou and Mathis suggest that one way activists express their voice 'is by sharing their stories. Experiencing acts of agency through reading and writing offers powerful ways to consider the potential for our own agency and to learn about other members of our local and global communities' (Panaou and Mathis, 2019: iii). When an activist advocates through sharing stories, they become the type of literary activist that Chakravorty says is 'fuelled by partisan positions in politics or aesthetics (for instance, the many forms of post-Marxist and radical feminist approaches to what in innocent times was called "literature")' (2016: 181). The author's voice, translated onto the page, is designed to change minds or gain support for a political cause.

I am particularly interested in the way that people advocating for various human rights causes used writing for children to further their aims, and in some way focused on Britain's (or the British Empire's) Black and Asian population. I use the word 'addressing' in my title because some writers addressed the issue of race as a part of their larger cause, and other writers deliberately tried to reach (or address) the young reader of colour. It is often the case that the reader (no matter what their skin colour) is less important than the activist's cause; if John Newbery's dictum to create books that combined 'instruction with delight' is a founding principle of modern children's literature, these books frequently have much more instruction than delight. This certainly could be part of the reason that some of the books I discuss have been 'lost' in history – although, as some of the didactic literature on causes like abolition survive while other causes, including anti-colonialism and British Black Power, have traditionally not been represented in children's literature histories, didacticism alone cannot be the only concern.

Kimberley Reynolds, who has done considerable work bringing to light texts buried by traditional histories of children's literature, writes in *Radical Children's Literature* that 'children's literature, since its inception, has been implicated in social, intellectual, and artistic change' (2007: 1). But histories of children's literature have often only reflected the concerns and values of dominant groups; abolitionist children's literature was considered on the fringe of acceptability until the British abolished slavery, at which time it was celebrated. On the other hand, being an anti-colonialist was never a valued trait in a British children's writer, either in terms of cultural or monetary value. Jesse Aberbach argues that, 'the worthy position that children's literature held as nurturing "children of the empire" also disguised monetary exchange' (2018: 177). The virtue of empire books, such as those written by G. A. Henty or Bessie Marchant, was that they taught readers the 'right' values of upholding the empire – but these values also made money for the authors and publishers of these books. Those children's books which took an anti-colonialist stance, such as books written by Sister Nivedita or Anthony Delius, have largely disappeared. And while books about multiculturalism in Britain, including Bernard Ashley's *The Trouble with Donovan Croft* (1974) and Mary Hoffman's *Amazing Grace* (1991), continue to be celebrated as evidence of the success of white British tolerance, anti-racist authors who criticize British institutional racism, past or present, including A. Sivanandan or Farrukh Dhondy have often faced censorship and their books have fallen out of print. This book sets out to reclaim and examine the 'vanished' children's books as part of the history of British children's literature, and compare them with the activist literature produced in the twenty-first century.

Finding 'lost' books is not an easy task, especially when you are not absolutely certain that they are there to be found. My previous research had shown me the influence of certain political movements (such as Black Power or Communism) on authors writing for Black British readers. I started with these, searching archives including Seven Stories (the National Centre for Children's Books in the UK), the Black Cultural Archives, the George Padmore Archives, the Institute of Education archives and the London Metropolitan Archives for any lists of children's books or references to authors. One of the best sources came from organizations who used books from or were part of local, independent publishing concerns, such as the book lists used by John La Rose's supplementary school in the George Padmore archive. I also examined histories of other left-leaning organizations, for example the Fabian Society, for any reference to children's books by their members. Some of these investigations were fruitful (like the material on the Afro-Caribbean Education Resource Centre in the Institute of Education Archives), and some were not (the Fabian writers proved to be disappointing in their depiction of race in children's books). Academics who work on any area of 'hidden' literature know that a serendipitous reference or phrase can lead to success (although often after hours, days or weeks of dead ends or fruitless searches). One example of this came as I was trying to determine whether Black Jamaican poet Una Marson, active in the 1930s, had written for children. A casual mention in an article by Delia Jarrett-Macauley of the poet Rabindranath Tagore's influence on Marson led me to discover Tagore's political activism and his writing for children. Articles on Tagore led me further to the Anglo-Irish writer Margaret Noble, who changed her name to Sister Nivedita and agitated for Indian independence while writing folktales for children. Networks of influence such as these were invaluable in discovering material from Britain's imperial era. In the 1960s and 1970s, many activists knew each other and wrote about these interactions. This led me to material I would not otherwise have found. Seven Stories, the UK's National Centre for Children's Books, was particularly useful in uncovering the way that writers in the late 1960s and 1970s, such as Rosemary Stones, Bob Leeson and Farrukh Dhondy, interacted with each other and reviewed each other's work. Without the help and access I was granted to Seven Stories archives, I could not have completed this project as successfully, particularly during a global pandemic.

It should be said that this is far from an exhaustive history, and that much work remains to be done – hopefully by a new generation of scholars who have an inside knowledge of the communities and activism that the literature embraces. As a white, middle-class scholar, I have tried to be mindful of my privilege, careful in my research and accurate in my presentation of this history of an under-researched area of literature. Much of the material in this book was first presented at conferences, seminars and symposia. Scholars of colour at these events, including Aishwarya Subramanian, Breanna McDaniel and Karen Chandler all graciously made suggestions or asked questions that furthered my thinking. Conversations with Darren Chetty, my colleague and co-author for 'Beyond the Secret Garden' articles in *Books for Keeps*; and with children's publishing expert Melanie Ramdarshan Bold, have been invaluable in thinking about children's books and power. Working with the Reflecting Realities research project led by Farrah Serroukh at the Centre for Literacy in Primary Education (CLPE), and acting as consultant for the Chartered Institute of Library and Information Professionals (CILIP) on changing judging guidelines for the Carnegie and Kate Greenaway medals, have made me conscious of how diversity is presented to and valued for young people in the UK today. Nothing, however, substitutes for the knowledge that can only come from lived experience and I look forward to the research that will follow, expand and sometimes correct my own.

Additionally, there are some noticeable gaps in what readers might expect from an activist history about children's literature and people of colour; in part, this is because I have published work in this area before. I have written extensively about Eric and Jessica Huntley and their independent Black publishing house Bogle L'Ouverture, Leila Berg's efforts to address working-class and Black readers through her *Nippers* series, and the efforts of Verna Wilkins, through Tamarind Press, to create literature for Black children, in *Children's Publishing and Black Britain 1965–2015* (Sands-O'Connor, 2017). I have also written about children's literature inspired by political movements such as Rock against Racism in 'Punk Primers and Reggae Readers: Music and Politics in British Children's Literature' (2018) and the Black Power movement in the UK in 'Power Primers: Black Community Self-Narration, and Black Power for Children in the US and UK' (2020). Although I mention all of these writers, publishers and movements in this book, if you are interested in a more extensive treatment, you may consult these previous works.

There are those who would contend that the invisibility of anti-racism in the history of British children's literature is not a matter of racial hierarchies or intentional erasure but simply a matter of demographics. If Britishness is equated with whiteness, it might be argued that this is because the population of Britain is now, and for all of its history as a nation has been, predominantly white. This is the argument that publishers have sometimes used in deciding not to publish more books by authors of colour; as the novelist Hanif Kureishi has pointed out, 'the social makeup of the industry (the editors, agents and so on) is almost always narrower than that of the artists. Therefore what the decision-makers think an audience will like is often quite limited' (Shukla et al., 2015). Yet Melanie Ramdarshan Bold adds in her report for Booktrust on *Representation of People of Colour among Children's Book Authors and Illustrators* (2019) that not only are there moral and ethical reasons for publishing children's books by and about people of colour, publishers (like publishers of books for children extolling empire) should be convinced that there are, increasingly, economic reasons as well:

> Although people of colour are not the sole audience for inclusive books, publishers will not realize the true commercial potential of 'BAME consumers' and their estimated £300 billion annual spending, if they do not publish books that reflect these communities. (Ramdarshan Bold, 2019: 17)

The economic value of publishing for child readers of colour will only rise over time; the government's population statistics indicate that in the ten-year period between 2001 and 2011, the population identifying as White British decreased from 87.4 per cent to 80.5 per cent while the population identifying as one of the government's minority ethnic categories rose in all categories ('Population of England and Wales by ethnicity over time' *gov.uk*). While the numbers are still small – Black British people, for example, only represent about 3 per cent of the population – much of the change is seen in the population of school-aged children. And while the Centre for Literacy in Primary Education's *Reflecting Realities* report (Serroukh, 2020) notes that in 2019, 33.5 per cent of school-age children come from a minority ethnic background, only 5 per cent of children's books had a Black, Asian or minority ethnic main character. Purely by numbers, British children's books are still invested in Britishness as whiteness.

But even if numbers of children's books with representation of characters of colour are increasing – and they are, however slightly – numbers are not enough. Farrah Serroukh points out that 'we should not just expect more but we should also expect better in terms of the quality of ethnic minority representation in children's literature' (2020: 8). The combination of being passionately committed to a cause and creating literature specifically for children of colour perhaps *should* result in better, more careful representation, but in the books I examine in this study, representation did not always prove to be better. In fact, it was continually complicated by issues of 'competing representations' and by whose voice the activist writer thought mattered most.

Competing representations: Anti-racism and …

As part of the steering committee for CLPE's *Reflecting Realities* reports since their inception in 2018, I know that one of the criticisms of the report has been that it only focuses on representation based on race, something that is acknowledged in the 'Reflecting Realities Year 2 – FAQs' on the CLPE website. People asked: Why not look at representation based on other protected characteristics, such as gender, sexuality, religion, socioeconomic status? Did we not care about all children being represented in books? One answer to this is, of course we care, but the time and effort it takes to examine all the children's books that would fall under these various categories is enormous, and CLPE's resources are limited. Another answer is that of course we care, but issues of racial representation are urgent. Particularly since 2020 with the global response to the murder by police of George Floyd in the US, but more broadly over the last decade, we have seen time and again the ways that people of colour still suffer from discrimination and oppression. In Britain, the Windrush scandal and the furore over the examination of national heritage sites embodied in the Colonial Countryside project are just two instances of institutional and public disregard for the concerns of British citizens of colour. The coronavirus pandemic has also had greater negative impact on Black and Asian communities, in everything from higher death rates ('Why have Black and South Asian people been hit hardest by Covid-19' *ons.gov.uk*) to educational disadvantage (Akpan, 2020) to mental health ('Existing inequalities have made mental health of BAME groups worse during pandemic, says Mind', 2020). All lives matter, but some people's lives are under considerably more immediate threat than others, and therefore deserve particular attention to justice for them.

Yet the idea that attention to racial justice is not important enough for consideration on its own is not new. The 1970s in Britain was a period in which many groups were fighting for rights, including gender-based rights and class-based rights. Often, liberal white activists interested in feminism or Marxist ideas would also advocate for rights for people of colour as well. While this might appear to embrace Kimberlé Crenshaw's idea of intersectionality, where race, gender and class 'intersect in shaping structural, political and representational aspects of violence against' people of colour (1991: 1244), white people's advocacy of racial justice was often secondary to or subsumed by issues that affected 'everyone' – gender equality for feminists and class equality for Marxists. This hierarchy of social justice tended to dismiss or ignore the specific ways that gender or class issues impacted people of colour. By universalizing white feminism and white Marxism, activists writing for or about children of colour often failed to present nuanced, complex and realistic representations of communities of colour. When Rosemary Stones argued in her sex education book, *Loving Encounters*, that the sexual permissiveness of the 1960s resulted in 'a generation of young people joined together to reject many of the stigmatising and stifling values of the "traditional" family' (1988a: 35), for example, she ignored the religious and cultural values of some Black and Asian communities. What may seem sexually liberating for (some) white women also ignores the way that Black and Asian women have been treated throughout history as sexually available partners for white men. Justice for one group does not automatically mean justice for all.

Voices matter

Activism (including radicalism) involves taking a public stand on an issue. When activists use their voice by writing for children, is it the adult's politics or the benefit to the child reader that is of utmost importance? I discovered that the answer was complicated. Like children's literature itself, activism on behalf of or directed towards children is nearly always initiated and produced by adults. What role does the child reader have in activist literature? When activists (especially, but not exclusively, white activists) purport to advocate for communities or individuals of colour, how do they approach this in literature?

This tug-of-war between the voice of the activist, the voice of the child (and children are not all of one voice) and the voices of the 'community' of colour (and there is never a single 'community' of colour) seemed especially evident in literature written by children of colour, such as that edited and produced by Chris Searle or Len Garrison's ACER project in the 1970s and 1980s. I have therefore paid attention to children's writing published by activists because of this tension between competing voices. In so doing, I considered Rachel Conrad's warning to consider 'adult mediation in selecting, editing, contextualizing, and interpreting children's words and statements' (2016: 198). Additionally, I have examined how the voices of activists (such as Len Garrison) differ from the voices of radicals writing at the same time (such as Ambalavener Sivanandan); and how white activists (for instance the illustrator Dan Jones) approached literature for children differently than Black activists (such as the illustrator Errol Lloyd). My aim is to understand how different voices are valued within activist children's literature.

History matters

The bulk of this study concentrates on a specific period of British children's literature history: the 1970s and 1980s. This is deliberate. For one reason, as Lucy Pearson suggests in *The Making of Modern Children's Literature*, it was an age when 'the changing social and political environment of Britain helped to expose some of the implicit ideologies in children's literature' (2013: 47). Aidan Chambers, as editor of Topliners, a young adult imprint for Macmillan, and Leila Berg, as editor of a reading series, *Nippers*, for primary school children, focused on reluctant, working-class readers beginning in the late 1960s. Rosemary Stones and Andrew Mann set up the Children's Rights Workshop in 1974 to expose sexist, racist and classist children's literature. Independent publishers as well as the Inner London Education Authority began to produce literature for and by Black and Asian British children. There was a sense that, as Bob Dixon put it in *Catching Them Young*, 'anyone interested in how ideas – political ideas in the broadest and most important sense – are fostered and grow up in a society cannot afford to neglect what children read' (1977: xv). Children's literature was, by its nature according to some writers in this period, activist.

Perhaps more importantly for my purposes, however, the 1970s and 1980s were also a crucial period for being young, Black or Asian and British, and how these groups were defined and defined themselves in literature still resonates today in everything from ideas about Britishness to ideas about who belongs in children's books. Whereas the previous generation, their parents, had been part of the Windrush Generation or arrived after the partition of India or the expulsion of Ugandan Asians by Idi Amin, young Black British and British Asians of the 1970s were the first to have to grapple with the idea of being two sometimes-oppositional identities, one based on citizenship and one based on skin colour. Nicole M. Jackson argues that in the 1970s, 'for Asian and African-descended students, understood as perpetual immigrants, this [British] education robbed them of the ability to relate to their ancestral histories and excised them from the British narrative as well' (2019: 123). Identity and belonging were urgent questions for this generation. Activists began to fight on behalf of this generation, organizing within the Black Parents' Movement, as Black Power and Black Panther activists, as well as through groups such as the All London Teachers Against Racism and Fascism (ALTARF), the Children's Rights Workshop and the British Communist Party. Black and Asian young people also, in this period, began to speak up for themselves, forming and joining groups such as the Black Liberation Front or Rock Against Racism, or adopting the symbols and beliefs of Rastafarianism. Many joined in protests about the under-investigated deaths of Black and Asian people, especially young people, as in the Black People's Day of Action in response to the New Cross Fire in 1981, where thirteen young Black people died in a fire at a birthday party and police indifference led to victim-blaming. The mistreatment of South Asian women factory workers that led to the Grunwick Strike of 1976, the increased powers given to the police to stop and search through the sus law from the mid-1970s and the day-to-day lived experience of racism were all reasons for young Black and Asian Britons to become activists, and sometimes activist-writers, on their own account. This period throws up for examination different forms of activism and writing produced by activists, as well as the response (when available) of readers themselves.

I have sandwiched the three chapters of discussion of the 1970s and 1980s between two additional chapters of historical contextualization. The first concentrates on pre-Second World War activism, particularly the fight for the abolition of British enslavement of African people and the fight against British colonialism and imperialism in the late nineteenth and early to mid-twentieth centuries. I have contrasted these two forms of activism because while one (abolitionism) produced, in Britain, children's literature written by white authors largely for white readers that has since become part of the standard histories of children's literature, the other (anti-colonialism) produced literature by a wider range of authors for a wider range of readers – but it has largely disappeared from canonical children's literature histories. I believe that, unlike abolition, anti-colonial children's literature did not fit the narrative of the empire that Britain wanted children – white, Black or Brown – to believe. Additionally, an understanding of activist literature before the end of empire helps to set the stage for the clashes of ideology that characterized the post-1970 period.

The final chapter looks at activism after 2012 when the British government instituted their 'Hostile Environment' policy. This policy, which I discuss in more detail in the chapter, helped create the conditions for a new age of activism for young people of colour. I wanted to think about what has changed – and what has stayed the same – in delivering activist messages to children through their literature. Issues of voice still matter, but an increased emphasis on Black and Asian people as a part of British history for hundreds or even thousands of years suggests a new focus for activism.

Finally, a note on terminology and capitalization. This is a fraught, and even contested, area for many people. As Jeffrey Boakye points out in *Black, Listed*, his examination of the different identifiers used for Black people throughout history, 'names are obviously a huge part of an individual's identity, but they have a far wider cultural resonance' (2019: 64). Many of the names white people designated for Black people in Britain placed them outside of Britishness. For example, Black and Asian people were often, in the first half of the twentieth century, referred to as 'colonial', as in A. Creech Jones's introduction to *Fabian Colonial Essays* where he writes that the book is part of 'the expanding pool of constructive ideas as public opinion in Britain and abroad becomes more definite and pronounced that colonial peoples must move to responsibility and enjoy social well-being' (1944: 9). By the 1950s and 1960s, they were 'immigrants' (even when many, as British subjects, were actually migrants or born in Britain). The term 'immigrants' again placed them outside of or less connected to Britain.

One of the hypotheses with which sociologist E. J. B. Rose begins *Colour and Citizenship*, is 'that immigrants despite the possession of a common citizenship would not be felt to have a claim to equal treatment' (1969: 5). By the 1980s, although many white writers had started to refer to Black people, they meant anyone without white skin, and therefore often had to qualify what they meant. These qualifications generally put distance between Britishness and Blackness, as when white librarian Judith Elkin wrote, in *Multi-racial Books for the Classroom*, that Len Garrison's *Black Youth, Rastafarianism and the Identity Crisis in Britain* was 'a sociological essay outlining the plight of Black Youth of West Indian parentage' (1980: 18). Blackness, in this phrasing, is connected with West Indian rather than British citizenship. The use of the term Black in the Black British communities began in the late 1960s, when Black Power and the Black Panthers, ideas and organizations that originated in America, came to Britain. As I have written elsewhere, however, 'there were some significant differences between British and American Panthers. Although the BBP concerned themselves with many of the same issues, including education and the treatment of Black people by police, they were a broader-based organization which included British Asians' (2021: 14). Nonetheless, there was still debate about these and other terms within and outside of Black and Asian British communities.

Since I started writing about Black British children's literature more than twenty years ago, I have used several different descriptors, paying close attention to the language of self-identification used by the communities drawn into my research. Inevitably – again, as Boakye points out – there is no agreement within local communities, since language is slippery, relative and idiosyncratic, while cultural context is changeable and complex. The individuals that I refer to in this book come from white British, British Afro-Caribbean, British Asian and British African backgrounds, although most often the authors and audiences of people of colour that I discuss are from Afro-Caribbean or South Asian heritage, the racially minoritized groups most frequently represented in British children's literature even today (see Serroukh, *Reflecting Realities* reports 2018–20). I use the terms 'white' to refer to white British people, 'Black British' to denote people of Afro-Caribbean or African heritage (although, where it is significant, I do indicate their heritage or country of origin) and British Asian to signify people from (mostly) South Asian heritage (again,

I try to be specific about heritage). Partly this is to emphasize their Britishness; for much of the history that I discuss in this book, Black and Asian people were not seen as British, and racism was something that happened (or was imported from) elsewhere – which allowed publishers of children's books to turn to American authors, like Ezra Jack Keats or Mildred Taylor, rather than seeking out Black British or British Asian authors who might respond to British readers' experiences.

When I discuss readers or authors from both African or Asian heritage, I use the term people (or readers or authors) of colour; this is not a perfect term, but it is preferable to the reductive acronym 'BAME', which, as former chair of the Commission for Racial Equality, Trevor Phillips has said, 'simply "tidied away" a mixture of real people who only shared the characteristic of not having white skin' (Ford, 2015). BAME does not individualize or highlight the many differences that exist within this term, and it is one of many ways of 'othering' British people who were born here but whose skin is not white, so I have chosen to avoid the term where I can. My use of capitalization of the words Black and Brown, but not of white, is to call attention to and reverse the centuries-long, historical hierarchies of domination that exist when those terms refer to human beings. In thinking about these aspects of language, I have been guided by the work of Kwame Anthony Appiah, who suggests that 'the persistence of racism means that racial ascriptions have negative consequences for some and positive consequences for others – creating, in particular, the white-skin privilege that it is so easy for people who have it to forget' (2009: 673).

Finally, some brief acknowledgements. The British Academy and Newcastle University co-funded my Global Professorship, which made this book possible. I could not have completed this work without the support of many people, including people at archives such as Kris McKie, Ros Bos, Michael Geary and Sarah Lawrance at Seven Stories, and Sarah Garrod at the George Padmore Institute, all of whom helped with sourcing materials and securing permissions; authors including Catherine Johnson, Patrice Lawrence, Corinne Fowler, and especially Errol Lloyd and Beverley Naidoo who provided kind permission to use the artwork from their books; academics and writers including Farrah Serroukh, Melanie Ramdarshan Bold, Darren Chetty and my wonderful colleagues at Newcastle University

Lucy Pearson and Hazel Sheeky Bird. Special thanks go to Lisa Sainsbury, whose editing of the original manuscript was stellar and vastly improved the final product. And finally, a grateful acknowledgement of my friend Paula Wride, who lent me her empty house when I needed space to write and think.

1

Empire and activism:
A pre-Windrush history of activist British children's authors and issues of race

In the schools, children have been told that the Empire is a big, happy, united, 'loyal' family, and that the burning ambition of every little Indian, African, and Malayan boy is to die for the Union Jack.

Alexander Campbell, It's Your Empire, 1945: 7

'I suppose the black people have schools which teach in their language too?' Dick said.

'Oh yes, there are Government schools for them as well, and there are big missionary schools, too', Cecil added. 'But, you know, there are such a lot of natives that they haven't got half enough schools to go round. Besides, the Government doesn't spend such a lot on educating the natives as it does on the whites.'

Anthony Delius, The Young Traveller in South Africa, 1947: 36

How can activist writers represent and advocate for the child of colour, in and out of the book? This question became increasingly pressing in the latter half of the twentieth century and early part of the twenty-first century as the population of Britain changed to include more people from former colonies in Africa, the Caribbean and South Asia. Beginning with attempts of the Windrush generation to provide literature for their children, books for and about British people of colour often responded to the violence and trauma of existing in a society that didn't welcome Black and Brown people, or didn't see people of colour as belonging in or to Britain. From housing, employment and education discrimination, 'sus' laws[1] and police oppression, to the Windrush scandal, activists have organized communities of colour to protest and take action against a racist society. While most of this book will examine post-First World War activism, it would be disingenuous to suggest that activism on behalf of Black and Brown people, and resultant literature for children, began there. Activist and radical left politics in Britain have long been concerned with issues of race, and with communicating these issues and potential solutions to child readers. Historically, the rise of children's literature in Britain and the rise of anti-racism campaigning are tied together; the mid to late eighteenth century saw the beginning of modern children's literature in Britain as a separate entity from adult literature (Grenby, 2009: 3), as well as an intensification and organization of anti-slavery protest (Olusoga, 2016: 203). Many early campaigns, such as abolitionist boycotts of West Indian sugar were translated to children's literature by white authors for a white audience (see Gleadle and Hanley, 2020: 97–117) – even if the literature, by abolitionists such as Hannah More and Amelia Opie, was ostensibly written *for* or *about* people of colour. While institutional Britain eventually embraced abolition – the 1832 Slavery Abolition Bill was supported by the majority of members of Parliament – anticolonial activist literature, also concerned with issues of race, has effectively been erased from the canonical histories of the field. It is therefore useful to take the time to consider what abolitionists did that ensured their longevity in the history of children's literature.

Abolitionist children's literature showcases the way that activism on behalf of Black children can still privilege whiteness. Abolitionist children's literature, which included Thomas Day's *The History of Sanford and Merton* (1783), the cheap repository tracts of Hannah More (*The Sorrows of Yamba* was published circa 1790), 'Master and Slave' (1796) by Anna Letitia Barbauld, 'The Grateful Negro' (1801) and 'The Good Aunt' (1804) by Maria Edgeworth, and Amelia Opie's 'The Black Man's Lament' (1826), was a highly successful genre of British children's literature; it actually increased in amount following the

---

[1] The 'sus' law, first enacted in 1824, was part of the Vagrancy Act. It allowed police to arrest anyone they suspected of loitering with intent to commit an arrestable offence. As debates over immigration grew, with Enoch Powell and others calling for repatriation of Black and Asian people in Britain, police (most of whom, in the late 1960s and early 1970s, were white) began to use the 'sus' law with ever-increasing vigour against Black and Asian youth.

abolition of the transatlantic trade in enslaved people in the British colonies (trade in enslaved people was abolished in 1807; the abolition of slavery was a process that began in 1833 but was not complete until 1838 due to concessions to plantation owners). In 1840, British campaigners turned their attention to the continued practice of enslavement in the United States and other nations through organizing the World Anti-Slavery Convention in London. They continued their work through missions and by helping to bring African Americans out of enslavement to England, such as William and Ellen Craft.

British abolitionists, such as Maria Edgeworth (Edgeworth and Edgeworth, 1867: 33), made a direct link between the children's literature that abolitionists produced and the success of abolitionist campaigns in engaging the public. One of these campaigns involved the boycott of West Indian sugar. Gleadle and Hanley note the number of testimonial accounts and autobiographies of children who gave up sugar, including the account of Mary Anne Schimmelpennick, who wrote that it was 'thanks to the antislavery literature which her (adult) cousin Lizzie Forster lent her that she was able to abstain' from sugar (2020: 105). Abolitionist activism translated well into literature for children, playing, as John Oldfield has said, 'a vital role in creating anti-slavery consensus' (1989: 44). However, this success in terms of widespread distribution, political influence and a place in the history of children's literature contrasts starkly with early twentieth-century activism concerning people of colour when the British Empire was at its height. Events such as the 1919 race riots in cities like Liverpool and Cardiff did not produce either mass protests in the white British community or a wealth of anti-racist children's books. Even events that did engender protests, such as the treatment of Sikh or First Nations regiments after the First World War, rarely if ever found their way into children's literature of the time. Although major anti-colonial movements and organizations, including Marcus Garvey's Universal Negro Improvement Agency (founded 1914) and the League of Coloured People (founded in 1931 in London by Jamaican-born Harold Moody) had members throughout Britain and the colonial empire, they did not (as, e.g. the NAACP did in America) produce literature for children. Left-wing members of British organizations with mostly white members, such as the Fabian Society, often reproduced stereotypes about people of colour in the children's literature they wrote. This chapter will explore pre-1945 British children's literature about people of colour written by activists, and examine why abolitionist literature succeeded where other kinds of activist literature failed.

'Nothing to direct her but GOD's grace': Religious activism, abolitionists and children

The late eighteenth and early nineteenth centuries had no shortage of radical and revolutionary causes in Britain. American (1776), French (1789) and Haitian (1791) revolutions spread desire for freedom and equality throughout Britain, and women's movements, working-class movements and anti-slavery movements were all part of the radical foment. Dissenting religious belief often fuelled abolitionism; David Turley discusses abolitionists as 'a religious coalition tracing its ideology and practice across Quakerism, Anglican evangelicalism, Methodism, and the evangelicalism of religious dissent. Rational dissenters, later Unitarians, were integrated too' (2011: 26). Abolitionist children's authors, such as Amelia Opie and Hannah More, were white Britons who had dissenting religious beliefs but little contact with actual enslaved people in the West Indies. Black British radicals, including Olaudah Equiano, a member of the Sons of Africa abolitionist group, and Unitarian preacher and abolitionist Robert Wedderburn, published abolitionist literature for adults but not for children. Activist children's literature by writers like More or Opie often aligned itself with traditional Christianity in ways that ensured its publication – and its continued place in children's literature history.

The evangelical Christians who made up the Clapham Sect were one of the groups who published literature for children in the late eighteenth and early nineteenth centuries. Evangelicals, who were part of the Anglican church, focused on spreading the word of God through mission work of various kinds. When John Venn became rector of Clapham's Holy Trinity Church in 1792, he preached an evangelical gospel on a global scale, arguing that religion needed to be brought to people throughout the world, not just in England. He was a driving force in the Clapham Sect, a group of parishioners (many of whom were members of parliament) agitating for societal reform. Education, prison and mental health reforms, and better sanitary provision for the poor, were among the causes that the Clapham Sect supported in addition to abolition. As well as Venn, other members of the sect included William Wilberforce, Henry Thornton and the writer Hannah More, who in 1795 began publishing the first of her Cheap Repository Tracts.

The Cheap Repository Tracts were, according to Alderson and Garrett, 'designed to look like popular chapmen's wares' (1999: 6), thus appealing to readers who purchased cheap editions of fairy tales, legends and greatly abridged novels such as *Jack the Giant Killer*, *Robin Hood* and *Robinson Crusoe*. Chapbooks, as these cheap editions were known, generally contained simple language and woodcut illustrations, and were designed to appeal to the whole family. More copied the successful publishing techniques of chapbooks to get religious stories into the hands of those who might not otherwise come into contact with organized religion. Clare MacDonald Shaw notes that More's tracts engendered enough subscribers to become self-funding, ultimately selling two million copies in the first year (2002: xxi–xxiii). From the beginning, the tracts included stories about slavery.[2] A 1795 tract, *Babay, A True Story of a Good Negro Woman*, was part of the first series of tracts that More produced. Taken from an earlier publication by James Ramsay (it first appeared in his 'An Essay on the Treatment and Conversion of African Slaves in the British Sugar Colonies' in 1784), it was one of several produced by More that included enslaved people as characters.

Although the Clapham Sect, and More herself, were activists who followed abolitionist principles, the Cheap Repository Tracts were not radical abolitionist literature. Indeed, in the tracts containing enslaved characters, most remain in human bondage throughout the tale (although Babay, the title character of More's early tract, is 'freed' to become a servant for the man who bought her freedom). *A True Account of a Pious Negro* and *The Sorrows of Yamba* regard enslaving others as a sin, but posit that human hope can only be found in religion. Because it has helped her find God, Yamba is able to 'bless my cruel capture' (1797c: 689); the pious negro, despite being enslaved, is able to relate to a white man 'great things God had done in the course of some years for his soul' (1797b: 345); and Babay 'had nothing to direct her but GOD's grace' (1797a: 341) in deciding to help out a white man who had been abandoned

---

[2] Claire Midgley's 1992 book, *Women Against Slavery: The British Campaigns 1780–1870* (Routledge), is an invaluable source for finding literature by female abolitionists.

with an infectious disease. Moira Ferguson argues that evangelicals 'agreed that spiritual salvation was the paramount concern of all humans, that worldly affairs were inconsequential' (1998: 153) *even if* these 'worldly' concerns were the oppressions and brutalities of enslavement. Ending British involvement in the enslavement system, either for individuals or for all people, is not the aim of these stories; rather, the conversion and saving of souls is paramount. The emphasis on waiting for a heavenly reward highlights the way that a lack of direct experience with enslavement makes freedom a philosophical argument rather than an urgent concern. The suggestion by white writers such as More, that Black people should look for heavenly rather than earthly freedom, would retain enough prominence throughout history that Bob Marley would criticize it nearly 200 years later in his 1975 song 'Get Up Stand Up', where he exhorts his listeners to 'look for yours on earth'.

In contrast to literature that emphasizes heavenly reward over physical freedom, Black abolitionist writers emphasize the relief of physical and emotional brutalization before religious conversion – if religion is mentioned at all. Robert Wedderburn, for example, details the rape of his Black mother by his white father before commenting that 'my father's conscience would stretch to any extent – and he was a firm believer in the doctrine of "grace abounding to the chief of sinners"' (1824: 7). Wedderburn published for adults, because topics such as rape were not considered acceptable for the innocent ears of white children – despite the fact that Wedderburn, like many other Black children, had to witness rape and other brutalities of the enslavement system from a very young age. As Robin Bernstein argues in *Racial Innocence*, this unequal treatment of children of colour extended to literary depictions in which 'white children became constructed as tender angels while black children were libelled as unfeeling, noninnocent nonchildren' (2011: 33). Innocence, like reading itself, was reserved for white children in the eighteenth century.

Mad, bad or dangerous: Radicals and abolition

Radicals demanding more immediate abolition of slavery tended to eschew links to state religion (the Clapham Sect were Evangelical, but still part of the Anglican tradition). Wedderburn was associated first with Methodism, then Unitarianism and finally rejected Christianity altogether in favour of the freethinking movement. He was imprisoned several times for his beliefs, which were considered dangerous. The Romantic poets, who believed that humans should be free to make their own choices, tended to be on the side of abolition, and were often, as a result, seen as having suspect morals and values by wider society – but this was truer for some romantics than it was for others. William Blake was 'known' to be mad; his fellow poet William Wordsworth famously wrote that 'there was no doubt that this poor man was mad' and Blake's first biographer, Alexander Gilchrist, wrote a whole chapter about Blake's state of mind titled 'Mad or Not Mad' (1863 [2005]: 341–54). Blake saw himself as a visionary, but it was not the fact that he had visions that made his contemporaries view him as mad, it was the subject of these visions, which were anti-religious and anti-establishment. Foucault notes, in *History of Madness*, that society 'identifies madness and designates it against a backdrop of all that is reasonable, ordered, and morally wise' (2006: 205); to his contemporaries, Blake was none of these things. Mark Barr notes that 'when Blake was writing ... lunacy and its association with radical discourse had been much in the public eye' (2006: 754). Blake's radical vision of human freedom, particularly his ideas about the hypocrisy of religion, placed him on the edge of society in ways that even his fellow romantic poets were not. Wordsworth, for example, may have championed the idea of liberty, yet it was a liberty of a limited sort. Like many of the abolitionist writers, Wordsworth never visited the Caribbean, but he was stirred by the events of the Haitian Revolution and its Black leader, Toussaint L'Ouverture. His 1802 poem, 'to Toussaint L'Ouverture', however, is not about the revolution itself, but about L'Ouverture's imprisonment by the French following the uprising. To suggest, as Wordsworth does, that Toussaint L'Ouverture should maintain 'in thy bonds a cheerful brow' (1802 [2002]: 583) suggests that – similar to the evangelical Christian writers – freedom of the body is unnecessary.

Blake's poetry, on the other hand, refused the notion that mental freedom was sufficient in an unjust world. Although Blake's radicalism can best be seen in some of his works for adults, such as *The Book of Urizen* (1794), it is also visible in his poetry 'for' children (some would say Blake wrote about, rather than for, children, but the poetry has been memorized by generations of children since its publication). In *Songs of Innocence* (1789), Blake highlighted the hypocrisy of British society by having his 'Little Black Boy' aspire to 'be like' the white English people who hold Black people captive. Blake's depiction of a Black boy with a 'white' soul continues to raise doubts today about the poet's intentions. A recent major exhibition on Blake at Tate Britain opined that Blake's poem 'associates whiteness with enlightenment and purity, and blackness with physicality and ignorance. It is impossible to say whether Blake is endorsing or questioning this viewpoint' ('William Blake' 11 September 2019–2 February 2020), but few adult readers in Blake's time were in doubt that he was ridiculing the morally superior attitude of the white (Christian) Briton. In fact, Lauren Henry argues that this particular poem uses the tradition of Black poetry (particularly the poetry of Phillis Wheatley) to critique the very people who thought themselves key to the abolitionist movement, that is to say, the Evangelicals. Henry writes that in Blake's poetry, 'confusion, contradictions, and irony are the necessary results of Christianity's involvement in Africa and the slave-trade, and, perhaps also of Evangelical involvement in the anti-slavery movement' (1998: 82). Christianity, for Blake, was a way for the white establishment to maintain power over the Black person (and perhaps white people as well), and therefore could not legitimately support the freedom of the enslaved. Blake's criticism of organized religion has not affected his poetic reputation, but he is labelled mad and his abolitionist credentials are left in doubt by his failure to accept the religious standards of his time.

A useful counterpoint to Blake's radicalism is that of Quaker writers against slavery. Quakers were considered to be Christians, but religiously odd; they were often described as 'queer' or 'quacks' (Sands-O'Connor, 2008: 38). Many in England were the earliest, however, to embrace the abolitionist cause. Quakers, including Elizabeth Heyrick and publisher James Phillips, led sugar boycotts and demanded full and immediate emancipation, rather than the gradualist approach favoured by the Evangelicals, such as Wilberforce and the Clapham Sect. While this put them outside the realm of the mainstream opinion on the ending of the British enslavement system, it did not hamper their ability to publish and distribute material for all ages, including children.

Amelia Opie was a romantic poet who moved in the same circles as Mary Shelley and the actress Sarah Siddons, and – later in her life – a fervent Quaker.

In 1826, she published an abolitionist poem (far from her first, but her first for children), 'The Black Man's Lament' with the firm Harvey and Darton, exhorting 'tender hearts, and children dear' (Opie, 1826: 2) to listen to an enslaved man's story in the hopes that it would encourage children to join the sugar boycott. A sympathetic contemporary wrote that Opie was 'an "ultra-liberal". Her sympathies ... were often exercised when advocacy of freedom was a crime, and there was peril even in the free interchange of thought' (Hall and Hall, 1865: 286). Opie, like Blake, criticized the hypocrisy of white people, but unlike Blake, her criticisms were directed at white West Indians and not white Britons. So, although the Sunday morning church bells may remind enslaved people 'that we must *work* while others *pray*' (Opie, 1826: 24; italics in original), British missionaries 'come o'er the main' (1826: 25) to explain 'true' Christianity to the enslaved people, which will save them for another world, while legislators in Britain (urged on by children boycotting sugar) would bring freedom in this world. Opie and Blake both advocated freedom and equality on a radical level, but Opie's alignment with some version of Christianity and the legislative system made her only mildly dangerous and not insane like Blake. The directing of criticism beyond British shores also made her radicalism more palatable to British readers; Gretchen Holbrook Gerzina notes that a slave 'paraded with padlocked collar in London ironically aroused far less sympathy than a white man or woman pretending to be a black person' (1995: 7) in bondage. Gerzina was discussing theatrical portrayals, but Opie's use of an imaginary Black man's voice in the Caribbean has much the same effect.

Activism against slavery played a significant role in British children's literature in the eighteenth and early nineteenth centuries, but activists who accepted the religious status quo were more likely to be celebrated in their own time and in the history of abolitionist children's literature. Paula Feldman notes in 'Endurance and Forgetting' that Opie's poems were anthologized throughout the nineteenth and early twentieth centuries (1999: 17–18), and Opie is regularly mentioned in books and articles about abolitionist writers for children (from Oldfield's 1989 article, 'Anti-Slavery Sentiment in Children's Literature 1750–1850', to Gleadle and Hanley's 'Children Against Slavery: Juvenile Agency and the Sugar Boycotts in Britain', published in 2020). Radicals such as Blake who wrote outside the mainstream may be remembered as poets, but rarely as abolitionists, both in their own time and afterwards. The need for radicals to continue to embrace elements of the status quo is even more evident when looking at children's literature about the end of the British Empire. Whereas abolition has a place in children's literature history, anti-imperialism has never been wholeheartedly celebrated by Britain itself (it still is not!), and children's literature that takes an anti-colonial standpoint has remained practically invisible in the history of children's literature.

Victorian and Edwardian England and the 'liberal' left

The major twentieth-century radical movement that addressed children of colour before 1945 was the fight against colonialism and empire, and the concomitant push for national self-determination. Unlike the abolitionist movement, which has a well-documented history (including as a part of children's literature – see the previous section of this chapter), anti-colonial literature has not had a significant role in standard histories of children's literature. While many scholars, including myself, have documented the pro-imperial and often racist children's literature at the height and twilight of empire, there is little extant scholarship about literature for children that was actively anti-empire. Kathryn Castle notes in *Britannia's Children* that from the 'late nineteenth century, a particularly strong relationship developed between education, the juvenile press and the imperial propagandists' (1996: 4). John MacKenzie, in *Propaganda and Empire*, comments that 'the same complacent self-confidence, sense of national and racial superiority, and suspicious xenophobia continued to be the principal characteristics of children's literature' in the twentieth century (1984: 224). The Empire League, the Empire Day movement, the Royal Colonial Institute and the Imperial Education Conference all pressed British educators and the children in their charge to learn about and celebrate the British Empire. Empire propaganda was entirely about the white British people, and what Empire could do for them: Thomas August, discussing the importance of youth to Empire, comments that 'in youth lay the colonial elite of the future, the consumers and producers to-be of the nation, the prospective settlers of still sparsely populated overseas territories' (1985: 107). The focus of British Empire children's literature was on the white, British youth and the voices of the colonial child of colour, the colonial subject more generally, and the anti-colonialist were rarely found.

Indeed, many radical groups in Britain campaigning for a more just society either did not have any members that produced children's literature at all, or had members that actually *re*-produced imperial stereotypes in the literature they did write for children. Perhaps the most obvious example is the Fabian Society, a group of liberal intellectuals and writers who formed the forerunner of the modern British Labour Party. The Fabians believed that socialist policies, including a dismantling of capitalism and an end to hereditary wealth and power, were the only way to reform Britain. They pressed for reforms in education and housing that would help eradicate poverty. But in terms of the British Empire, Fabian Society policies did not differ greatly from those of broader British society. George Bernard Shaw, writing in 1900, argued in favour of maintaining the British Empire, though not entirely without reform. 'The British Empire, wisely governed, is invincible. The British Empire, handled as we handled Ireland and the American colonies, and as we may handle South Africa if we are not careful, will fall to pieces without the firing of a foreign shot' (1900: 15). There is no question in Shaw's discussion that Britain should continue oversight of the empire, even when some limited power may be shifted to local control, and there is certainly no need to consult those subjects of empire.

Edith Nesbit, who helped found the Fabian Society, certainly aligned with the imperial view in her children's books. Some of her most popular stories, including the trilogy beginning with *Five Children and It, The Phoenix and the Carpet, and The Story of the Amulet* (1904 [1979]), are filled with stereotypes about people of colour. With Nesbit, it is always necessary to add that her characterizations tended to be ironic, and could be read as criticisms of middle-class white British ideas about the world beyond its shores; however, her use of direct address, non-human descriptors of human characters, and reference to other Empire literature belies such a reading. In the sequel to *Five Children and It, The Phoenix and the Carpet* (1904 [1979]), specifically the chapter 'The Queen Cook', the children are transported by the Phoenix to a desert (but not deserted) island. They realize they are in the presence of 'savages' (1904 [1979]: 234) once they see huts, and debate introducing themselves as missionaries (they decide against it) before a 'savage' actually appears. Nesbit describes him thus:

> He had hardly any clothes, and his body all over was a dark and beautiful coppery colour – just like the chrysanthemums father had brought home on Saturday. In his hand he held a spear. The whites of his eyes and the white of his teeth were the only light things about him, except that where the sun shone on his shiny brown body it looked white, too. If you will look carefully at the next shiny savage you meet with next to nothing on, you will see at once – if the sun happens to be shining at the time – that I am right about this. (1904 [1979]: 235)

Nesbit goes on to talk about the savages playing 'strange-shaped drums' (1904 [1979]: 240) and singing 'odd-sounding songs' (1904 [1979]: 240). Her dehumanization of the person she calls a savage, her excessive focus on his skin colour and nakedness, typify racist attitudes of some British Edwardians who saw colonial people, particularly people of colour, as uncivilized and subhuman. By addressing the reader directly ('if you will look carefully'), Nesbit makes that reader, whom she presumes as white, complicit in this racism.

In the next chapter, 'Two Bazaars', the children go to India. 'They knew it was Indian at once, by the shape of the domes and roofs; and besides, a man went by on an elephant, and two English soldiers went along the road, talking like in Mr Kipling's books – so after that no one could have any doubt as to where they were' (1904 [1979]: 248). Here, Nesbit uses a white, British standard (Kipling) to measure, define and understand colonial people of colour. Nesbit, who never left Britain, had many progressive ideas, particularly about what she argued was a stultifying British education system. But though she argued that children needed 'every possible liberty, of thought, of word, of deed' (1913: 10), such liberty only extended as far as the white child. Nesbit's writing was typical for left-leaning writers of the time, and the acceptance of this paternalistic and hierarchical view of Empire in Britain and British children's literature helped ensure that anti-colonial, anti-imperial writers either did not find an audience in Britain, or had to use indirect means of delivering their message.

Nesbit, like many white Britons of the time, had little or no contact with people of colour. Liberal white writers who had direct connections with people of colour were far more likely to produce work that challenged stereotypes, and to be active in social justice causes. A good example of this is Mary Pamela Milne-Home, who published a book of Jamaican Anansi stories from her home, Wedderburn Castle, in the Scottish borders. *Mamma's Black Nurse Stories* (1890) came directly from Milne-Home's own experiences growing up in Fort George, Jamaica, which becomes clear when reading the text. Unlike the work of folklorists (and anthropology and folklore were in fashion in the late Victorian and Edwardian periods), Milne-Home had grown up with Jamaicans and Jamaican patois (or Creole, as she called it). Therefore, her consideration for the people and rendering of the language is much better than most folklorists. Her contemporary Andrew Lang, for example, whose 'colour' fairy books are still in print, writes casually of 'outlandish natives' (1904 [1965]: viii) whose stories must be revised 'in the hope white people will like them' (1904 [1965]: viii). Even Walter Jekyll, who tutored future Harlem Renaissance poet Claude McKay and was interested in Jamaican folktales and the people who told them, was not skilled in the representation of patois. In the introduction to *Jamaican Song and Story*, he writes that his 'method of procedure has in every case been to sit them down to their recital and make them dictate slowly' (1904: liii). Even living in Jamaica, he has to have patois dictated slowly; Milne-Home produced her work from childhood memory.

Comparing Milne-Home's use of patois to the much later publication of Black Jamaican storyteller Louise Bennett's *Anancy and Miss Lou* (1979) is instructive. Both collections have a story about Anansi and Tiger; the language is very similar. For example, Milne-Home depicts Anansi boasting, 'What me tell you? Me no tell you, say Tiger is me fader fus' riding-horse?' (1890: 53) and Bennett's reads, 'Shame ting me tell yuh, Miss Quashiba! See, ah prove i seh Tiger is me fada ole riding-horsh!' (1979: 20). Though not a native speaker of patois as Bennett was, Milne-Home was surrounded by it in childhood, and could therefore depict it naturally – even though she was writing from a castle thousands of miles away. Milne-Home's interest in people under Britain's imperial control made her pay attention to their voice – what they said and how they said it. Milne-Home would go on to fight for the rights of First Nations tribes – to whom she was distantly related (see Alison Norman's *Race, Gender and Colonialism: Public Life among the Six Nations of the Grand River 1899–1939*). Familiarity and kinship increased the chances that white British writers would produce accurate representations of people of colour, as well as the likelihood that they would write about them and speak on their behalf. However, while Andrew Lang's fairy books have never been out of print and Walter Jekyll's work has been reprinted several times (including in picture book form for children, the 1994 *I Have a News*), Milne-Home's work has rarely been discussed in critical scholarship or reprinted for children.

Nationalisms in the colonial (Celtic) twilight

Milne-Home was not an anti-colonialist, despite promoting ideas of equality throughout the British Empire. Perhaps unsurprisingly, those who objected most strongly to the British Empire were the people who were subjected to it, and most anti-colonial literature published in Britain for children came from these quarters. At the end of the nineteenth and beginning of the twentieth centuries, many Irish and Indian people found common ground through myth as well as anti-colonial movements. But anti-colonialist authors were fighting an uphill battle in the Edwardian period. John MacKenzie writes that imperial propaganda societies, such as the Royal Colonial Institute, pushed the government to include 'imperial studies at all levels of education' (1984: 149) throughout the empire. According to him they succeeded, as much of the Edwardian school-based material was 'replete with racial, cultural, and economic values' (1984: 149) of empire. Writing against the imperial domination of formal education was a difficult hill to climb, but two anti-colonial activists who channelled their ideas into literature for children were Margaret Noble, later known as Sister Nivedita, and Rabindranath Tagore.

Margaret Noble, an Anglo-Irish educator, became interested in Indian education through her work with Swami Vivekananda; she followed him to India, changed her name to Sister Nivedita, and became a fervent Indian nationalist who encouraged the Young India movement. She also started a school for girls in Calcutta [Kolkata] and, during her most political period, published a book of *Cradle Tales of Hinduism* (1907). Nivedita inspired another Indian nationalist with ties to Ireland, Rabindranath Tagore. It was Tagore's connection to the mythic tales of India that brought him to the attention of Irish poet and nationalist William Butler Yeats; Yeats would go on to champion Tagore's work and helped get him noticed by the Nobel

Prize Committee who awarded Tagore the Nobel Prize for literature in 1913. During this same year, Tagore produced a book of poetry for children, *The Crescent Moon*. Both Nivedita's and Tagore's children's books were published in England, so I want to consider the books in light of Indian nationalism, which the British government was trying to actively suppress at the time (see Sukla Sanyal, 2008: 764–5).

The British government was slow to release its grip on India, despite appearing to move towards self-government. Although the British government had allowed the formation of an Indian National Congress in 1885, the body was overseen not by Indians but by British liberal reformer A. O. Hume, and most of the delegates were moderates utilizing peaceful tactics (prayer, protest, petitions) to press for more self-government. But with the partition of Bengal and subsequent departure of Lord Curzon, the Viceroy of India who had overseen partition in 1905, radical movements strengthened. Verney Lovett, a British civil servant in India during this time period, wrote that following the death of Queen Victoria and the decision by Lord Curzon to push through Bengali partition, 'numbers of publications were alleging that the British were cunning oppressors' (Lovett, 1920: 65). Many of those against British involvement in India had been inspired by the teachings of Swami Vivekananda, 'whose words inculcating nationalism and religion had sunk deep into the minds of many of the educated classes' (1920: 64). Vivekananda did not just inspire his own people, however. On a trip to England in 1895, Vivekananda visited the Sesame Club, a literary and education reform salon that attracted many white liberal thinkers of the day including George Bernard Shaw and Aldous Huxley. One of the founders of the club, Margaret Noble, was intrigued by Vivekananda's ideas, and after a few years of studying his teachings, she followed him to India and became a devotee.

That a woman with Irish heritage would feel sympathy with Indian nationalism is not surprising. The Irish, like other colonised people, had long been considered in need of an English version of civilization; Sean Donnelly notes 'the widespread scepticism that was expressed ... regarding the Irish people's ability to govern themselves reflects the historic belief in English/British superiority' (2019: 501). Noble was unusual, however, in the lengths to which she went: leaving London, changing her name to Sister Nivedita and sympathizing with the Young India movement. After the death of Vivekananda she continued to promote his work, including a commitment to Indian self-rule, that she called 'the Indianising of India' (Iyer, 1922 [2000]: 209). Despite her radical speeches against British rule, however, her children's book *Cradle Tales of Hinduism* (1907) does not, at first glance, seem to hold particularly radical views. A collection of religious stories which one British review called 'pleasant and interesting' but which 'exhibit too much of the dreamy mysticism of the East' (Hewlett, 1908: 605) to be successful in 'English nurseries' (1908: 605), *Cradle Tales* in fact embodied Nivedita's ideas about the route to Indian independence, which she based on Vivekananda's version of nationalism.

In a speech in Madras soon before he died, 'The Work Before Us', Vivekananda argued for 'the conquest of the whole world by the Hindu race' (Lovett, 1920: 65). This Hindu conquest would not come about through military action, nor through the kind of capitalist imperialism practiced by countries like the United States. Instead, 'Spirituality must conquer the West' (1920: 65). Writing a few years later, Nivedita echoed Vivekananda's sentiments, but added that it was up to Indians to 'translate ancient knowledge into modern equivalents' (Iyer, 1922 [2000]: 209) that 'must voice the past, translate the present, forecast the future' (1922 [2000]: 210). The idea of national mythologies as important to the understanding of national character as well as that nation's success in global influence was not limited to Indian nationalists. As I have written elsewhere, the Scottish folklorist Andrew Lang, also working at the turn of the twentieth century, felt that 'understanding contemporary "savage" thought would help civilized people – adults and children – to understand their own methods of reasoning, leading them to a more scientific understanding of the world' (Sands-O'Connor, 2009: 179). A book like Nivedita's *Cradle Tales*, therefore, would serve two purposes for two different audiences. As published in India, it would teach Indian children moral values informing their ability to lead India in the future. As published in Britain, it would offer readers 'proof' of a great culture with a mythological heritage equal to or surpassing the cultures of the West, a culture worthy of self-rule.

Nivedita's *Cradle Tales*, despite being mediated through her non-Indian voice, are 'genuine Indian nursery-tales' (Nivedita 1907 [1988]: v) according to the author, told to her 'by word of mouth' (1907 [1988]: v). When these oral tales conflicted with other accounts (such as those by Greek writers),

Nivedita argued (without irony) that 'I doubt that alien opinions could ever be much more than interesting speculations' (1907 [1988]: viii). While in her preface she discounts the value of foreign writers to understanding Indian culture, a clearly anti-imperialist sentiment, in the actual tales she provides links between Indian and Western literature. She does this through her chapter titles, which label 'Savitri, the Indian Alcestis' (1907 [1988]: 51), 'Krishna, the Indian Christ-Child' (1907 [1988]: 141) and the story of Privthi Rai as 'The Indian Romeo and Juliet' (1907 [1988]: 268). In these literary allusions, Nivedita shows a keen understanding of children's books and child and adult readers. Paratextual material, such as prefaces, are not designed for child readers but adults; this is where Nivedita emphasizes the necessity for Indians to control their own literature. But by connecting Indian myth with Ancient Greek and Christian mythology and with Shakespeare in the naming of the tales, Nivedita suggests to her British (and British-educated Indian) child readers that Indian literature is not 'savage' or 'primitive' but on par with what they have been taught to think of as the most important literature of the Western world.

The text of the stories themselves do not include these direct references to western literature – only the chapter titles. For readers familiar with the western literature, Nivedita's phrasing occasionally echoes western phrasing. In 'The Birth of Krishna', for example, Krishna's parents are threatened by 'Kamsa, the tyrant king of Mathura' (Nivedita, 1907 [1988]: 141) and one night soon after Krishna's birth they hear voices that tell them, 'Arise! Take the young Child, and leave Him in the house of Nanda, Chief of the Cowherds, in the village of Gokula' (1907 [1988]: 143). For white British readers raised in the Christian tradition, this passage has clear parallels to Matthew's account of the flight into Egypt, where 'the angel of the Lord appeareth to Joseph in a dream, saying, Arise, and take the young child and his mother, and flee into Egypt, and be thou there until I bring thee word: for Herod will seek the young child to destroy him' (Matthew 2.13 *KJV*). However, in the *Srimad Bhagavatam*, Krishna's father Vasudeva hears the voice of the Supreme Lord in his own baby, and 'as instructed by the Supreme Lord carefully wanted to carry his son away from the place of delivery' (Canto 10.3 verse 47). By altering the story of Krishna's exile slightly to make a more direct parallel with the Biblical story of Jesus's flight into Egypt, Nivedita allows British readers a way to connect with the stories initially before being immersed in something that they might otherwise have seen as foreign or uncivilized. Nivedita's *Cradle Tales* is not perhaps as radical as books by later children's authors; like most of the rest of the literature discussed in this chapter, she had to tread extremely carefully in promoting nationalist sentiment, especially in order for the work to be published for white British children, and a sense of Christian morals (even if only by comparison) remained necessary. But by advocating the authentic Indian voice and comparing Indian myth with great Western literature, Nivedita attempted to plant the seeds of Indian self-rule in the minds of her readers.

These readers included the future Nobel laureate, Rabindranath Tagore, who once asked Nivedita to become tutor to his daughter. Tagore did not always agree with Nivedita, finding her too spiritual at times, but he admired her, writing in an introduction to Nivedita's *Web of Indian Life* (1904 [1917]) that 'Nivedita has uttered the vital truths about Indian life' ('Introduction'). Rosinka Chaudhuri suggests that Tagore's admiration for Nivedita was rooted in his romanticism: Nivedita, according to Tagore, could see that 'the garden, or India, is poor, miserable, indigent, but possessed of true beauty once the veil is torn, or seen through, at a particular moment' (Chaudhuri, 2004: 112). Supriya Goswami agrees, arguing that 'Tagore's validation of folklore … echo[ed] the romantic nationalism of the British Romantic poets who glorified children and common folk as embodiments of purity and innocence' (2012: 141). Like Nivedita, Tagore believed that a transcendent vision of India, beyond the real, was necessary to lead Indians out of a colonial mindset that could only see the poverty and 'backwardness' of India.

Elleke Boehmer notes that Indian nationalism, as a cultural movement, was marked by an emphasis on 'a romanticized, pastoral past and a yet unblemished spiritual essence in order to mould a coherent identity in the present: an identity, that is, independent from industrialized Europe in its traditionalism and inner "truth," yet also modernizing' (2005: 53). She compares romanticized Indian nationalism to a similar sentiment in Irish nationalism. Indeed, in the early twentieth century, as Joseph Lennon points out in *Irish Orientalism*, Irish nationalists often linked Celtic and Asian myth (2008: 5). Nowhere is this more obvious in the relationship between William Butler Yeats and Rabindranath Tagore.

Interestingly, most critics who write about the Yeats–Tagore relationship focus on Yeats' view of Tagore. In part, this may have been because, as Ana Jelnikar points out, Tagore was far advanced in his career by the time he met Yeats, while Yeats 'was yet to write what are considered to be his greatest works' (2008: 1016). Yeats therefore looked to Tagore for inspiration; but as Jelnikar points out, it was not Tagore the anti-colonialist, but Tagore the Oriental that Yeats saw. 'The Celtic sensibility that Yeats reconstructed as an alternative to the imperialist (materialist) culture espoused precisely those qualities that he attributed to Tagore: simplicity, naturalness, spontaneity, imagination, spirituality, and innocence' (2008: 1021). By adopting these qualities from Tagore, Erin Sheley suggests, Yeats takes on 'what he considers to be the Eastern sensibility as a more authentic identity for an intellect alienated by the world' (2012: 110). Tagore's value, for Yeats, is as a model of authenticity, not as an anti-colonialist. Or, as Roderick McGillis puts it, 'the Celt may know the Indian without understanding that person's culture. To know is to enter into, but in a manner that appropriates' (1999: 225). Tagore is 'known' by Yeats, but only in a way that is useful to the poet; whiteness remains central to Yeats' understanding of Tagore. Edward Said argues that Orientalism worked by 'converting instances of a civilization into ideal bearers of its values, ideas, and positions, which in turn the Orientalists had found in "the Orient" and transformed into common cultural currency' (1979: 252); in short, the 'Oriental' is what the Westerner wants to see.

This romantic vision of the 'Oriental' may have masked Tagore's anti-colonialism, but it also allowed him a certain measure of success as a poet in Britain. Because the British did not see Tagore's Indian (and more specifically, Bengali) nationalism, he was celebrated as a mystic. In Yeats' introduction to Tagore's *Gitanjali* (1913a), the book that was used to make the case for giving Tagore the Nobel Prize that same year, he writes, 'we fight and make money and fill our heads with politics – all dull things in the doing – while Mr Tagore, like the Indian civilization itself, has been content to discover the soul and surrender himself to its spontaneity' (Yeats, 1913: xx). Yeats seems deliberately blind to poems in *Gitanjali* that are obviously about politics, such as poem thirty-five, in which Tagore prays that his country might awake to 'a heaven of freedom' (Tagore, 1913a: 28) 'where the world has not been broken up into fragments' and 'knowledge is free' (1913a: 27). Tagore, it is important to note, was not a nationalist but an anti-colonialist; unlike Nivedita, Tagore did not involve himself in political groups such as the Young India movement. His ideas were universalist – nonetheless, part of his universalism was a critique of the colonial system, particularly in terms of its education system and emphasis on commerce rather than appreciation for the natural world. British readers, like Yeats, saw Tagore's critique as romanticism rather than anti-colonialism, and thus Tagore could be celebrated by the neo-romanticism of the Edwardian literary world.

Tagore's children's collection, *The Crescent Moon*, is similar to Nivedita's *Cradle Tales* in that it is not an overt critique of imperialism. Many British reviewers did not understand it as a critique at all, seeing only, as one unnamed reviewer put it, 'images and ideas which are comfortable rather than stimulating' ('A Poet of the Lotus', 1913: 816). Put in the context of Tagore's ideas about universalism, colonialism and education, however, as well as measured against the most popular book of children's poetry in England at the time, Robert Louis Stevenson's *A Child's Garden of Verses*, the book is highly critical of a British system that moulded children into imperialists and separated them from their natural ties.

Education of children was a major focus for Tagore throughout his life. He wrote several essays on the subject, always favouring a Rousseauian education based in the natural world over, as Alicia Alves writes, 'textbook learning that was associated with British colonial efforts in India' (2018: 47). Alves continues, 'the child protagonist in Tagore's poems unsettles these structures of colonial education models in his emphasis on the education of the natural world as opposed to the space of the school' (2018: 47). In *The Crescent Moon*, adults use knowledge of the natural world only to build up wealth, but the child lives in nature and is a part of it. In 'The Sailor', the boatman's boat is 'uselessly laden with jute' (Tagore, 1913b [2017]: 35) but the child speaker says that if he owned the boat, 'I should never steer her to stupid markets' (1913b [2017]: 35) but to fairyland. Similarly, 'On the Seashore' has children ignoring the pearls in favour of pebbles that they gather 'and scatter them again' (1913b [2017]: 4). When sent to school, the child chafes and longs to get out into nature again, as in 'Twelve O'Clock'. In his 1933 essay entitled, 'My School', Tagore argues that in colonial education, 'we are made to lose our world to find a bagful of information instead. We rob the child of his earth to teach him geography, of language to teach him grammar' (Tagore, 1933). An important aspect of Tagore's anti-colonialism was to write about the child in nature in a way that directly contrasted with the formal education brought to India by the British.

Another way in which Tagore subtly counters colonialist attitudes is in the parallels between his *Crescent Moon* and Robert Louis Stevenson's collection, *A Child's Garden of Verses*. Both books of poetry are about the child's world and play, and there are several poems in Tagore's collection that seem to be direct responses to poems in Stevenson's collection. Both Stevenson and Tagore, for example, have poems about making paper boats. Stevenson's 'Where Go the Boats' and Tagore's 'Paper Boats' concern children making boats and watching them sail away down a river where, perhaps, they will be found by another child. But whereas Stevenson's child is relatively incurious about the receiver of the boat, saying only 'other little children/shall bring my boats ashore' (Stevenson, 1885 [1921]: 27), Tagore's child speaker uses the boats to try to connect with the natural world as well as with other humans. The child writes her name and village on the boat in the 'hope that someone in some strange land will find them and know who I am' (Tagore, 1913b [2017]: 34); but also the child looks for playmates in the clouds and wind who 'race with my boats' (1913b [2017]: 34). In Stevenson's 'At the Seaside' the child speaker has imagination and play shaped by others; first 'they gave' (Stevenson, 1885 [1921]: 12) a spade to the child, 'they' presumably being adults; then the sea itself interrupts the child's play by filling up the holes dug with the spade. The child is alone, confined to one space, and his activity is neither chosen nor directed by himself. Tagore's 'On the Seashore' is a much different affair. Many children meet at the seashore 'with shouts and dances' (Tagore, 1913b [2017]: 4); the only adults present are in boats far out to sea, and the children are deliberately disconnected from the adults' money-making activities. They do not, like Stevenson's child, have manmade tools to interact with the sand, but use shells and leaves and pebbles. They have no set activity, and no one tells them what to do. The sea is their friend rather than their enemy: 'The sea plays with children, and pale gleams the smile of the sea-beach' (1913b [2017]: 5). Stevenson's child, despite being surrounded by consumer goods throughout the course of the poems, is alone and disconnected from the wider world; the child speakers in Stevenson's collection are often looking out of windows or playing in isolation. Tagore's child speaker is always with other people and a part of the natural world. Tagore's poetry uses natural imagery and childhood play to subtly criticize colonial education and consumer society, both of which discouraged Indians from dissent against the British. Sanjay Seth writes in *Subject Lessons* (2007) that the British believed 'instruction in western, rational knowledge was surely likely to lead to the greatest improvement in the Indian character' (Seth, 2007: 47) and that 'a sign of [the western-educated Indian's] intellectual and moral superiority would be his recognition of the virtues of British rule, and his secure attachment to the continuation of that rule' (2007: 47). Tagore's advocacy of the rejection of 'western, rational knowledge' formed a critical part of his anti-colonial children's poetry.

Neither Nivedita nor Tagore present a direct challenge to the British Empire in their literature for children. Instead, they present alternatives to the colonizer's literary and education standards, offering readers non-western values and viewpoints and making space for a world not ruled by the British. Celebrated as mystics and neo-romantics by British critics of their time, their work soon fell out of print (in Britain)[3] in the face of the hardened imperialism that accompanied and followed the First World War, the Amritsar Massacre and growing anti-British sentiment in the colonies.

Spheres of influence: Anti-racist activism in London 1930–60

Tagore's poetry and his conviction that India could bring something to the world if it could shake off the shackles of colonialism impressed many, including a young Jamaican poet, Una Marson. Writing in the 1930s, Marson suggested that culture was more important than commerce in creating a nation. Delia Jarrett-Macauley comments in *The Life of Una Marson* that, 'Indian cultural nationalism, traceable in the writings of nineteenth-century poet

---

[3] The British Library Catalogue lists only one British edition of *Cradle Tales of Hinduism*, from 1907, and an Indian edition from 1968 (reprinted in 1972; my personal copy is from the same Calcutta publisher, Advaita Ashrama, but the date is 1988). The same catalogue does not contain any print edition of Tagore's *The Crescent Moon*, although Macmillan published an edition, printed in London and New York, in 1913, which was reprinted several times, probably due to Tagore's Nobel Laureateship. However, in 1930, the year of Gandhi's Salt March, Macmillan ceased publication of Tagore's work.

Rabindranath Tagore, had become for Una an ideal for Jamaicans' (1998: 117). Marson arrived in England in 1932, the same year as the Trinidadian activist and cricket commentator C. L. R. James. Like many colonial writers during this period, Marson had already had a successful career in her homeland before she came to the metropole. In Jamaica, she had edited a journal, *Cosmopolitan*, and written successful plays – one of which, *At What a Price*, first performed in Kingston in 1931, not only funded Marson's trip to London, but became the first all-Black colonial play to be produced in London's West End (1998: 54). Marson is best known for her work at the BBC, producing the show that would become *Caribbean Voices*, but she was also a poet and activist. On her arrival to London, she lodged at the home of Harold Moody, who had founded the League of Coloured Peoples in the previous year. She became the League's secretary, interacting with the Gold Coast king Sir Nana Ofori Atta Omanhene, the future leader of Kenya Jomo Kenyatta, and the communist singer Paul Robeson as part of her work. These encounters, Anna Snaith suggests in *Modernist Voyages*, 'crystalliz[ed] her interest in Africa, and her anti-imperialism' (2014: 156).

Marson's anti-imperialist work took a number of different forms. She often publicly criticized white feminists (including those in an organization to which she belonged, the British Commonwealth League) for their use of the term 'primitive' to refer to colonial women (Snaith, 2014: 170–1), and for their patronizing attitudes towards the 'charity' required by colonial people from the British (Jarrett-Macauley, 1998: 151). In films, such as 'West Indies Calling', a war propaganda film, Marson narrates the story of skilled, hard-working Caribbean people helping the war effort to counter stereotypes of West Indians as lazy or unskilled. And she confronted the British with their role in creating the negative conditions in places like the West Indies. Writing in *The Listener* in 1939, Marson suggested that the people of Britain pay attention to the Moyne Commission report, which she had taken part in preparing: 'I hope you will read the Report of the Royal Commission on the West Indies to be published shortly. We Britishers in the West Indies are your poor relations. … But even if we embarrass you at times, the bonds formed in prosperity should not be broken in adversity' (1939: 167). Diplomatically, Marson avoids mentioning that the prosperity belonged almost entirely on the white, British side and the adversity on the Black, Caribbean side; yet Marson suggests throughout her work the civilized nature of Caribbean people *in spite of*, and not because of, British colonization.

Marson did not write for children, although she raised money on their behalf (in a Jamaican branch of the charity Save the Children) and occasionally wrote about them, as in her poem 'Little Brown Girl' (1945) which, as I have written elsewhere, 'demonstrated the loneliness of being' (Sands-O'Connor, 2017: 15) a Brown child in London mid-century. The book of poems which included 'Little Brown Girl', *Towards the Stars*, was dedicated to the white writer and Marson's friend, Stella Mead. It was through Mead that Marson would have the most direct influence on British child readers. Mead seemed to be a woman of independent means. She never married (she is always referred to as Miss Stella Mead in newspaper accounts, including her *Times* obituary from 14 April 1981), and travelled the world (in August, 1933 she sent verse to *The Daily Mail* about her trip to 'The Khyber Pass') and is socially significant enough to be mentioned as one of the guests at a reception for the foreign ministers of Nepal, Saudi Arabia and Afghanistan ('Reception' *The Daily Telegraph,* 31 July 1936: 15). Although she began by writing somewhat stultified verse for the British papers (including one on the 1931 general election for the Daily Mail) – through her travels she became a storyteller for children. In London during the late 1930s and early 1940s, Mead read her fairy tales on BBC children's programmes. Mead and Marson may have met through either diplomatic or journalistic avenues; the reception that Mead attended in 1936 was hosted by R. S. Nehra, who had at one time been a treasurer for the League of Coloured Peoples; and of course, Marson met many writers through her work with the BBC (see James Procter's 'Una Marson at the BBC' for more on Marson's career there; and Delia Jarrett-Macauley's *Life of Una Marson* for more on her friendship with Mead).

However they met, they were friends by the mid-1940s, when Marson published *Towards the Stars*. In fact, as Delia Jarrett-Macauley points out, Mead 'helped Una select poems for the collection, and in June 1945 *Towards the Stars* was published by the University of London Press, which had also brought out several of Stella's books' (1998: 161). Marson's *Towards the Stars* contains about half of its poems reprinted from earlier works. Alison Donnell comments that 'although only a handful of significant revisions occur, they would seem to suggest that Marson, aided by her English friend and fellow writer, Stella Mead, was aware of the need for some cultural mediation in order to present her poems to an English audience' (Donnell, 2011: 15). These descriptions of the publishing process for *Towards the Stars* imply a lopsided relationship between the women, but reading Mead's stories for children suggests that their editorial exchange was more mutual, as Mead's fiction changed in both subject matter and attitudes following her meeting of Marson.

Mead began publishing for children in the late 1920s. Her early work included folk tales and animal fables from around the world, retold for children. *The Land Where Tales Are Told* (1931) contains mostly European stories; and while *Great Stories from Many Lands* (1936) has a more global focus, both books are set in the vague mists of long ago, and do not therefore challenge the ideas British readers might have of African and Caribbean people as primitive. After she becomes friends with Marson, however, Mead's collections of stories change. *Travellers Joy* (1952) might seem to be a continuation of Mead's collections from the 1930s, but this book depicts a modern, even technological Caribbean and African space. The characters in 'A Boy and his Dog in Jamaica', 'The Missing Necklace' and 'The Rain-Maker's Gifts' all live in recognizably middle-class homes, with western-style clothing, two-parent families and village or town communities. Hamu, the 'young Zulu farmer living in a mountain valley to the north of Natal' (Mead, 1952: 35) has been to agricultural college, and uses his knowledge to improve his father's farm. Similar settings and characters can be found in Mead's *Adventures of Peter and Tess Through the British Commonwealth* (1944) and *Bim, A Boy in British Guiana* (1947). This may not seem particularly revolutionary, and Mead was certainly not the anti-imperialist that Marson was. Her white characters, like Peter and Tess, travel the world in a private plane and, at best, see the adults of colour that they meet as equals *thanks to past British intervention* and not as naturally capable on their own merit. But because many African and Caribbean people were depicted in British children's literature of the time as savages in jungles and huts, still reliant on the knowledge of the British to save and protect them, Mead's children's stories after meeting Marson suggest an ability of colonial people to survive without the continuing help of the British. Her efforts were noticed; a review of the *Peter and Tess* books in the *Times Literary Supplement* points out that 'the text is attractively garnished with the small human bits of information which children like' ('Children's

Books: Entertainment and Education', 1942: 394). Mead's literature is not problem-free, and she continues to employ some stereotypes, but it is clear that contact with the anti-imperialist Marson influenced her storytelling in a way that she could bring to her (presumably mostly white) readers.

Upon Marson's return to Jamaica in the last decade-and-a-half of her life, she became more conservative; Imaobong D. Umoren suggests that 'while she was not against Jamaican independence, she cautioned against blaming Jamaica's problems on British colonialism' (2018: 107). Yet in one way, Marson's views did not change. Her experiences in London during the 1930s made her critical of the colonial system of education. Umoren quotes Marson in a speech before the British Commonwealth League in 1934, in which Marson suggested that 'the child using books which upheld the glory of Empire grew to manhood and womanhood knowing nothing and caring less, for the land of his forefathers – Africa – and the race to which he belonged' (2018: 29). In 1949, Marson partnered with *The Gleaner*, Jamaica's biggest newspaper, to found the Pioneer Press, a publisher of youth literature. Arthur Calder-Marshall, writing in the *Times Literary Supplement* in 1952 that the press's 'main concern is the creation of a cultural tradition' (Calder-Marshall, 1952: 348) for its young readers, including through retellings of history and of Anansi stories. This cultural tradition was aimed squarely at Black child readers, and the choices that Marson made in publishing reflect this.

As editor, Marson rejected the British influence that had guided Jamaican publishing throughout modern history. Alvona Alleyne notes that 'the authors included in its list were steeped in the Jamaican way of life and were not interested in the area merely for geographical colour. Financially some of its volumes were quite successful. S. A. G. Taylor's historical novel *Capture of Jamaica* (1951), sold over 12,000 copies, an excellent figure by any standard' (Alleyne, 1978: 246). In addition to history, Marson's press published folktales. The acknowledged authority on Jamaican folktales in Britain after the Second World War was Jamaican-born, British-educated white Philip Sherlock, then-secretary of the Institute of Jamaica (and on the advisory board of the press); he had already published books of Anansi stories for educational and mainstream publishers. Marson, however, chose to publish a book of Anansi stories told by another (like herself) under-acknowledged Black Jamaican female poet, Louise Bennett, also known as Miss Lou. Bennett was known for celebrating Jamaican patois; whereas white Jamaican Philip Sherlock had published Anancy stories in standard English, Bennett's *Anancy Stories and Dialect Verse* (1950) encouraged cultural nationalism of a kind that rejected the British colonial tradition as the nation headed towards independence. Bennett, who had trained at the Royal Academy of Dramatic Arts in London and who could speak with a cut-glass British accent when she wanted, rejected British ideas of what Jamaicans should become through her celebration of patois.

Marson's editorship of Pioneer Press would have an indirect effect on British children's literature, as well as providing Jamaican children with a literature of their own. As part of her work to promote Pioneer Press's publications, Marson formed a book club in Kingston for young writers. One of the writers she encouraged and was first to publish was the young Andrew Salkey, who would go on to play a major part in establishing independent Black British publishing in 1960s Britain, as well as writing novels, published in Britain, of historical and contemporary Kingston that dispelled racist stereotypes of Jamaicans. Although definitely anti-imperialist in her views, Una Marson did not publish her own anti-imperial stories for children. Nonetheless, she used her influence with other writers, both as friend and editor, to change the way that the Caribbean and Caribbean people were presented to children, both in and out of Britain. She championed the voice of Black Jamaicans, and young readers – including Salkey – were able to see themselves in the book world because of it.

The young traveller in the end of empire

As the Second World War came to an end, the British Empire's end seemed imminent as well, especially for many in the colonies who had long been agitating for freedom. Anti-colonial sentiment became less of a radical notion and more of a given fact, something that Britain needed to understand and prepare for. To that end, the publisher J. M. Dent (through its Phoenix Books imprint) began publishing a series called *The Young Traveller*. The series, which ran to over forty books, had different authors assigned to each country or region, from Geoffrey Trease writing about England and Wales to Arthur

C. Clarke writing about the young traveller in outer space. Not all books in the series were about colonies or former colonies of Britain, but the ones that were frequently used local, rather than British, authors. This marked a considerable change from typical 'round the Empire' series (like Mead's *Peter and Tess*) that had existed since the nineteenth century, in which white British authors produced white British characters who surveyed the tourist areas or civilized the 'savage' areas, generally as they enriched themselves through business propositions. The history included in this earlier type of book was most certainly from a British perspective; often, periods before the British (or European) colonization were depicted as non-existent or prelapsarian. *The Young Traveller* series, in contrast, highlighted history from a localized perspective; pointed out the problems as well as the benefits that came with colonialism; and painted a picture of the country's future as largely independent from imperial rule (even when actual independence turned out to be several decades away). But crucially, some of the authors used by the series were critical of both British imperialism and colonial governments, and the books that they wrote for the series not only took an anti-colonial stance, but also portrayed people of colour with much less prejudice than other authors in the series

In fact, one of the earliest books in the series, *The Young Traveller in South Africa* (1947), was written by Anthony Delius who would eventually be exiled by the South African government for his views. Delius, a South African-born white journalist and playwright, advocated throughout his life for the rights of all South Africans. Unlike many liberals, Delius did not just press for education of Black South Africans, he highlighted what Black South Africans had to give to the education of all young people, specifically through the oral literary tradition and history of tribal South Africans. Writing in an African literary journal that 'the darkest part of the Dark Continent for the white man is the black man's mind' (Delius, 1955: 268), Delius goes on to enlighten his readers with a discussion of Bantu poetry and literary tradition that includes the oldest versions of the fables told by Aesop and the Brer Rabbit folktales. The highlighting of the Black South African's humanity fuelled Delius's conviction that the government-sponsored racial segregation had to end. He contributed to the *New African: The Radical Monthly*, which 'looked ahead to the ultimate collapse of white racial supremacist strategies and the dawn of non-racial democracy in South Africa' (Vigne and Currey, 2014: 56). In his work for the *Cape Times* and the *Port Elizabeth Post* (which he helped found), Delius criticized the Nationalist government, which ruled from 1948 to 1984 and made the segregation of people in South Africa official under apartheid. By 1964, *The New African* could talk of the likelihood of the government 'gagging' Delius ('Words Words Words', 1964: 116) and other journalists who objected to government policies, and indeed, this soon became the case. He was suspended from reporting on Parliament, and because of this, Delius – who won the Roy Campbell prize for poetry in 1959 and met Robert F. Kennedy on his official visit to South Africa in 1966 – was forced into exile in 1967.

Many have argued that British children's literature about South Africa rarely told the facts about South Africa – see, for example, fellow South African Beverley Naidoo's *Censoring Reality: An Examination of Books on South Africa* (1984) where she writes that 'materials endorsing apartheid are still widespread and … endorse the gross exploitation of millions of black people in South Africa, a country with which we in Britain have close connections' (Naidoo, 1984: 43). But Delius's volume in *The Young Traveller* series is remarkably frank, and does not hesitate to criticize the government or the colonial system that put such a government in place. Early in the book, the main character's father, Mr Wisley, 'was talking about some business matter in South Africa and used the word "colonial"' (Delius, 1947: 15). A South African objects, telling him that 'we run the Union ourselves and we don't take orders from anybody' (1947: 16). Despite this, however, the influence of European colonialism is felt throughout the book. Dick Wisley stays for a time with his father's friends, the Blacksons, who take him to visit sites in Johannesburg. One day they visit the Blacksons' uncle who manages a gold mine. Uncle Willie, who is white, manages a mine that employs both Black and white miners. However, Delius makes clear the hierarchy that is in place in the mine. Dick sees 'a white miner and his black assistants' (1947: 45); the 'assistants' did the hardest work. The gold they mine goes 'to the Rand Refinery, and from there they are sold at a fixed price and sent to the South African Reserve Bank. The Bank in turn sells them to the Bank of England' (1947: 47). Dick notes the wealth of Johannesburg and not only thinks that 'Without gold you wouldn't be here' (1947: 48) but also he 'would find himself thinking of gold, about Uncle Willie sitting in control in his big office and of Jonathan the Zulu, stripped to the waist and sweating, guiding the shuddering rock-drill on his little shelf in the reef many thousands of feet below all the big buildings and busy crowds' (1947: 49). White people are literally on top of the hierarchy, which was created and remains in place because of colonialism. Although he has little power to alter this hierarchy and disparity, Dick – and the presumed-white reader – is forced to at least recognize the inequality.

This disparity is underscored by Dick's visit the next day to Bantu mine workers compounds and Bantu villages. Alice Blackson tells Dick that 'there were Government regulations to ensure that the natives were fed and housed properly' but that 'all these men in the compounds live away from their families – sometimes for years' (Delius, 1947: 51). Dick is shocked to find women and young children living 'in a wilderness of shanties and mean little dwellings, mostly in a dilapidated condition' (1947: 51). Dick is certain that these houses could not be part of the same Johannesburg of wealth and prosperity he had seen, but Alice points out that 'Johannesburg is responsible for it and so is the rest of South Africa … in South Africa, if you're black and want to live in a city, whether you're poor or not, you must live in a location' (1947: 52). Delius's text also points out the difference in education (1947: 35–8, 130–5) and wages (1947: 52) between Black and white South Africans, the imbalance always favouring white South Africans.

Unlike many accounts of South African racial segregation, however, Delius does not put the divisions down to white superiority. Although there are white people who discuss 'civilization' as something belonging only to white people, they are shown to be prejudiced; Dick's friend Paul Blackson uses racist terms for Black people and his sister Alice corrects him: 'Don't pick up Paul's attitude to the Bantu, Dick, it's as behind the times as the Kaffir wars of the last century' (Delius, 1947: 50). She reminds both Dick and Paul that it is the poverty and lack of education that keeps the Bantus from succeeding as the Europeans have done. And a Bantu teacher points out that Bantu civilization produced 'irrigation works … Bantu pottery and music' (1947: 133). A Bantu woman whose husband worked in the mines, 'told the group of children one of the innumerable fables with which Bantu folk-lore abounds' (1947: 140). When Dick notes that the story is similar to Brer Rabbit tales, Dinah points out Brer Rabbit's African origins (1947: 141). Black African civilization is highlighted and underscored for the white character and reader whose typical reading described Black Africans as primitive and uncultured.

Delius also showcases moments of resistance. In Durban, Dick sees some South African Indians being arrested and asks Paul about it. Paul is indignant, saying that 'just because we won't let these coolies buy land anywhere they start passive resistance movements' (Delius, 1947: 144). Dick's father later explains that passive resistance 'is disobeying a law you object to without being violent. Gandhi started this sort of thing when he was a young advocate in South Africa and didn't like the Union's laws about Indians' (1947: 144). The reader is left to puzzle out the morality of this episode, but the fact that Dick's father does not condemn the Indians as Paul does suggests that he, like Alice, feels that the injustice of South African society must be resolved, and this will never be accomplished by leaving it to the good will of white South Africans like Paul Blackson. As Delius would later write, 'there is a growing realization that all the peoples of South Africa can only be saved or lost together' (1963: 24).

Writing about this series some years later in *Books for Children: The Homelands of Immigrants in Britain*, anti-racist librarian Janet Hill was critical of Delius's book, finding it 'a superficial travelogue' (1971: 19). However, it is notable that Hill refers to the 1959 revised version of the book. The revisions, which include references to the apartheid system that became law after Delius wrote the first edition, also include specific alterations that soften the depiction of white people's racism. For example, in the scene where Dick is thinking about his uncle and the workers in the gold mine, the text is changed from Uncle Willie being in 'control' to 'working with figures' (Hill, 1959: 47) and Jonathan the Zulu is merely 'guiding the rock-drill' (1959: 47) without all the sweat and hard work. Everyone is just doing their job in the revised version, and no one is oppressed. It is not clear who made the revisions to the second edition of the book, Delius or the editors at Phoenix, but either way it is easy to concur with Hill's opinion that 'it is a pity that a fine writer should be circumscribed in this way' (1971: 19).

Sentiments of equality and (some) anti-colonialism are expressed in another of *The Young Traveller* series, *The Young Traveller in India and Pakistan* (1949) by the white English historical writer, Geoffrey Trease. Trease, whose Marxist version of the Robin Hood story, *Bows Against the Barons* (1934) had brought him to prominence, was given the task of writing about the former jewel in Britain's imperial crown because he had spent time in the Army Education Corps during the Second World War (Powling, 1994). Early on in the book, Robert and Carol Woodstock are sent to Ellora 'to see something really ancient – something to remind them (as Mr Gupta said with a twinkle behind his glasses) that India had a great civilization before Julius Caesar had heard of Britain' (Trease, 1949: 26). India's modernity and problems associated with that modernity are also emphasized: one man points out to the Woodstocks 'Bombay's greatness as a port and a centre for cotton and other textile mills' (Trease, 1949: 23) but adds that 'one must be fair: if the luxury flats were shown, so too must be the slums in which tens of thousands of mill workers existed rather than lived' (1949: 23). Girls are being educated, 'but here in India not many people worry about fun and freedom for girls – in fact most of them are shocked at the idea' (1949: 72). Trease argues that the problems arise from two sources: first, India and Pakistan's conservative religions. Each religious group is given space to explain their point of view, but Trease has a clear bias:

> 'There are so many differences between us', a Muslim man tells the children, 'Islam is democratic and holds all men equal; Hinduism has the caste system. Any man can become a Muslim if he wishes: you must be born a Hindu, you cannot be converted. We believe in one God, they have many. We consider that ours is a pure religion, and theirs is full of abominations. We are disgusted by their idols. We are offended by their music, which our holy book, the *Koran*, forbids'. (Trease, 1949: 125)

The children have already stayed with a Hindu family, the Guptas, but they are 'quite westernized' (Trease, 1949: 19) and agree that the caste system is 'the bane of India' (1949: 19). Mr Gupta, unlike the Muslim the children meet later, does not have such prejudices against his Muslim neighbours: 'There are many millions [of Muslims] in the new Dominion of India and we hope they will stay. Most of us in the Dominion did not want to split the country at all, because we believe in one nation for all Indians, whatever their religion' (1949: 27). This sentiment mirrors that in Delius's book about South Africa; however, it is too late for India to be 'one nation' by the time that Trease is writing.

Trease puts the blame for the disunity and violence in the country squarely at the feet of the British. Although he writes that 'Britain had given many important things to India – railways and irrigation, schools, hospitals, and law courts' (Trease, 1949: 113), he also argues that the British did not want to deal with Indians as humans. A Sikh they meet points out that the British rarely consulted Indians on matters that affected them: ' "For example," he said, "when Britain went to war with Germany in 1939, India was not consulted. She found herself automatically at war, because London said so. Canada and Australia and the other Dominions were not treated like that. They declared war by their own decision"' (1949: 114). Britain's abrupt abandonment of the country, the book argues, caused the violence and religious tension that existed between India and its new neighbour Pakistan. A Pakistani explains it to the children by saying, ' "Imagine if Britain or America decided one day to split into halves! Picture the scenes in Washington if the old division between North and South was made again – or in London, if all the Yorkshire and Lancashire Civil Servants had to go off and start a new government in Manchester!"' (1949: 145). The chaos of starting a new country 'almost overnight' (1949: 145) would have been bad enough, but Britain's religious division of India caused 'the riots when the great movement started, Muslims passing into Pakistan, Hindus and Sikhs travelling the other way … Those were terrible days. Trains were stopped by the mob, there were atrocities and counter-atrocities, sometimes hundreds of passengers from a single train were murdered' (1949: 146). The violence of empire is laid bare in Delius's and Trease's books in *The Young Traveller* series, but a plea is made in both for the colonial people to rectify what the British have torn asunder, and create unified nations.

Anti-colonialism in *The Young Traveller* series is certainly present, and it makes the series unique in books of this sort. But Trease's anti-colonialism did not extend to Britain itself. In 1953, he wrote *The Young Traveller in England and Wales*. In this book, a white South African and a white Australian come to visit friends in England. ' "We'll be the natives"' (Trease, 1953: 15), the English father tells his children. But unlike English visitors to other countries, Australian Sally and South African Jim do not see the negative, problematic or even changing parts of Britain. They are introduced to the London underground, but most of the rest of their time is spent in 'historic' England, visiting castles and abbeys and natural areas, with the occasional factory or school thrown in. The wealth of these places is never connected to Britain's colonial past.

Sally finds England '"all so *tidy*"' (Trease, 1953: 18) in its '"neat hedges hemming the pocket-handkerchief fields"' (1953: 18). Jim, despite being more reluctant to come to England, quickly compares it favourably to South Africa:

> I'll have to mend my ways, Jim told himself. At home he was used to space and untidiness. He could throw his clothes down on the floor and a black servant would pick them up, fold them, and put them away. In England, he quickly learnt, very few people had servants now. Even fathers and sons took their turn at washing up. Jim was soon doing his share, and polishing his own shoes for the first time in his life. (Trease, 1953: 23)

The wealth and order of Britain is unconnected in this book with empire; the country is entirely made up of white people and the children do not even see any Black Britons driving or collecting tickets on London buses, despite this being an extremely likely occurrence by 1953. A possible cause for Trease's caution can be found in another of *The Young Traveller* series, written by white writer Lucille Iremonger (born in Jamaica but later to become a London County Councillor for the Conservative Party). Iremonger represented a different type of white Jamaican from Mary Pamela Milne-Home. Whereas Milne-Home saw Black Jamaicans and First Nation Canadians as people, Iremonger wrote about 'treacherous Indians' and 'ignorant Creole' girls in her books ('Lucille Iremonger', 1989: 19). In *The Young Traveller in the West Indies* (1955), Iremonger's main characters ask their father why out-of-work West Indians don't just move to the UK. He replies that 'there's a tricky point. There's no colour bar and no colour problem in England, and we hope there never will be one. But can we be absolutely certain that if she imported a really large number of Negro people, her own people would be so wise and so tolerant that a colour problem would not arise?' (Iremonger, 1955: 39). In fact, 'colour problems' were already evident enough in London that the newsreel film company, British Pathé, had produced a film in 1955 entitled 'Our Jamaican Problem'.

By the end of the Second World War, anti-colonialism had become more than a movement; it was an accepted fact in most of Britain's former empire. Nonetheless, the British government continued to see anti-colonialism as a threat, long after nations started gaining their independence. In 1955, the Conservative Commonwealth Council published a pamphlet entitled *Colonial*

Rule: Enemies and Obligations. In it, the Council argued that the dangers of anti-colonialism include 'the building-up of a myth of perpetual white imperialism' (1955: 9); in fact, the Council argued, colonial powers 'are among the bulwarks of liberty' (1955: 3), helping people 'who previously were incapable of fending for themselves in the modern world' (1955: 4). This defensiveness shows why anti-colonial children's literature needs to be reinserted into children's literature histories, because these attitudes would continue to dominate in children's literature after the war. As Adam Elliott-Cooper has said in *Black Resistance to British Policing*, 'anti-racism must be rooted in anti-colonialism and the capitalist exploitation which connects them' (2021: 52). To understand post-war activists producing anti-racist literature for children, it is necessary to contemplate how economics of empire would continue to shape the relationship between Britain, Africa, Asia and the Caribbean after former colonies had gained their freedom. *The Young Traveller* series, along with the work of Nivedita, Tagore, Marson and Mead showed countries which had until very recently been colonies of Britain, but were moving forward with independence and modernization. But books depicting people of colour as intelligent, capable and cultured *outside* of Britain, including Nivedita's *Cradle Tales of Hinduism*, Stella Mead's *Bim, a Boy in British Guiana* and even Tagore's *The Crescent Moon* often fell out of British print within a few years, while racist depictions such as those found in Nesbit's children's fantasies remain in print today. Representations of such capable people of colour within Britain were almost impossible to find in children's literature prior to the end of the Second World War. Additionally, the education and self-esteem of white British readers often remained central even in books promoting the education and self-esteem of Black readers and characters. It would be some time before British activists and radicals, white or Black, began writing children's books about and for Black Britons living in the country and actively participating in British life.

2

Black, white, unite and fight: Children's books and activism across racial lines

The child is entitled to receive ... an education which will promote his general culture.

UN Declaration of the Rights of the Child, Principle 7

What's the reaction when black comrades get together on their own to have a meeting? Some white comrades take strong objection to it. They want to be in there, maybe dictating to black people how they should play the game. They assume that blacks can't do anything, can't control anything, can't organize themselves.

Dorothy Kuya, '100 Years of Abuse', 1981: 18

Activism concerning the rights of children intensified in Britain following the Second World War: the horrors of the Holocaust led to the creation of UNICEF (1946) and the UN Declaration on the Rights of the Child (1959); Britain's social welfare system was overhauled including the introduction of universal health care and an extension of compulsory education for children; and the market economy increasingly targeted the child (and, more particularly, the newly defined 'teenager'[1]) as consumer. Childhood was not only extended through keeping young people in education longer, children were also thereby under increased surveillance by the state. Although the school curriculum

---

[1] A term imported from America, the concept of the teenager occurred with increased frequency after 1945. A notable example is the *Picture Post* article from March 1957, 'The Truth About Teenagers', where Trevor Philpott argued the importance of paying attention to the moral education of the teenager because 'tomorrow, for better or worse, they will be Britain' (1957: 11). Their spending power quickly became of interest to the media; see for example Mark Abrams' 1959 article in *The Financial Times*, 'The £900m. Teenage Market'.

was not nationalized until much later, education, and particularly reading and literacy, were seen as levellers for society. Distinctions based on class, gender and (somewhat later) race could, it was felt, be erased by universal literacy. Amy Palmer notes that in the 1940s, 'calls for education reform were linked strongly with left-leaning ideals to improve the life chances of poorer children' (2011: 141); Phillida Bunkle discusses how wider access to free education helped girls stay in school longer (2016: 791–811). Geoffrey Crowther's 1959 report underscored these values in the 1944 Act (*The Crowther Report*, 1959: 15–18).

But post-war reading in Britain was designed for the white middle-classes; and gender roles, class distinctions and racial prejudices were generally reinforced rather than challenged in everything from reading schemes like Ladybird's *Peter and Jane* books, adventure and school stories by authors such as Enid Blyton, and fantasy from writers like C. S. Lewis. All children might be taught to read, but the book world in Britain belonged to white middle-class (and, in terms of power and authority, male) readers. At the same time, however, post-war changes in education, such as the rise in school-leaving age to fifteen in 1944 and sixteen in 1964 and the introduction of the comprehensive and secondary modern schools designed to serve the needs of working- and middle-class students, contributed to an increase in children's publishing generally, and allowed space for activists concerned with children's rights to bring their activism to a child readership. Many of these activists on behalf of children were themselves white and middle-class, educated into the British system. They often had multiple 'causes' about which they wrote. It is therefore useful to examine both the conditions that encouraged such activism in white Britons as well as how far they were willing to go to advocate change, particularly for readers of colour. Chris Searle, a white London teacher, was primarily concerned with children having the right to a voice, and his activism on his students' behalf led directly to his career as a writer and publisher of work by and about children of colour. Community activist and very early Amnesty International advocate Dan Jones fought against racism and for children's voices and published illustrated books that reflected his involvement in activism for the multiracial community in which he lived. White journalist Bob Leeson became increasingly interested in readers from working-class and 'immigrant' backgrounds through his work at the communist newspaper

Morning Star; he went on to write some of the earliest British historical novels featuring Black protagonists. White children's book editor Rosemary Stones' feminist advocacy extended to a concern for other under- and misrepresented children in books, including both working-class children and children of colour. This chapter considers issues of voice, agency and intersectionality in activists' writing for young people.

The extension of childhood and publishing for children

The 1944 Education Act began a revolution in British ideas about childhood, in terms of its longevity and requirements. The raising of the school leaving-age to fifteen, combined with a post-war baby boom, meant more students in full-time education and a greater need for and interest in teacher training. I. G. K. Fenwick notes that 'During 1948 secondary schools had to cope with nearly 400,000 more pupils remaining in full-time education' (Fenwick, 1976: 39); the question was how to educate a much larger segment of the population, spread across the social classes. The provision of bursaries for working-class students to grammar schools, and the establishment of the British comprehensive school aimed at working- and middle-class students, led to questions of curriculum and access. David Kynaston writes that access to grammar schools, particularly, through examinations, 'was the crux if significantly more of the working-class – especially the semi-skilled and unskilled working-class – were ever to have the chance fully to exercise their talents' (2009: 141). In reality, however, most British children would not be (and still are not) educated at grammar schools, and would have to be taught skills to serve a nation that could no longer rely on its far-flung empire. Literature designed for new populations of readers became an important element of educating post-war Britain.

At the same time, the children's book world was becoming increasingly professionalized. The first full-time course in children's librarianship (offered by North-Western Polytechnic in London; the course was six weeks in duration) was advertised in the *Library Association Record* in 1955 ('Children's Librarianship Course' 1955: 322). The increase in British children in full-time schooling meant that courses such as these soon burgeoned; by

1966, an article by C. D. Batty in *Library World* was calling for specialized university courses:

> The practice of librarianship for children implies a concern for their reading possibly even greater than the ordinary librarian's concern for the reading of adults; care must be exercised in the selection of material and in the guidance of children, but how can this be done without a fundamental understanding of child psychology, of children's literature and the world of children in general? (Batty, 1966: 156)

White librarian Eileen Colwell, in 'At the Beginning' discusses early attempts to organize children's libraries, saying that when she and a fellow children's librarian 'formed the Association of Children's Librarians in 1937, there were very few librarians available to join it' (1974: 36) but within a few decades, the professional organization in Britain was 'several thousand strong' (1974: 37). Similarly, the Library Association's Carnegie Medal, established in 1937, did not at first have the active participation of children's librarians. Pearson et al. notes that there were 'only a handful of children's librarians … on the committee up until the 1960s' (2019: 94), at which time the children's librarians took greater control over the award.

Children's publishing was also becoming a professionalized industry. New children's and teenage lists were introduced during and after the war. The extension of compulsory schooling meant that there was an increased demand for 'quality' books for children. A slow decline in British people living in poverty during the 1950s meant that there was more money to spend on books, and many children were choosing their own books thanks to the increased availability of cheaper paperback editions. This was spearheaded by Penguin, who in 1941 introduced their Puffin Story Books (the 'chapter book' Puffins that appeared a year after the first Picture Puffins appeared) under the editorship of Eleanor Graham. Cheap and accessible paperbacks, drawn from books published in hardback elsewhere, made reading available to a new generation of children; this would only increase in the 1960s when the Puffin Club, which advertised and promoted reading through a magazine and activities for club members, began. Linda Lloyd Jones argues that Kaye Webb's 'commitment to making reading exciting for children led to the forming of the Puffin Club in 1967. By 1972, one hundred thousand Puffineers had been enrolled' (Lloyd Jones, 1985: 71).

Yet Puffins, and many of the other new paperback imprints that sprung up in the 1960s, including Armada and Fontana Lions, were still aimed very specifically at middle-class, white children. Leila Berg talks about how the children's book 'confirms middle-class people in their own human identity' (Berg, 1967), but leaves working-class children feeling alienated. Berg was interested in children's rights, the rights asserted by the UN Declaration as well as the right 'to keep animals and … grow flowers' (Berg, 1964), to play on bomb sites and eat fish and chips. In short, Berg – and a growing number of other writers, including Bob Leeson and Chris Searle – did not feel that childhood should belong only to the middle classes. And part of that childhood was based in their reading, where Berg felt their lives should be reflected. 'Most people', she wrote in 'Moving Towards Self-Government', 'think of progressive education as belonging axiomatically, with fee-paying and generally boarding schools, to the well-to-do' (Berg, 1972: 22). Berg set out, with her writing for adults and children, to create a progressive education that preserved children's rights.

However, although Berg edited and introduced the reading series *Nippers* to Britain (about which I have written in *Children's Publishing and Black Britain*, particularly Chapter 2), she extended children's rights in her *own* children's books to working-class white children only. Like many liberal white activists of the time, Berg championed the rights of all children – including children of colour – as her attempt to find Black British writers for *Nippers* attests. But she never interacted at length with what was then called the 'West Indian' community, and did not attempt to speak for them. Thus, Black characters in Berg-authored *Nippers* were visible, but only in the background of white working-class family life. They did not have a voice, only a presence.

How to include and advocate for the rights of children of colour as well as white children's rights has long been a dilemma for white liberal writers. Berg's solution, to include Black characters visibly in her own writing but to find Black writers to speak about their specific needs, is rooted in her desire for all children to have the right to a voice. The idea of the voice of the child, representing their own experiences, was very much a concern in the educational community at the time, and continues to be so today. Connie and Harold Rosen commented in *The Language of Primary School Children* that, 'Children's language emerges from the lives they lead and we cannot hope to make sense of it without understanding their lives' (1973: 21). Many advocated listening to young children's conversation and basing reading and writing programmes around their experiences, as in the Breakthrough series edited by David McKay, Brian Thompson and Pamela Schaub. Other white British activists and writers for children solved this problem of representation in different ways, and the remainder of this chapter will examine different approaches to advocating for Black children's rights in British children's fiction.

The voice of the Cockney Sparrows

Like Leila Berg, Chris Searle was white British, interested in education, and advocated for children's rights through his teaching and his writing about education. He and Berg did not agree about methods; Berg wanted to break down the system of compulsory state education to let children create their own learning and complained that Searle's 'teaching is based, like the teaching of any Tory teacher at any state school, on different levels of coercion' (Searle, 1998: 89). Her concern arose from the fact that Searle did not leave children to do their own investigations, but directed their learning (as he would have been required to do in any state school). His response was that,

> An understanding of our history – as long as it is *our* history, the history of the ordinary people of this world and all its struggling communities – gives us a secure confidence that just as those who came before could act to make things better, in conditions that were harder, more fraught and challenging, then so can we now. (Searle, 1998: 91)

Searle encouraged his students to make their own stories part of 'our history'. His ideas about education may not have been radical enough for Berg, but they were certainly too radical for the school governors where he worked in Stepney; Searle was fired from his teaching job in 1971 for embracing the 'history of the ordinary people' and insisting on publishing his students' poetry that reflected those histories. *Stepney Words* (1971), the collection that Searle created from his students' poetry about the surrounding area, was condemned by the school governors. Searle commented, 'These governors did not want the children to write about the real world. As I said later, they wanted the cockney sparrow to sing cheerfully from his cage' (2017: 66). It was perhaps the version of the real world to which the governors objected, which described poverty and racism in the local area.

Searle's use of the term 'cockney' might suggest that he, like Berg, was more focused on the white Briton than the Black or Asian Briton. It is true that for Searle, race was not the main focus. As a committed communist, Searle sought an end to class hierarchies that divided his students from access to education and opportunity, as well as from each other. For him, class was a bigger barrier than racism, raising a question about whether or not Searle, as a white activist, really understood just how 'hard, fraught and challenging' the lives of his Black and Asian British students were. They were faced with, not just education discrimination and poverty (as were the white working-class students), but housing and employment discrimination and police oppression as well. In *This New Season* (1973), which contains poems from *Stepney Words* and the follow-up collection, *Fire Words* (1972), Searle writes, 'Although for our self-respect we must accept and affirm our race, black or white, it is imperative that we more strongly and committedly affirm our class loyalties together, black and white workers. It is the strongest social factor that unites us' (Searle, 1973a: 83). Focusing on class rather than race had specific ramifications for Searle's publishing projects and how he viewed both race and children's rights.

An emphasis on class did not mean that Searle ignored race entirely. He spent time before coming to Stepney teaching in the former British colony of Tobago, and wrote about the negative effects of colonialism that he saw in Caribbean education on Black identities. He saw how racism affected his students, both Black and white, every day, calling it 'one of the most effective demobilisers of our strength, unity and capacity to defeat our common enemies' (Searle, 1986: 52). For Searle, racism was a tool used by institutions to divide the working-classes and keep them from unified protest. 'The differences between races are normally created by outside social pressures forced upon the working-class: unemployment, bad housing, low wages, failure and impotence of the 'race relations industry', and historical bigotries and dominations' (Searle, 1973a: 83). In order to eradicate racism, Searle believed that all working-class voices had to be heard – including that of the racist. Racist comments by white children were evidence of the success of the leisured classes in sowing working-class division. Therefore, on the same page, Searle can publish a young person's poem entitled 'Racial Harmony' that doubts its possibility, commenting that 'Illegal entries to this country from India and/Pakistan, disgust me' (Searle, 1973b: 40), and another young writer's poem that suggests people should treat the immigrant 'like you/Treat your mother' (1973b: 40). Searle believed that allowing the child an unedited, a literally 'un-adult-erated' voice, would 'build a unity and comradeship' (Searle, 1986: 52) that would bridge the gulf of racism and allow for a working-class revolution.

Searle's early books of young people's poetry were successful, although not necessarily for the young writers. The young illustrator for the second collection featured in a BBC documentary entitled 'Born to Fail?' in 1974, in which he attempted to remain an artist after having left school (Searle, 2017: 75). Searle sees his story as a success, but it is success on a limited scale: Searle describes him as 'a teacher of art' (2017: 75), but the programme shows him teaching only members of his own family. There is little evidence of any child poets published in *Stepney Words* going on to writing careers. *Stepney Words* received extensive media coverage, and though not all of it was favourable, it did help sell books. After the initial print run produced by Searle ran out, local community publisher Centerprise published the first two collections in a single volume in 1973, in an edition that sold 5,500 copies. The *Times Literary Supplement* praised *Fire Words* (the volume that followed *Stepney Words* and was later published with it) for 'The children's sense of social injustice' ('Poetry for Children', 1972: 1329) but also wonders, 'how much of this is editorial policy' (1972: 1329). There is a lingering concern in many of the reviews that, while the voices of the students were authentic, it was Searle who directed the ideas behind their poetry, and thus the benefit for them in having their voices expressed was minimal. This sense that Searle as editor was benefiting more than his students only increased over time.

For Searle, the success of *Stepney Words* and the media attention that it brought him emboldened him to do more. His next anthology, *Classrooms of Resistance* (1975) was less about the local area and more about the world in which the students lived. They showcased Searle's teaching methods which, as he describes them, are about giving students 'the knowledge of resistance to, and organisation against exploitation and subjection, and contact and empathy with the oppressed of the world, whether in your own street or lands or oceans away' (Searle, 1975: 9). Focusing on current events, Searle taught the students about exploitation or violence – from the opening of a luxury hotel in their area when local residents were waiting to be rehoused, to the coup d'état in Chile in 1973 that put Pinochet in power. He then had them write response pieces – sometimes poetry, sometimes plays, sometimes essays – that were anthologized in the book. But the children's voices heard in *Classrooms of Resistance* are not the varied voices of *Stepney Words*. There are no National Front viewpoints, for example, in the section on South Africa. Andrew Retter, aged fourteen, imagines himself a Black South African who witnesses the Carletonville Massacre in which eleven Black miners were shot during a strike for higher wages. Searle suggests that 'The sympathies and solidarity of the children went out in their writing directly to the oppressed, breaking through the false barriers of race and nationalism' (1975: 59). Andrew's response is almost gleeful in its violence: 'While I was in jail I had to blow up some of the boulders from the sides of the mountains, now I blow up buildings … Once we blacks have overthrown the white men we shall make them work on the same pay and conditions we have had to bear with' (1975: 62). There is a sense of vengeance in these poems which Searle sees as solidarity. Other people were not so quick to believe that the children's voices were their own; the right-wing columnist for the *Daily Telegraph*, Peter Simple, commented sarcastically that the work in *Classrooms of Resistance* was 'all produced with stimulated spontaneity by these keen working-class child students of world politics' (Simple, 1975: 14). He called for an end to the 'systematic indoctrination of our children' (1975: 14). And John Izbicki, also in *The Telegraph*, argues that 'Nowhere in [*Classrooms of Resistance*] is there the faintest ray of pleasure or of the innocence of a child's humour' (Izbicki, 1976: 14). While the school governors had merely complained about the negative view of life produced by Searle's students, the media was more concerned about 'condemnation of the police, the British Army in Ulster, apartheid, and the rich in general' (Worsthorne, 1975: 18) in *Classrooms of Resistance*. The concern that Searle was teaching anti-authoritarianism was often couched in the idea that the students' voices were inauthentic – or were authentically Searle's alone.

More importantly, *Stepney Words* led to Searle's own move into publishing (and away from teaching) at a higher level. The communist publishing company, Liberation, and its white journal editor Kay Beauchamp, decided in

1980 to set up a children's book imprint following a successful 'Education for Multicultural Society' project. Beauchamp had been involved with anti-racist activity for decades. In 1973, she produced a pamphlet for the communist party entitled *Black Citizens* in which she argued that Black people required the help of the white-working-class: 'black workers have to face the fact that they cannot win alone. They cannot alone destroy capitalism and win socialism ... this can only be achieved through joint united struggle of all workers, black and white' (Beauchamp, 1973: 13). She played a part in organizing the Red Lion Square demonstrations in 1974 against a National Front gathering. During the march, a 21-year-old student was killed (at the time, the left-wing groups felt that he had died as the result of police brutality, though this has never been proved). Beauchamp testified at the subsequent inquiry, run by Lord Scarman, that she hadn't expected violence (Rowan, 1974: 7). The incident clearly affected her over the rest of her life and influenced her education projects especially. In 1979, she produced a pamphlet entitled 'One Race, the Human Race' in which she wrote about her hopes for schools to play a role in breaking down racism through the teaching of history. 'Schools need to include black history in their courses, not just so that we can know what really happened, but also so that white people understand the dangers of imperialism and racism' (Beauchamp, 1979: 6), she wrote. Critically, although maintaining an anti-racist stance, Beauchamp centralizes the needs of white readers over Black readers.

But like many anti-racist activists of the time, Beauchamp didn't like the literature that was available for children – so she set up her own imprint with the help of Chris Searle, who had the previous year published *Beyond the Skin*, a pamphlet on anti-racism in Mozambique with Liberation, in which he described racism as 'an ideology coming to justify a reality already accomplished ... as capitalism evolved and transforms itself into imperialism ... racism became the main ideological weapon of imperialism' (Searle, 1979: 9). Beauchamp was interested in transforming Searle's vision into one that children could understand. Describing the reasons for doing this in a grant application to the Greater London Council, Beauchamp wrote,

> We believe that one of the reasons for the underachievement of some sections of black people is that they are presented with images of children and young people in Africa and the Caribbean as inferior to white people,

both in text books and in fiction. We have deliberately set out to counter this. (Beauchamp, 1985–6: 2)

Underachievement is not connected with institutional Britain, but with images and books set outside of Britain. Initially, Young World produced stories from and about Africa and the Caribbean, particularly from regions where revolution and anti-imperial activities were taking place. Searle's earliest contribution for the press was *Tales of Mozambique* (1980), a book singled out for recognition by the Other Award, which celebrated work that highlighted issues of race, class and gender.[2] Beauchamp notes that the book 'was sold out for two years until an order from the ILEA enabled us to reprint it' (1985–6: 3). Clearly there was a market for books which portrayed racial struggle and racial strife outside of Britain, but like Leila Berg's *Nippers*, Young World's early publications shied away from depicting Black experience in Britain.

While *Tales of Mozambique* is about anti-racism and anti-imperialism in Africa, Searle would return to anti-racism in Britain with Young World in 1984, when (in cooperation with the Greater London Council) Searle organized a competition for London school students to write poems on the theme of 'our city' for the GLC's Year Against Racism. The poetry was judged by Searle, the Black British sociologist, documentary film-maker Colin Prescod and the African writer Ngugi Wa Thiong'o. Although the poems could be on any aspect of London, Beauchamp did assure the GLC's cultural committee, from whom Young World received a grant, that 'We shall stress the anti-racist content in the book' (Beauchamp, 1984). Searle, in his preface, does highlight the theme of racism, but only as one of several themes:

> The poems, in truth, organised themselves around such critical themes as were conceived by the poets to be the signal issues of the times in their city: the decay of urban infrastructures, the contrasts of wealth and poverty, racism and the struggle to eradicate it, crime and its relationship to unemployment, housing, the need for world peace. (Searle, 1984: 5)

Notably, racism comes third in Searle's list, and is surrounded on both sides by class issues. This contrasts with Ngugi Wa Thiong'o's introduction, which suggests that 'The London that emerges from these poems ... is full of people

---

[2] I discuss the Other Award in more detail later, when I focus on its founder Rosemary Stones.

struggling against degrading living conditions, against pollution, against harsh conditions imposed on them by others, and *above all against fascist and police terror*' (Searle, 1984: 7; italics mine). While anti-racist activity both within and without the institutional government is of prime importance to Thiong'o, Searle focuses on class issues as well as the unity across different groups struggling to eradicate racism, writing of a generation 'expressing the will for unity and action' (1984: 6) to solve the difficult problems. Black and Asian Britons, in Searle's vision, need to unite with white people and fight in the class struggle to free all Britons. The unique struggles of being British and Black or Asian are decentralized in favour of (white) Britons' need to restructure the economic system.

This side-lining of Black and Asian Britons' concerns accords with the general attitude of the British Communist Party. When they held a conference entitled *Black and Blue: Racism and the Police* (Cook and Rabstein) in 1981, several Black scholars and activists told them to listen to Black communities: Stuart Hall, in 'Policing the Police' argued that 'If you allow the police the kind of latitude which you have permitted in the black areas, they will come into your parish too' (Hall, 1981: 10); Dorothy Kuya took them to task for 'the lack of response' to 'our feelings and our experience' (Kuya, 1981: 18). But the 'Charter of Demands' (Cook, 1981: 28–32) created by the white conference organizers focused only on the negative actions of the police, not the white communists. Evan Smith, in *British Communism and the Politics of Race* said that Black activists rightly criticized the BCP for 'forgetting about the problems of Britain's Black communities' (2018: 253), particularly after the New Cross Fire, a fire in which thirteen young people died. The protests which followed were attended by many sectors of the Black community, but the BCP did not have an organized presence.

Our City was a book, like most of the Young World publications, produced mostly for a school market. Beauchamp noted that by 1985, 'More than fifty schools have now ordered copies of it' (Beauchamp, 1985–6: 3). These schools were mostly in London, and were purchased through the ILEA. But although the book succeeded in reaching school children in the 1980s through the ILEA, it was also to play a part in the ILEA's downfall. Like the anti-racist texts of A. Sivanandan (see Chapter 4), Young World's publications were part of the dangerous reading material brought up in Parliament as one of the reasons for abolishing the ILEA. In March 1988, conservative MP for Battersea John Bowis complained that Labour leader Neil Kinnock 'has been supporting books by the Marxist organisation Liberation for use in London's schools' ('Abolition of ILEA', 28 March 1988' Volume 130, Column 763). The push for the abolition of the ILEA was led by the conservative government, but also the popular press – particularly the *Daily Mail*, who reported two days earlier that Lady Olga Maitland, the coordinator of a group called Schoolwatch, had called for *Our City* and other books published by Young World to be withdrawn because, 'They are an absolute disgrace ... They are totally biased and undermine every aspect of authority' (Neil Thompson, 1988: 3). Searle continued to champion children's poetry, but it is perhaps significant that his last publication with Young World came in 1989, a ten-year anniversary tribute to the teacher (and Searle's friend) Blair Peach, who had been killed by police at an anti-racist rally in 1979. The collection contains poems ranging on topics from racist murders to education to the dignity of work and the beauty of nature and includes Black poets such as John Agard, Linton Kwesi Johnson, Merle Collins and white poets including Mike Rosen, Adrian Mitchell and Searle himself. Searle comments that the poems 'share a common inspiration that stretches to all humanity in every part of the world' (Searle, 1989: v) because 'Blair's devotion was to the classroom, but the classroom of the world' (1989: ix). As with *Our City*, Searle's introduction focuses more on the universal qualities of both humanity and childhood, but his selection tries to teach children rather than celebrate their voices. Unlike his other anthologies for Young World, *One for Blair* (1989) was an anthology of poems *for* young people, not by them.

The art of anti-racism

Chris Searle did note Blair Peach's commitment to anti-racism, arguing in *One for Blair* that 'What concerned Blair Peach more than anything was the growth in organised racism in East London all through the seventies. He didn't just speak out ... he organised against their poison' (Searle, 1989: vii). Blair Peach was well-known to another East End activist, the illustrator Dan Jones, who joined Peach on many anti-racist marches and protests. Like Peach, Jones organized against racists in a variety of ways. He grew up valuing both art and activism. His mother was the artist and children's book illustrator, Pearl Binder, and his father Elwyn Jones founded Amnesty International when Jones was a young man. But whereas his father built up an organization concerned with global injustice, Dan Jones focused very much on his own local community. As a youth worker, he hosted dances and events for the multiracial young people who lived in and around Stepney. And he tried to keep them out of trouble with the police. This aspect of Jones's life is depicted in the 1973 'Tunde's Film' by eighteen-year-old film-maker Tunde Ikoli, for which Jones created the opening credits made up of busy, vibrant paintings of the East End that would become his trademark. Ikoli's film portrays Jones as a concerned but hapless white liberal, whose artwork can encompass the Black and Asian British experience but who cannot keep Tunde and his friends from being beaten up by the police. In the film, Jones tries to get the young Black youth to follow the rules; they agree when Jones asks them to call it a night at the community centre, but refuse to allow the police to push them around.

In real life, while Jones marched and protested against fascists and skinheads who regularly invaded the East End, his work with children and young people tended – as in 'Tunde's Film' – to follow the lead of young people. He became a collector of their rhymes, from Bengali versions of Twinkle, Twinkle Little Star (Gentle Author, 2010) to rhymes that 'use the tune of the pop group Aqua's Barbie Girl' (Thorpe, 2007). Jones deliberately 'squashes any comparison with the revered royal couple of children's folklore, Iona and Peter Opie' (Ward, 2007), partly because he does not claim to be a scholar. But his collection, much of which is now catalogued in the British Library, allows children a voice without censorship; he collects from all children and about any subject that they care to share with him.

Jones's refusal to be the authority, instead giving children that role, has caused some controversy particularly connected with the struggles between youth of colour and the police. When Jones's 1977 mural of East End school children and their rhymes was displayed at Bethnal Green Museum of Childhood, some complained that his inclusion of a rhyme about wanting to attack the police, 'Cop, Cop, Copper', was 'turning East End youth against the police force' (Gentle Author, 2012; the mural itself can also be viewed here). But Jones knew that the Black and Bangladeshi youth in his neighbourhood were regularly attacked by the fascist National Front, and when he tried to help, he would arrive 'to find angry Bengali victims standing amongst the broken glass, the police often "did nothing", he said, "Or it was the victims who ended up getting arrested"' (Fuscoe, 2020). Jones included a version of the mural as endpapers to the nursery rhyme collection *Mother Goose Comes to Cable Street* (edited by Rosemary Stones and Andrew Mann in 1977); the book version also includes the 'Cop, Cop, Copper' rhyme. But whereas the public mural has three children, two white and one Black, pointing offstage (presumably towards the copper on the corner), the book version moves the rhyme further from the edge of the painting, next to four children playing a game of 'chicken' (where a smaller child is held on the shoulders of a bigger child, and the smaller child fights another small child in a similar pair). In this case, the rhyme is next to a pair of Black children. The smaller Black child has his hands up while across from him, a white child on top of another white child prepares to punch him. Given the publication of *Mother Goose Comes to Cable Street* during a time of increased tension with the police, Jones's depiction of the children makes a political statement about what Eddie Chambers in *Roots and Culture* called the 'mutual hostility and antagonism between youth in the Black community and the uniformed agents of the law whose policing of these youth was openly unfair, aggressive and deeply racist' (Chambers, 2017: 159). Actual police are rarely depicted in *Mother Goose*, but there are two instances when the police are focused on Black youth. In 'Little Tommy Tittlemouse' a lone Black boy is fishing and a white policeman across the canal is shaking his fist at the boy (Stones and Mann, 1977); and in 'One misty, moisty morning' a march of predominantly white dockworkers is going on, but the policeman on his motorcycle is eyeing a lone Black boy who is not part of the march, and is tipping his hat politely to the police. The sense of constant surveillance of Black youth and the threat of violence against them by the police is a theme that runs throughout the book's illustrations, although most of the rhymes' texts do not indicate police involvement in any way.

Jones not only depicted the surveillance by police, he was increasingly sympathetic to the attempts of Black youth to assert their identity in an age when Black expressions of identity were seen by institutions as political. The politics of Black British hair and clothing, for example, became an issue in the 1970s with the rise of Rastafarianism and Black Power movements. Paul Gilroy, in *There Ain't No Black in the Union Jack* quotes from the 1981 Scarman report. Lord

Scarman led the inquiry into the 1981 Brixton riots; Scarman suggested that 'young hooligans' (Gilroy, 1987 [2005]: 135) had appropriated the symbols of the Rastafarian religion, 'the dreadlocks, the headgear and the colours' (1987 [2005]: 135) to excuse their destructive behaviour. Scarman was not the only one to believe that dreadlocks were associated with criminality; Sally Tomlinson, in *Race and Education*, points out that schools debated whether or not to ban dreadlocks (2008: 49) in the late 1970s and early 1980s. A young person's hair and dress were not simply reminders of a (possibly negative, possibly positive, depending on your point of view) past history, but a political and particularly anti-authoritarian statement, one that faced censure from official government institutions such as the police and the schools. In Jones's follow-up to *Mother Goose Comes to Cable Street*, *Inky Pinky Ponky* (edited by Michael Rosen and Susannah Steele in 1982 [1990]), Jones showcases several children with Rastafarian tams of green, gold and red, and Black children with locs. These children often are shown interacting with the police, and although the same is true for white people in the book, the end result is different for Black children. A double-page spread in the middle of the book demonstrates this clearly. On the left-hand side is the poem, 'Don't go to granny's' (Rosen and Steele, 1982 [1990]); the reason not to go to granny's is that 'There's a great big copper' waiting there. The picture by Jones shows a white child in a cowboy outfit being held by a policeman. On the right-hand side of the page is 'I'm a little bumper car' (1982 [1990]); the accompanying illustration has a child with dreadlocks riding in a bumper car and being confronted by the police. However, whereas the white child, according to the rhyme, will get off with a fine (or possibly a bribe) – the policeman will 'charge you half a dollar' (1982 [1990]) – the Black child is jailed for drinking 'a small ginger ale' (1982 [1990]). Jones uses the texts chosen by Rosen and Steele (and earlier, by Stones and Mann) to portray the unequal treatment by the police towards Black youth, despite the harmonious multiracial community of the East End of London.

A feminist anti-racism

At the same time that Dan Jones was looking out for the youth of Stepney and Chris Searle was working with multicultural classrooms there, another educational activist was advocating for the rights of another group of children: girls. In 1974, a group of parents in London set up the Children's Rights Workshop to help other parents find – and, when they couldn't find, *found* their own – free schools. Free schools were community-based centres for education, outside the mainstream system, that focused on child-centred education and connections to the local surroundings. The Children's Rights Workshop was set up to address 'the need for information on Free Schools and alternative education generally (*Children's Rights Workshop Newsletter* no. 1, 1974: 15). However, in addition to advice (legal and practical) about Free Schools, the workshop had several other working groups, including one on children's books. 'The Book Project of the Children's Rights Workshop has been under way since September 1973 when we first compared notes and ideas with a number of other groups who had been looking at the portrayal of women in children's literature' (1974: 17). The Book Group had as one of its instrumental members a feminist campaigner for children's rights: Rosemary Stones, who was the children's book buyer for the Hackney community organization Centerprise.

By the time the first newsletter was published, the group had already published a pamphlet on 'Sexist Stereotypes in Children's Books: A List of Principal References and Contacts' which was designed to 'coincide with a picket of a children's book exhibition for teachers' (*Newsletter*, 1974: 17). The group had wider aims than sexism; the newsletter goes on to comment that 'Together with other British groups, we are currently approaching publishers and librarians about the sexist, racist and class bias of most children's books' (1974: 17). The Children's Rights Workshop had already had an impact; Bob Leeson, the book editor for the *Morning Star* wrote in September of 1974 that 'There are a number of groups, like Children's Rights Workshop, critically concerned with class, sex and racial bias in children's books, and their reception (in public) by the trade industry has not been friendly' (Leeson, 1974a: 4).

But although they published material on sexism early in the group's history, their work on racism was initially more limited. In order 'to encourage the development of a critical approach to children's literature that can confidently rely on social as well as aesthetic criteria' (*Newsletter*, 1974: 17), the group started 'actively importing and distributing the best foreign material in the field, in particular the publications of the Council on Interracial Books for

Children (U.S.A.)' (1974: 17). The Council on Interracial Books for Children (CIBC), directed by Bradford Chambers, was a radical American group who argued that 'The children's book publishing industry's loyalty to the white middle class is largely based on financial considerations ... most white parents who buy children's books are subconsciously committed to myths of white superiority and black inferiority' (Paul Cornelius, 1971: 112). They published essays, which the Children's Rights Workshop reprinted, about classic children's books with racist attitudes, including British children's literature like *The Adventures of Doctor Dolittle* (1920) and *Charlie and the Chocolate Factory* (1964). Just as many white publishers argued that racism was an American problem, the Children's Rights Workshop saw the solution as being led by Americans as well.

That the Children's Rights Workshop created their own material on feminism but had to 'import' critical approaches on race from the Unites States is not surprising. Many white Britons remained largely unaware of the good work that Black Britons were doing to promote positive depictions of Black people in children's literature. Mainstream publishing houses continued to import American children's books, such as *The Snowy Day* (1962) by white American Ezra Jack Keats or *To Be a Slave* (1968) by African-American Julius Lester, rather than support Black British writers, and many cultural commentators saw Black empowerment movements as being responses to the American civil rights movements and racial unrest rather than originating from Black British-specific concerns (see Chapter 4). Even Rosemary Stones, whose efforts to focus on racism meant examining British books closely, argued that Americans did it better: 'United States publishers appear much more sensitive than their British counterparts. Their insistence that biased passages in British children's books they wish to buy for the American market be omitted or altered is seen here as little more than an irritating eccentricity' (Stones, 1979a: 83–4). For white Britons, racism was an imported concern (this is still true to some extent; see Chapter 5 for more on this) while classism and sexism were basic and endemic to British society. This tended to make racism something of an 'add-on' to white scholarship about sexism and classism, and side-lined Black British concerns about lack of reading material for Black children.

Rosemary Stones spent most of the 1970s and early 1980s as an activist scholar writing for teachers and librarians in publications like *Where: The*

Education Magazine for Parents and *Children's Book Bulletin*, which she founded with Andrew Mann. In 1980, she launched the journal *Books for Keeps*, also aimed at teachers. Girls' rights were her major concern, something which becomes clear even in her writing about embracing non-racially biased children's literature. For example, in 'Radically Revised Reading Schemes?' which she wrote for *Children's Book Bulletin* in 1981, she discusses racist and sexist depictions in Ladybird and Breakthrough reading schemes, and attempts that the two publishers had made to improve their books. One of the rare Breakthrough titles that Stones praises from the original, unrevised series is *the wendy house* (1970; capitalization in original) by David Mackay, Brian Thompson and Pamela Schaub with illustrations by Kenneth Brooks. Stones calls it a 'sensitively told, amusing non-sexist' story (Stones, 1981: 4) that portrays 'a girl and a boy inviting children to tea and then clearing up after them. Domestic tasks are shared' (1981: 4). This may be the case, but Stones's analysis leaves out the fact that the one child of colour in the story is consistently sidelined or absent from the action. Additionally, in book reviews for *Children's Book Bulletin* Stones speaks up for white women in books by writers of colour, commenting for example that Farrukh Dhondy's *Siege of Babylon* was 'marred by its sexist depiction of the white women' (Stones, 1979c: 23), and she and Mann praise the changes made to US versions of Petronella Breinburg's *Doctor Sean* 'for the alert US market with the qualification of the sexist assumptions' (Stones and Mann, 1980: 3). Sexism, for Stones, often trumped racism, just as class trumped racism for Searle. The press would sometimes use this hierarchy to portray white feminists and anti-racists as opposing forces, as in Andrew Purvis's article 'Book Boat' which praises Petronella Breinburg's *Sean's Red Bike* as 'highly recommended by "thinking" educationalists and anti-racist groups' (Purvis, 1986: 62) before being 'seized upon by one LEA stormtrooper because of its outrageous sexism' (1986: 62). While feminists and anti-racists often had different concerns, it was rarely an either/or proposition.

Indeed, as with Searle, Stones did not ignore racism. She made a sincere effort to help eradicate it from children's books through her critical scholarship, even if her discussion of racism is sometimes limited in scope and lacking in nuance. Thus, while she might focus on white British girls in *'Pour Out the Cocoa, Janet': Sexism in Children's Books*, a 1983 publication for the Schools Council, she does, in her list of 'Questions to ask about children's books', include a section on 'Sex roles in other cultures and in British ethnic minorities' (Stones, 1983: 22). Her examples, however, are from books that discuss African cultures (in Africa) and not Black British characters.

Perhaps Stones's most important contribution as a critic of children's books was her establishment, with Andrew Mann, of the Other Award in 1975, an award designed to promote books that presented an anti-racist, anti-sexist and anti-classist world to child readers, and as a direct provocation to awards like the Carnegie Medal. The Carnegie and Kate Greenaway medals were offered by the Library Association, and in Andrew Mann's view, favoured the '"social consensus" so sought after by the middle classes' (Mann, 1975: 143). Although in the criteria that Mann and Stones and their fellow Children's Rights Workshop members came up with, 'literary merit' is still a focus, it is an inclusive literary merit that considered social concerns and marginalized people. And even though anti-racism is the last of these concerns (the sixth out of six criteria), the award itself was notable, not only for recognizing anti-racist children's books, but also for highlighting authors of colour. The first awards included two that featured Black British characters, although the books were written by white authors; but in 1976, the award went to Farrukh Dhondy, an Indian-born teacher who wrote about multiracial London in his book of short stories, *East End at Your Feet* (1976). The Other Award would continue to recognize children's books with anti-racist depictions (including Chris Searles's *Tales of Mozambique* and his Young World Press) for thirteen years, when, as Stones put it, 'We no longer think an award is an appropriate way to promote "other" concerns' (1988b: 53). The Carnegie Medal had, over the thirteen years of the Other Award, gone to books that met the Other Award's criteria. Gene Kemp's *The Turbulent Term of Tyke Tiler* (1977) was hailed as a feminist classic because the book did not reveal Tyke's gender until the book's end. Both Peter Dickinson's *Tulku* (1979) and Susan Price's *The Ghost Drum* (1987) featured characters of colour. Significantly, Stones and Mann saw their work as having succeeded by 1988. But while the 'feminist' winner of the Carnegie was written by a British woman, the 'anti-racist' winners of the Carnegie were about non-British subjects, and were created by white writers. Racism and racial concerns, remained largely 'other', outside of Britain and outside of Black British or British Asian children's experiences despite the Other Award.

Near the end of the Other Award period, Stones began publishing her own works for children and young people, sometimes as an editor and sometimes as sole author. In Stones's own publications for children, it is possible to see the changes – and the continuing blind-spots – in her thinking as she began to consider racial issues along with feminist ones. A case in point is the interaction between her edited collections *More to Life than Mr Right: Stories for Young Feminists* (1985) and *Someday My Prince Won't Come: More Stories for Young Feminists* (1988c) and her nonfiction guides, *Too Close Encounters and What to Do About Them* (1987) and *Loving Encounters* (1988a). Both fiction collections and non-fiction guides are feminist by nature, and both include voices from many different British communities.

More to Life than Mr Right contains two short stories by Londoners of colour involved in community publishing projects. Ravi Randhawa, the author of 'India', was the coordinator of the Asian Women Writers' Workshop, and Stella Ibekwe, originally from Nigeria, published 'Everybody Else Does It' with Centerprise before Stones included it in her collection. Randhawa, like Stones, was interested in feminist causes, and helped to set up one of the first women's shelters for Asian domestic abuse victims (Randhawa, 2020). The Asian Women Writers' Collective that she also helped found had an unusually broad (for the time) anti-discrimination policy that opposed 'writings and attitudes which are racist, sexist, or communalist, or are oppressive to others on the grounds of sexuality or disability' ('Asian Women's Writers Collective', 1989). Ibekwe's story was written when she was a teenager, and published as part of *Teenage Encounters* in 1978 by the Centerprise Writers Workshop, which supported young writers through workshops and in poetry collections like *Talking Blues* (1976). Stones worked in Centerprise's community bookshop, and likely came across several young writers and their work there, but Ibekwe's collection of short stories was also reviewed by Stones and Mann's journal, *Children's Book Bulletin*, in Autumn of 1979. Reviewers Maggie Hewitt, Neil Martinson and Jean Milloy write that Ibekwe's work is 'Very entertaining and full of humour [and] many stories have a twist at the end which leaves the reader with a lot to think about' (1979: 10). It was not uncommon in the 1970s and 1980s for larger publishers to mine community and independent presses for talent; the poet Grace Nichols first published her short story 'Babyfish' with Islington Community Press in 1983 before Ladybird picked it up and Lorraine Simeon's

Marcellus, about a boy with dreadlocks being nervous about his first day at school, was initially produced by the Peckham Publishing Project in 1984 before it was reproduced with new illustrations by Writers and Readers. But in the move from independent publisher to more mainstream publisher, changes in the original text often occur. While in most cases, it is unclear who initiates the changes, author or publisher, they are often made to suit a presumed-to-be-white reading audience. For example, Grace Nichols's original version of 'Babyfish' included mild patois words and phrases that were removed in the Ladybird edition. Surprisingly, Stones reprinted Ibekwe's story almost word for word when she published it, only adjusting the grammar slightly in a few spaces.

Stones's experience of editing *More to Life* affected her own writing for young people. In her guide on how to deal with unwanted sexual encounters, *Too Close Encounters and What to Do About Them*, Stones gave voice to teen fears and concerns. Sometimes these were presumed fears and concerns, but often Stones included quotations from teenagers as well. The names of the teenagers (including Parminder and Ravi) indicate that Stones did her best to include the voices of teenagers of colour. But although her book welcomes in readers from all backgrounds, none of the quotations directly address unwanted sexual encounters that intersect with racial expectations or stereotypes, and no section addresses religious responses to sexual behaviour (presumed or actual) or sexual assault. In her follow-up book, *Loving Encounters: A Book for Teenagers about Sex*, the lack of discussion of racial and cultural issues is even more pronounced. All the illustrations are of white people, and Stones celebrates a permissive society that allows young people to express their sexuality without any commentary on how racism or cultural values might impinge upon this sexual freedom. Natalie Thomlinson, in *Race, Ethnicity and the Women's Movement*, comments that 'British Black feminists argued that many of the critiques of patriarchy so long clung to by white feminists could not translate on to the realities of Black women's lives precisely because of the effect that racism had on their lives' (Thomlinson, 2016: 2). Sexual permissiveness, for many groups of British women, did not equal freedom.

Stones's feminism is ultimately uncomplicated. She does not discuss relationships that cross racial lines and the questions or concerns that might arise from racial differences. She writes that the new freedom has 'not come about by magic, but by years of brave campaigning by social reformers; in recent years the tenacity and determination of groups from the Women's Movement have been particularly important' (1988a: 47) but there is little indication that women of colour have played a role in this universalizing statement. In fact, deliberate racism in children's books is a non-issue for Stones; she and Andrew Mann editorialize in 'Are Children's Books in Britain Still Racist?' that 'We at Children's Rights Workshop believe that British children's book writers, illustrators and publishers are in general anti-racists of good will and that continuing manifestations of racial bias in children's books are therefore inadvertent – the result of a lack of understanding about the nature of racial bias in literature, a reluctance to confront white racism' (Stones and Mann, 1979: 3). Hazel Carby, in 'White Woman, Listen! Black Feminism and the Boundaries of Sisterhood', had brought up the difficulties of interaction between white and Black feminism as early as 1982. Carby wrote that, 'Feminist theory in Britain is almost wholly Eurocentric and, when it is not ignoring the experience of black women "at home", it is trundling "Third World women" onto the stage only to perform as victims' (2009: 451). Feminist issues and racial issues both require addressing, according to Stones, but often her feminism is one that preferences the needs and values of white Britons.

This hierarchy of justice is also evident in Stones's own short story included in the second feminist collection she edited, *Someday My Prince Won't Come: More Stories for Young Feminists*. 'Stilettos' is told from the point of view of a white British girl, Nicki, who works in a shoe shop part time. Her manager is a young Black British woman named Lynette. Stones places the shoe shop near a street market; this allows for market traders to help in the apprehension of thugs who try to rob the shop, but it also gives Stones an opportunity to introduce Nicki's thoughts on racial issues of the day:

> Our shop's just off Mere Street market and there's always some group or other at the end of the market selling their newspapers or handing out leaflets. […] It's … sometimes this black couple from Anti-Apartheid, with their kids, telling you not to buy things from South Africa. I go along with them. I never buy Outspan oranges or grapes. (Stones, 1988c: 9)

Nicki's anti-racism is evident, but it is also tenuous. She goes on to say that she finds it hard to keep up her boycott in the market 'because a lot of the stuff's not labelled and they think you're mad when you ask where it's from' (Stones, 1988c: 9). Additionally, Nicki dislikes it when the protestors are the National Front, and complains that they try to crowd black people off the pavement, but she takes no action to protest the crowding or to aid the people who have been pushed off. Stones introduces anti-racist issues, but following this paragraph these issues disappear and the story returns to one of female empowerment. Although Nicki's manager is Black, there is no discussion about racism she might have faced; Nicki sees and actively supports anti-racist causes only as long as they are far distant (South Africa) and not on her own sidewalk. Racism, for Nicki, is something that happens outside of Britain. This is very different to how many Black British people felt about apartheid. Elizabeth Williams writes that 'the brutality and dehumanisation of the system of apartheid was just a harsher form of the racism black communities faced on a daily basis' (2012: 686). Stones may include Black British characters, but like Nicki, she does not fully commit to anti-racism in her fiction.

Stones continues to portray racial issues with hesitation and some, perhaps unconscious, ambivalence in her later publications. While she generally presents a racially diverse Britain, even at a time when other authors do not, she does not always accept the deep structural racism of British society and how it permeates multiple issues. For example, in her 1998 nonfiction book, *Gangs and Bullies*, Stones includes a section early in the book about 'Racist Bullying'. This section focuses on a Childline Study indicating that 'Of the 430 callers who had experienced racist bullying, more than half had encountered racism within their families, had suffered racist street violence and racism at school from teachers or other school staff' (Stones, 1998: 10). However, the section gives no real-life examples as in other sections of the book; the box below the 'Racist Bullying' section is about a young woman with cerebral palsy who was bullied. While of course bullying towards any individual or group is unacceptable, the placement of this particular example suggests that it is easier to sympathize with disabled white people who are bullied than Black children who are bullied by adults.

This suggestion that racist bullying does not promote a sympathetic reaction in the reader is underscored when, in a section on 'Bullying in Britain', one of the examples listed is that of '13-year-old Mark Perry [who] cycled into the path of an oncoming van after being continually harassed by a group of boys' (Stones, 1998: 28). The incident is not described further, but newspaper accounts of Perry's death suggest that the bullying was race-related. His mother described him as 'coloured' (Warner, 1989: 4) and said that he and his twin sister were often called specific racial epithets. It seems curious that Stones would choose not to include this information (at least in some form), especially as the other example in the section, that of Katherine Bamber, gets her own box on an earlier page where she describes in her suicide note that people called her 'a tart and a slag' (Stones, 1998: 23). Vijay Singh's suicide note is given, but it does not mention racism – just 'names are called' (1998: 20), and Stones's description calls him a 'Thirteen-year-old Mancunian' who 'wanted to be a footballer' (1998: 20). Nothing is mentioned about the bullying being racially motivated, and yet the BBC made a programme in 1997 about Singh's death that focused on the 'reluctance on the part of schools to admit that racially motivated bullying exists' (Waymark, 1997: 46). Stones too seems reluctant to highlight the racial component of being bullied.

On the other hand, her section on 'Gangs and Crime' focuses much attention on race. Stones suggests that Asian gangs were a direct result of 'racial attacks against the Asian community' (Stones, 1998: 44); these gangs initially got together, Stones argues, 'to set up defence groups' (1998: 44). However, the passage immediately continues:

> In recent years with the spread of drug-dealing, more and more gangs have become involved in crime and violence, including those apeing the Chinese triads and the West Indian yardies (criminal gangs). In 1996 London headmaster Philip Lawrence was knifed through the heart when he went to help a pupil attacked by a triad-style gang outside his school. (Stones, 1998: 44)

While Black and Asian victims of racial attacks are not given space in Stones's narrative, white victims of Black and Asian gangs like Philip Lawrence are. In her overall discussion of gangs and bullying, Stones could have included well-reported racial attacks on Black and Asian people. These might have included the racially motivated playground murder of Ahmed Iqbal Ullah in Manchester in 1986 by a racist classmate. Ullah, like Philip Lawrence, was defending a student being racially attacked when he was murdered. Alternatively, she could have mentioned the murder of Stephen Lawrence by five racist thugs in 1993 while he was waiting for a bus. The fact that she does not include these examples, or discuss the racial component of Black and Asian bullying victims, does not suggest Stones is deliberately racist; rather, it suggests the way that British society understood racism and racial attacks in terms of aggressor and victim. John Solomos that the link between Black youth and criminality goes back at least as far as the beginning of the twentieth century (Solomos, 1988: 89), but despite a 1972 report that suggested that Black British and British Asian people were as likely (or unlikely) as white people to be involved in crime, 'The public debate about "mugging" helped to amplify and popularise the perception' (1988: 107) that Black British and British Asian youths were criminals. Stuart Hall et al. (in *Policing the Crisis: Mugging, the State, and Law and Order,* 1978) and Paul Gilroy ('Police and Thieves', 1982) also discuss white British perception that Black British and British Asian youth were perpetrators, rather than victims, of crimes. Stones's understanding of gangs and bullies in Britain is a reflection of this common understanding of race.

Ruth Frankenberg, in *White Women, Race Matters* (1993), discusses her own experiences in the 1980s as a white feminist who 'knew that I had not previously known I was "being racist" and that I had never set out to "be racist". I also knew that these desires and intentions had had little effect on outcomes. I ... was at best failing to challenge racism and, at worst, aiding and abetting it' (Frankenberg, 1993: 520). Bryan, Dadzie and Scafe, in *The Heart of the Race: Black Women's Lives in Britain* (1985) generally avoid criticizing white feminists directly, but are keen to point out that 'For us to campaign for non-sexist textbooks or career guidance, when the racism in those areas has already pre-determined what our daughters could do ... would be a denial of reality' (1985: 59). Feminism without a consideration of the insidious power of structural racism allows white women to ignore the privilege they have that Black and Asian woman don't. As Reni Eddo-Lodge suggests in *Why I'm No Longer Talking to White People About Race* (2017), 'White feminism in itself isn't particularly threatening. It becomes a problem when its ideas dominate – presented as the universal, to be applied to all women. It is a problem, because we consider humanity through the prism of whiteness' (2017: 169). Intersectionality only works when those involved are aware of their privilege and how it affects the choices they make.

Rosemary Stones once wrote that 'Most of the material found to be racist is probably inadvertently so, put out by publishers who are simply not sensitive to racial bias in books, nor indeed to the social consequences of their publishing policies' (1979a: 84). Her forgiving attitude towards publishers concerning racism does not extend to publishers who publish misogynist materials; racism is an accident, but sexism is deliberate. In an article about reading schemes, she points out that 'There can be no doubt that both *Ladybird* and *Breakthrough* were aware of the complaints about sex bias in their schemes voiced by teachers and others and of the specific research carried out' on gender bias (Stones, 1981: 3), but she does not mention any research or pressure on publishers to make them fully aware of racial bias. As an activist, Stones worked tirelessly in her attempts to eradicate misogyny and racism from children's books, and her attempts produced some potent results. However, her push for feminist viewpoints in children's books often unconsciously preferenced white viewpoints and cultural values, to the detriment of Black and Asian Britons.

An eye on history: Robert Leeson

In addition to sexism and racism, Stones and the Children's Rights Workshop were concerned with class as well. The Other Award that Stones and Mann created was, in its first year, given to two books about multiracial friendship (Jean MacGibbon's *Hal* and Dorothy Edwards's *Joe and Timothy Together*) and to Susan Price's story of the 1851 Dudley Miners' Strike, *Twopence a Tub*. Their work promoting working-class issues was praised by the children's book editor of the *Morning Star*, Britain's long-running communist paper. Bob Leeson commended the Children's Rights Workshop in 1974 for being part of a push for change in children's publishing, adding that 'If the children's book publishers can draw the right lessons, the "phenomenal" sales can lead to something much wider. But this means accepting the public as an active, not a passive partner' (Leeson, 1974a: 4). Leeson was invited by Andrew Mann to discuss this 'active partnership' between publishers and book readers at a Children's Rights Workshop summer course in 1975 (Leeson, 1977: 6). The lecture he gave there was later combined with a 1976 piece that Leeson wrote for *Signal* into a Children's Rights Workshop follow-up to *Sexism in Children's Books*, *Children's Books in Class Society*.

Leeson's concern with the working-class stemmed from the idea that they had not been given a voice in literature of any kind. One of his earliest (adult) books, *Strike: A Live History 1887–1971*, gave miners a chance to tell the history of the strikes they had experienced in their own words. Explaining his motivation for compiling the book in his introduction, Leeson comments, 'Strikers do explain themselves and have done for decades in leaflets, pamphlets and booklets, most often to fellow trade unionists. But these works do not find their way into the "official record"' (1973: 14). A similar sentiment is expressed in *Children's Books and Class Society* a few years later, when Leeson writes, 'The working-class majority may figure in children's books, but for the most part have done so as outsiders, not as central figures' (1977: 11–12). Leeson praised the work of groups like the Children's Rights Workshop and Centerprise, but unlike Chris Searle, who was content to publish the voices of working-class people through independent publishing, Leeson wanted to champion those voices in the mainstream, middle-class world of children's publishing. In *Strike*, Leeson had transcribed miners' stories and included them in their entirety, but in his children's literature, he was keen to create stories that could rival middle-class classics. Leeson embraced community publishing and community projects that gave children a voice, including those he helped run. In 1986, he wrote about his local Racial Harmony Committee, who 'invited children from seven to fourteen to write about themselves' (Leeson, 1986: 258). They received nearly 300 entries, 'marvellous stories in words and pictures' (1986: 258) which gave Leeson hope for the future of children's book writing. However, Leeson did not work, as Chris Searle had done, to publish these children's voices, but wrote his own stories for children. This necessitated different approaches to inclusion of working-class voices.

In some ways, Leeson's children's books look back to the past and emulate the elements of middle-class genres that made them successful. However, he also changed them to suit working-class politics. One area that this is evident is in his historical adventure novels. Daphne Kutzer suggests that historical fiction after the Second World War tended to be conservative in its values: 'Nostalgia for a vanished and powerful Britain takes many forms in children's books both during and after World War II, but is most likely to show up in either historical fiction or in fantasy works' (Kutzer, 2000: 129). Leeson agreed, writing in *Children's Books and Class Society*, that historical adventure stories

> Offered a means of confirming in each generation the unconscious acceptance of a certain type of person from a certain background as leader in any aspect of life. The blending of the conventions into a kind of ritual, an assumed background to excitement and adventure in the 'Empire' story, enabled the two most apparently opposed elements, the moralistic and the mindlessly violent, to join together. The muscular upper class heroes and their endless victories over 'lesser breeds without the law' … made for a confident extrovert literature. (Leeson, 1977: 30–1)

Leeson did not *like* these books, but he recognized their success. He tried to use those successful elements – excitement, adventure and child-agency – in his own historical fiction series, beginning with *Maroon Boy* (1974), a series that spanned roughly seventy-five years in the sixteenth and seventeenth centuries. In these books, Leeson gave his own unique perspective on Elizabethan imperial expansion, the slave trade and the English Civil War, but he retained middle-class adventure story elements such as moralistic and violent episodes.

The hero of *Maroon Boy* is Matthew Morten, stubborn and impulsive but also hard-working, loyal and brave. These could be the qualities of any boy's adventure story hero; but unlike the heroes of the novels of G. A. Henty, H. Rider Haggard or W. E. Johns, Morten questions the inherent superiority of the English (particularly the English of the upper classes). As Geoffrey Trease had done successfully in books like *Bows Against the Barons* (1934), Leeson combines elements of the middle-class adventure story with an embrace of working-class politics; but unlike Trease he indicates how these politics do not always intersect comfortably with anti-racism. John Stephens points out in *Language and Ideology* that 'The ideologies implicit in historical fictions are an important dimension, since the socio-cultural values of a writer's period will determine which "universals" are inscribed within the fiction's teleology' (1992: 238), and this is very much the case with Leeson. He creates in Matthew a protagonist who is reluctant to give up the comfortable old ways, even if he disagrees with the values that underpin them – paralleled, for many readers, by the reluctance to accept a new, multiracial society after growing up with the privilege that the British Empire brought white Britons. In many ways,

Matthew is a hesitant rebel; he defies his father and leaves his home because of it, but becomes apprenticed to his father's friend. He does not agree with the trade in enslaved Africans, yet joins a slaving ship as quartermaster – in part to win a fortune that might make him an eligible match for the daughter of one of the ship's investors. On the ship, he befriends the 'blackamoor' who accompanies them, thinking himself the virtuous defender of the weak. Matthew is therefore surprised when, after Satan is whipped and Matthew tries to put palm oil on his wounds, 'Satan spat full in Matthew's face' (Leeson, 1974b: 115). Matthew, and perhaps Leeson's reader as well, expected gratitude and received the opposite.

It is the first time that Matthew must confront his white privilege, and Leeson does not let the reader wonder why Satan spat at the young hero. He continues with Matthew sitting by himself to

> ponder soberly why the black man's hate had sought him—who had wished Satan no harm. Then, in a flash, he recalled the day when the slaves were loaded. Satan had stood in the crowd and watched him – Matthew – number his own people like cattle, shove them, force them to rise, even beating their children. (Leeson, 1974b:115)

Matthew realizes in this segment that as much as he might do individually for one person, he is still complicit in the sale of other humans. In reality, one young boy would not be able to overturn the system, but in typical boys' adventure story fashion, Matthew manages to help all the kidnapped people on board escape. He must pay the cost for betraying what his father calls 'thine own kind' (Leeson, 1974b: 177). In helping the enslaved people escape, he ruins the hope of fortune for the sailors – and the ship's investors, including his former employer (and the employer's daughter whose hand he'd hoped to win). Matthew's father tells him when he arrives home at last,

> Speak not to me of liberty. Thou hast taken too much liberty to thyself. Had no thought for Abraham Combe, that did give thee a place in business and home. Had no thought for Sir Henry Ferrers, a kind patron. Had no thought for shipmates, men with wives and little ones, who waited for a share of that cargo, which thou did wantonly let go. (Leeson, 1974b: 177)

Matthew cannot upset the capitalist system without being also labelled a traitor to his 'race' and his father bids him go back to 'the savages whose good fortune thou cared more for than that of thine own kind' (Leeson, 1974b:177). Matthew tries to remain in England, going to his employer's daughter to ask for her hand, but she tells him that he is 'wilful and violent' (1974b:180) and she would prefer to marry his rival, or no one. Following this, 'Matthew Morten left the tavern and next day went from his native town forever' (1974b: 190), returning to the encampment of maroons in the Caribbean. By acting outside societal rules, Matthew becomes 'mad, bad and dangerous' and cannot be allowed to participate in his own society anymore. Leeson shows that it is possible for white people to reject the status quo and rebel, but not without huge personal costs. Matthew must give up his fortune (he gives it to the families of his fellow sailors), his family and home. He joins the 'others', people of colour outside of Britain and outside of Britishness. While Leeson does offer a different understanding of the hero in historical fiction, it is one that 'rewards' its hero with exile from Britain and its values.

Leeson did not just write historical fiction; indeed, he wrote in multiple genres. Brian Alderson may have called Leeson's historical fiction 'portentous' (1982: 10) and his 1975 *The Third Class Genie* 'lightweight entertainment' (1982: 10), but they both had serious purpose. Alderson wrote, 'For 10 years now Bob Leeson has argued with patience and good humour for children's books which will take account of changes in society and serve as a counterweight to (not a replacement of) the "middle class" literature of times gone by' (1982: 10). The *Maroon Boy* series took account of changes in society by offering an alternative version of historical events that allowed the recently expanded Black British population to see themselves as part of, even heroes in, a history that had long seen them only as victims. In *The Third Class Genie*, Leeson indicated how colonial histories continue to affect the present – and suggested that white Britons needed to examine the ways their everyday actions made them complicit in racism. The book begins with Alec, the protagonist, participating in racist bullying – even though everything else Leeson tells us about Alec is to put the reader in sympathy with him. Alec is presented by Leeson as a victim of disasters: 'Today disasters were away down the field while the other team was still in the changing room' (Leeson, 1975: 7). However, he is happy to let someone else be the victim of Sam Taylor's bullying, and even 'started to snigger' (1975: 7) when Sam makes a racist comment to a new boy in the class. He regrets his sniggering, not because it is wrong, merely because it gets him in trouble with the new boy, who threatens him, and the senior master of his school. Alec is, like Aladdin, the protagonist of the story, who finds a genie to help him with his problems – but he is not the story's hero. Leeson makes Alec sympathetic, but at the same time he must learn how his abuse of white privilege affects others.

The change in Alec's behaviour is affected through the person (rather than the power) of the genie in Leeson's book. Abu Salem, a 'third rank genie' (Leeson, 1975: 25), was created in revenge by the magician who opposed Aladdin. Abu tells Alec that the magician 'used his powers to make hundreds of small lamps, each one with a third rank genie, and he gave these to people in the city' (1975: 25) so that they could become as rich as Aladdin. This was the magician's way of breaking the capitalist system, but Aladdin sent troops to take the lamps away from the people. Leeson, using the familiar story of the Arabian Nights, indicates the way that those in power will use force to maintain that power against those of lower classes. Alec, whose family is working-class, does not immediately appreciate this story. Indeed, he mimics the megalomania of Aladdin, demanding multiple wishes from the genie and delighting in the fact that 'Ginger Wallace, Mr Cartwright and all infidels would bite the dust from now on. Flash Bowden, Scourge of the Cosmos, Defender of the Faith, Keeper of the Kan, was on the warpath' (1975: 33). Like Matthew Morten, he eagerly accepts a system when it promises to profit him, no matter what the cost to others.

At first, Alec receives his wishes without seeing the genie, who remains in the beer can in which Alec found him. Alec is aware that the genie does not see things from his point of view (the genie, e.g. provides Alec with Arabian Nights-style slippers instead of plimsolls as the fulfilment of a wish) but does not really consider what this means for the genie – or for him. Alec does not see the genie, physically, and he does not see how his actions affect others until he asks Abu Salem to redo a ruined history project on the crusades. Abu grants the wish – but writes the essay from the point of view of the Muslims rather than the Christians. Alec's history teacher belittles him in class, asking, 'now that you have started on your career of rewriting history, what next may we expect? My regrettable failure to blow up the House of Commons, by Guy Fawkes; my victory over Wellington at Waterloo, by Napoleon' (1975: 39). Alec uses Abu's retelling of tales in his English class as well, seemingly unconcerned that Abu is doing his work for him. 'Now that he had Abu Salem, genie of the light brown ale on his side, nothing was too much. From now on, triumphs would hammer disasters' (1975: 32). He thinks he is allowing the genie to do the thinking for him. But his interaction with Abu begins to change Alec's point of view. He is sent to the headmaster's office, where Mr Cartwright questions Alec about his 'interest in things Arabian' (1975: 71), adding that his time in the Middle East made him 'realize that the Arabs have quite a different view of history from ours' (1975: 71). Alec agrees with this, but when Mr Cartwright suggests that the West replaced the East as the most civilized society, Alec protests. 'I don't see why any civilization should be up while another's down, sir. It'd be better if they were all on the same level' (1975: 72). Alec is able, through his interaction with Abu Salem, to accept an idea of global equality even though this could potentially result in England's loss of power. Leeson's depiction of Alec's refutation of national superiority was not unique; Les Back, in 'The Fact of Hybridity: Youth, Ethnicity and Racism', argues that it is interaction with other cultures that caused white youth in the 1970s and 1980s to reject 'the national chauvinism so prevalent in Britain' (2001: 443). 'The engagement [by white youths] with black culture also led in some circumstances to a political opening with regard to issues of multiculturalism and racism' (2001: 443), he says. This indeed is exactly what happens for Alec; while Mr Cartwright is stuck in nostalgia for a powerful Britain, Alec starts to think beyond nationalism.

The idea of equality eventually extends to ideas about race and class on a societal level as well, but this only happens after Alec sees Abu Salem outside of the can. Alec is at first surprised by the genie's appearance: 'his face was coal black. The silly thought went through Alec's head. I thought he was an Arab or something, but of course he was a slave from Africa' (Leeson, 1975: 84). Alec's surprise turns to dismay when he realizes that Abu might be blamed for a 'mystery sickness among immigrants in Bugletown' (1975: 78). These 'immigrants' are West Indians (many, like the bully threatening Alec, British-born). When Abu is not only grouped with these 'immigrants' but potentially labelled a threatening 'illegal immigrant', Alec realizes that his just global society has to begin much closer to home: 'the more he thought of Abu as a slave, the more ridiculous it seemed. Abu was a friend, a mate. […] now the boot was on the other foot and Alec Bowden had to work the magic' (1975: 87). This magic includes not only saving Abu, but reconciling with the local bully, Ginger, who is 'British, even if we are black' (1975: 96). Alec does not change until he has experience of another culture, first through its history and literature, and then by interacting with a member of that culture. Racism and inequality are not problems that exist (only) in the past or outside of Britain; Leeson's *Third Class Genie* argues that white Britons must understand their own history of brutal colonialism and begin to interact with people different from them in order to recognize the ways that brutality continues to replay itself within Britain itself.

Critically, Matthew and Alec's change of attitudes towards empire, race and white superiority were changes that Leeson himself had to make. In *Children's Books and Class Society*, Leeson discusses how his own white privilege threatened his success as a writer in both *Maroon Boy* and *Third Class Genie*. With *Maroon Boy*, Leeson 'wanted to write an Elizabethan story of an apprentice who discovers that his fortune depends on sailing on a slave ship, who sets the slaves free' (Leeson, 1977: 56) but he could not make the story work until he recognized the humanity of the enslaved people. 'It was the slaves or rather my own prejudiced view of them as people to be pitied and set free' (1977: 56) that kept him from making progress on the story; this did not change until 'As people who claimed their own freedom, they stood out suddenly in my mind as real characters' (1977: 56) and Matthew Morten, no longer the central figure, was a helper in the freedom fight of others. Similarly, Leeson's *Third Class Genie* was stuck until he realized that 'A good deal of the magic of European and Arab civilization has been made by the labour of black genies. It wasn't insight on my part, simply hindsight. Once the genie materialized, he did so into the tensions already existing not only in my story but in every real school and community in the country' (1977: 58). Understanding history, and white Britons' place in it, allowed Leeson to write stories focused on an equal society – both in and out of Britain.

Leeson won critical success for his historical fiction and for his books of magical fantasy. But his real commercial success came through his creation of three novels based on the popular children's television series, *Grange Hill*. Leeson embraced technology in a way that other writers in this chapter (and indeed, this book) did not, particularly television. Leeson argues that 'TV is not out to destroy the book. It feeds off it and promotes it' (1986: 259). He might have added, "and vice versa," since Leeson produced some of the most successful television spin-off books for children when he wrote books based on the BBC television series, *Grange Hill*. The first, *Grange Hill Rules, OK?* was published in 1980; by the time Leeson published his third Grange Hill book, *Grange Hill for Sale* (1981), book sales had reached a million copies, a huge number for any children's author in the UK but especially for one the *Guardian* called 'a card-carrying communist' ('Willingly to School', 1982: 11). Journalist Bob Fischer added that the Leeson *Grange Hill* books 'perfectly captured the "Thatcher's Britain" grimness of the TV series' (Fischer, 2020). Leeson uses the medium of the Grange Hill series to discuss the prospect of an equal society when magic cannot intervene to save the day. While on the one hand, this makes the *Grange Hill* books darker than Leeson's *Genie* stories, it also allows him to explore the practicality of his ideas within British society.

In *Grange Hill Rules, OK?*, the child characters and their parents are predominantly working-class. Those in the middle classes – the teachers and the police – make often negative, stereotyped judgements about the Grange Hill students and their parents. The teachers are concerned about the new parent advisory committees; as one teacher puts it, 'In the old days, we used to tell *them*. Now we're supposed to listen while they discuss … we'll have the blooming school run by parents and pupils' (Leeson, 1980: 10). The parents are a threat to the teachers' authority.

However, it is not the parent-teacher conflict that is the focus of the class conflict in Leeson's book. The main villain of *Grange Hill Rules, OK?* is Detective Constable Houston, referred to as Det-Con Houston. Det-Con Houston is looking for someone on whom to pin a series of break-ins, and he starts with the Grange Hill kids because, as he says, they are 'characters' that 'bear a little detailed observation' (Leeson, 1980: 20). Leeson shows the way that class and race are tied together through Houston's main suspect, Benny Green. Houston identifies him as 'a little dusky boy' who had been 'messing around the shops' (1980: 21). When Houston finds out that Benny's dad is 'on the Social' (1980: 21), that is, receiving welfare because he is out of work, his suspicion increases. The combination of Blackness and working-class status is sure to be trouble, according to Houston. In 1980, when Leeson's book was published, tensions between police and Black Britons were high, with Margaret Thatcher's 'sus' laws affecting the Black British population much more than the white British. Leeson suggests that equality cannot be achieved only on an economic basis as long as racial inequality also exists.

As a writer, Robert Leeson was concerned to promote ideas of race and class equality. He was also interested in narrative, and in what the reading audience wanted to see in a story. Like nineteenth-century abolitionists whose success depended on an alliance with the status quo, Leeson did not reject a history of successful middle-class literature, but tried to understand what made that literature successful. He embraced narrative traditions in familiar and popular forms, including the boys' adventure story, the magical realist story, and the school story, and used what these forms had to offer to put across his ideas. In *Reading and Righting*, Leeson said that child participation in the creation of his stories 'helped me in my search for a balance of interests between what I want to say and what they want to hear' (Leeson, 1985: 169). Rather than rejecting popularity in literature, Leeson embraced it, arguing that by listening to what his audience liked, he could find success. However, he did not embrace all aspects of genre fiction, especially the classist and racist aspects often found in British genre fiction before the end of empire. Instead, his white characters gain maturity and a sense of self through learning to accept and learn from what other communities have to offer.

The right to a voice in literature?

The driving motivation behind the four-white author-activists I discuss in this chapter is that children have a right to a voice in literature. Traditionally, children's literature has been seen as a space where middle-class, white and mostly male children get stories, and readers from working-class backgrounds, female, and children of colour – when they are addressed at all – get told how to behave. Literature was, for all children, viewed as something the adult created for the child, and the voice of the real child was seldom heard. Children's rights activists such as Chris Searle, Dan Jones, Rosemary Stones and Robert Leeson wanted to create a new hierarchy within children's literature, one that would allow child voices to be heard and would promote equality between race, gender and class. Searle and Jones focused mainly on promoting the child's voice, but Searle was specifically focused on class division whereas Jones collected the child's voice without censor. Stones was concerned with the messages that children received in their books, and the books she wrote and edited attempted to replace racist, sexist and classist messages with new, non-biased ones. And Leeson looked to narrative, using traditional forms to tell new stories and incorporating the suggestions of children into his own stories.

In championing children's rights as white authors, however, all of these writers faced difficulties in giving the Black and Asian Briton a voice in literature. Searle and Stones both published the work of young people of colour, but in their own work, issues other than race were foregrounded. Searle's commitment to economic equality often came across as economic sameness, in that his work suggested that all working-class people – Black, Asian and white – had the same concerns and goals. Similarly, Stones's focus on girls' issues often disregarded the complications of racism in achieving gender equality. Robert Leeson confronted racist attitudes directly in many of his stories, and discussed the idea of confronting his own white-privileged assumptions before being able to make a story work; but a reliance on popular forms of narration meant maintaining a white character at the centre of a narrative. Jones illustrated multiracial communities and collected their voices, but his children's literature is not necessarily explicit in its anti-racist views. Thus, while all these writers champion the idea of an anti-racist society, their literature is about a white response to racism rather than a focus on Black or Asian British voices. But Black and Asian British voices were being heard, emboldened by the empowerment movements that swept Britain during the 1970s and 1980s. The following chapters will look at the ways that activists of colour became authors to give readers of colour a place in the children's book world.

3

To be young, British and Black: Writing for a new generation of British readers

These people who are themselves experiencing all these things will one day produce the artist.

Errol Lloyd, qtd in Walmsley, *The Caribbean Artists Movement 1966–1972*, 1992: 181

While white political activists in Britain, anti-colonial, communist, feminist, or anti-racist, tried to bring their overtly political views to child readers of colour, many Black people during the 1970s and 1980s grew up and lived with day-to-day institutional oppression that triggered their activism in the careers they had already chosen. Oppression, long visible in the educational system where Black students were relegated to Educationally Sub-Normal classrooms at a much higher rate than white or Asian students, was exacerbated by other governmental and institutional racism beginning with the 1968 Race Relations Act. The act, which was celebrated for banning discrimination in housing, employment and public services, exempted the government – including the police – from having to follow the regulations.

For a young generation of Black Britons who had either been born in the country or come to the UK as children, police oppression became increasingly visible as they reached their teens and twenties. Events such as the 1971 trial of the Mangrove 9 (in which nine Black young people were charged with inciting a riot after protesting police persecution of the Mangrove restaurant in Notting Hill), the oppressive police presence at the 1976 Notting Hill Carnival and the death of thirteen young people in the 1981 New Cross Fire – likely begun by white racists but never properly investigated by the police – all raised hostility between the Black community and the police. Many young Black Britons felt disconnected from both their Caribbean and African roots and from their Britishness, and this rootlessness only threatened to increase and intensify uprisings and clashes between Black Britons and the police.

Concern for this young generation – or the experience of being part of it – led many Black Britons who were established in other careers to become writers for children during the 1970s and 1980s. Some of these would-be authors had already participated in radical activities, including protests and anti-police action; others expressed their rebelliousness and desire for positive change for Black people in different ways. However, for all the writers I will discuss in this chapter, it was the absence – and sometimes violent erasure – of Black people from British society, historically and contemporaneously, that motivated them to produce children's books despite beginning from radically different careers. Errol Lloyd trained as a lawyer, Ziggi Alexander was a librarian and historian, Ambalavaner Sivanandan worked for a think tank funded by multinational companies. And while none started out as activists and children's book creators, their experiences in racist Britain helped them become activist artists and writers for children.

The legality of racism, the art of community: Errol Lloyd's artistic response

In 1963, twenty-year-old Errol Lloyd arrived in the UK from Jamaica to study law. In doing so, he followed a friend from Kingston, Richard Small who was also studying law at King's College in London and who had arrived in Britain four years earlier. Small, who by the time that Lloyd arrived was working for the Campaign Against Racial Discrimination (CARD), may have advised Lloyd to come as a student. The 1962 Commonwealth Immigrants Act in Britain decreed that 'the only Caribbean people able to enter Britain freely were students and schoolchildren' (Walmsley, 1992: 28). Small, alongside CARD, was already protesting the immigration restrictions, but he would have been able to help Lloyd navigate the system as it was, possibly before Lloyd left Jamaica and certainly after he arrived; they shared a flat together early in Lloyd's university days. Small became the Press Officer for CARD, and his connections to Black political and intellectual radicals provided Lloyd with a scholarly and challenging community where he could find his feet in Britain. Small was a founding member of the West Indian Students' Centre (WISC), and it was there that Lloyd likely encountered the Caribbean Artists' Movement (CAM) for the first time, as they had their meetings there. WISC 'had a lively arts and educational programme driven by a radical political agenda. Richard Small was among those actively leading this agenda' (Andrews, 2014: 101). Aware of Lloyd's talent for art, Small often asked him to design pamphlet covers or produce other artwork for political handouts.

Initially, Lloyd did not have to choose between his legal and artistic vocations. In 1966, he and Richard Small gave legal advice to two WISC members, Jessica and Eric Huntley, on setting up and registering their publishing concern, Bogle L'Ouverture Press. In 1967, Lloyd participated as the junior member of one of the first CAM artist exhibitions, along with Aubrey Williams, Ronald Moody, Karl Craig and Althea McNish (all of whom were already established artists). Lloyd was not a complete novice; he had taken art at A-level and had done quite well but, as he wrote, 'few made a living by art, so it was law for me' (Lloyd, unpublished email 25 November 2020). However, Anne Walmsley notes that Lloyd was aware of his 'beginner' status, acknowledging that his work was 'very much in the embryonic stage' (1992: 81); also that his work was focused on people and faces, particularly how the face represents 'the person's essential quality and character' (1992: 81). His association with CAM and WISC would pay off artistically more than legally, however; he was asked to produce a bust of C. L. R. James, and to create greetings cards for sale in the Huntleys' bookshop. He also illustrated some of the earliest work that Bogle L'Ouverture produced for children, including Odette Thomas's *Rain Falling, Sun Shining* (1975); however, by the time he did these illustrations, he had been away from the Caribbean for more than a decade and was beginning to think about the new generation of Black British readers for whom the Caribbean was only someplace their parents talked about.

He would soon get his chance to illustrate for this new audience. Rosemary Stones notes that 'it was being shown Bogle's series of greetings cards featuring Errol's paintings in another Black bookshop, New Beacon Books, that led Bodley Head children's editors to invite him to illustrate his first full colour picture book for children' (1979b: 3). Lloyd was one of the first Black artists in Britain to illustrate books for children, and the first to be nominated for a Kate

Greenaway medal, for his work on Petronella Breinburg's 1973 *My Brother Sean* – one of the books he produced for the Bodley Head. The reviews for the Sean books (there were two others) were warm, and the books were reprinted by Puffin and (later) Red Fox, underscoring Breinburg's and Lloyd's belief that books about Black children were for all readers, and not just Black readers.

But even though Lloyd felt that the Sean books were 'relevant to all British children' (Stones, 1979b: 4), his art never left his politics behind. The early 1970s saw an increase in media stories about Black British youths mugging white Britons – often elderly white Britons. Statistics offered by local police stations and reported on by newspapers suggested that, as in this opinion piece in the *Daily Mail*, 'in a few areas, like Brixton and Wandsworth, the great majority of muggers are young West Indians' ('The First of the Second Generation', 1972: 6). Brixton and Wandsworth had large populations of young Black Britons at the time, many of whom suffered from the scandal of being placed erroneously into ESN (educationally sub-normal) classrooms and who subsequently left school without qualifications. Even though the media reports often pointed out that the increase in crime was due to a lack of employment and prospects, the selective media coverage raised fears among white Britons. *The Times* diarist reported a claim by Detective Chief Superintendent Sugrue of Brixton that 'the age of offenders is surprisingly low. Sugrue said that a woman of 70 complained that she had been set upon by three or four boys under 12, the youngest about seven' ('Black People and the Police Cont'd', 1973: 14). Despite the fact that *The Times* diarist was largely sympathetic to the Black community (the article also quotes extensively from both residents and local community rights activists), it was stories about elderly white women beset by young Black muggers that would dominate news reports.

In fact, the image of the elderly white woman in fear of her Black British neighbours goes back further than the 1970s, and was given credence by the infamously racist 'Rivers of Blood' speech from conservative MP Enoch Powell. Paul Gilroy argues that the 'centrepiece' (1987: 106) of Powell's speech is a letter he received from an elderly white constituent afraid to leave her house because of the Black 'immigrants' who have moved in nearby. Gilroy adds that 'the moment at which crime and legality begin to dominate discussion of the "race" problem is thus also the moment when "black youth" become a new problem category' (1987: 106). The year of Powell's speech, 1968, is also the year of the

Race Relations bill that made discrimination illegal but allowed the police to continue to make decisions based on race. If white Britons lived in fear of Black British youth, Black Britons lived in fear of government institutions.

Errol Lloyd's illustrations provided images for both Black and white readers that challenged the idea of the criminal, unemployed and dangerous Black British youth. Whereas Dan Jones painted crowded, multiracial outdoor scenes, Lloyd focused on the intimate and domestic in order to remove the aura of danger often attached to Black male children at this time. This is immediately evident on the cover of *My Brother Sean* (1973), which depicts the head and shoulders of a young Black boy centred on the cover. Despite his centrality (to both cover and narrative), Sean is not defiant or angry. Instead, his wide eyes are looking shyly away and slightly downward. It is impossible to think of this boy as a threat to even the most elderly of white ladies. Indeed, it is the world that is a threat to Sean rather than the other way around. He is eager to be a part of the institution of school, but also frightened of being left by his family. Uncertain of his welcome, Sean is pictured again in the centre of a page, with head and shoulders only, with mouth wide open, eyes shut and hands in fists up to his face. The text indicates only that 'Sean cried' (Breinburg, 1973) but Lloyd's illustration is of a boy who is bawling, sobbing and terrified. Several children are glancing at him, mostly indirectly. The text goes on to indicate various aspects of school (nice kids, a swing, a kind teacher) that should allay Sean's fears, but the key to these illustrations is the number of people (the teacher, other kids, Sean's sister) *who are looking at Sean's face*. It is being seen, and accepted for who he is, that makes Sean feel comfortable in and accepted by institutional Britain.

The two sequels to *My Brother Sean*, *Doctor Sean* (1974) and *Sean's Red Bike* (1975), have similarly empowering-without-threatening storylines by Petronella Breinburg. *Doctor Sean* has both Sean and his sister acting out roles in the medical profession, positions of importance but also a historical reminder of the role of the Black Caribbean 'immigrants' in the establishment and good maintenance of the National Health Service, which benefited (and still benefits) all Britons. *Sean's Red Bike* has Sean, not just longing for a red bike, but working for it; when he finally achieves it, the neighbourhood children suggest it is 'too big' (Breinburg, 1975) for him, but Sean is undeterred. Just as he earned enough money to purchase the bike, so too he puts in the work to learn how to ride it. Lloyd's illustrations depict Sean as capable and self-assured, again placing Sean as the lone and central figure on the cover of each book.

One illustration in *Sean's Red Bike* sums up Lloyd's attitude about what a children's illustrator should do. In an interview with Ann Thompson, Lloyd argued that 'the black child in this society suffers a real disadvantage that has its roots in housing, education and job opportunities for parents' (Thompson, 1980: 5) and that 'the media makes [Black children] aware of racial differences and attitudes' (1980: 5) even from a very young age. The double-page illustration of Sean at the bike shop with his mother and the shopkeeper goes a long way to counter media images about Black people in Britain. Sean is in the very centre of the spread, with his back towards the viewer. He is looking at the shopkeeper, an older white man, and holding up coins. A piggy bank, a symbol of careful saving, is between them. The shopkeeper is smiling, and certainly does not appear afraid of Sean (indeed, the text indicates that he knows Sean and sees him every week). Sean's mother, to the left of both Sean and the shopkeeper, is looking at her son and also smiling; she holds a purse indicating that she is not without means herself. She and the shopkeeper reach the same height on the page, a suggestion of equality between them. Lloyd's image is in stark opposition to that of the media's and Enoch Powell's fearful white elderly Britons surrounded by Black youth disconnected from their families and intent on stealing what they cannot earn.

Lloyd went on to author picture books as well as illustrating them. His *Nini at Carnival* (1978), as Ann Thompson points out, 'showed black children walking confidently through the streets (particularly important since many authorities wanted to remove West Indian carnival from the streets)' (Thompson, 1980: 5). This is an understatement; the 1976 Notting Hill Carnival is infamous for its heavy police presence and descent into clashes between the police and Black British young people. But although Thompson places Lloyd's story in London, neither Lloyd's illustrations nor his text indicates this. In fact, as I have written elsewhere, 'his carnival is set nowhere at all, as the characters are set on blank pages with no background, and there are no adults present' (Sands-O'Connor, 2008: 123). Lloyd himself commented about this, 'somebody asked me the other day why I did not include the buildings etc, to place the carnival in a specific locality. The reason I didn't was that I wanted the story to have a timeless quality free from everyday reality, in which it could take on a fairy tale aspect' (Lloyd, unpublished email 20 November 2020). Like Lloyd's image of Sean with the shopkeeper, the illustrations in *Nini at Carnival* provide a contrast to media depictions, which included white Notting Hill residents barricading themselves into their homes amid police surveillance and brutality at the 1976 carnival (see, e.g. the BBC documentary 'Summer of Heat: 1976' first broadcast 3 June 2006). Lloyd's carnival is both peaceful and joyful because of the absence of fearful white onlookers and police who, as Darcus Howe put it in his 'Is a Police Carnival', had 'come expecting a confrontation' (1976 [2019]: 53) in 1976. The closest Lloyd comes to depicting law enforcement in *Nini at Carnival* is the figure of a boy dressed up as a cowboy with a sheriff's star; however, he has his arm around his traditional (media-created) enemy, another child dressed as an American Indian. Lloyd, in his illustrations for *Nini at Carnival*, reclaims carnival for Black British children.

In 1981, Lloyd published a sequel to *Nini at Carnival*, *Nini on Time* (Bodley Head). This book tells the story of Nini and her friends trying to get to the zoo. Though this book is clearly set in London (the bus is the Route 74 that at the time went between Camden Town and Putney), it is also 'no place' because Lloyd draws shops that existed in various parts of London in close proximity to each other. For example, New Beacon books, run by John La Rose and located in Finsbury Park, is in Lloyd's book just around the corner from Honest John's, a Notting Hill record shop known for its Afro-Caribbean clientele (there was also a branch in Camden Town, but this is nowhere near New Beacon either). The Black British community is in this way the background to Nini's life and the lives of her friends. Lloyd designed the illustrations by taking photographs around the city and walking, with his own child, the route that Nini might take. The children in the story, from different ethnic backgrounds, all wander the streets without fear and know the everyday 'helpers' in their neighbourhood (postman, firemen, ambulance driver) well enough to ask for a ride to the zoo. Nini and her friends never get lost in the crowd, even if they can't find their way to the zoo. They belong in the city, and the city streets belong to them. The book, published just three months before the Brixton uprising, highlighted an ideal version of London – and one that would soon become impossible to imagine for many in Britain (Figure 1).

Figure 1 Lloyd creates a multiracial and inclusive Britain that emphasizes the belonging of Black Britons; note New Beacon Bookshop in the background. Illustration copyright Errol Lloyd, used with permission.

Lloyd, who had got his start through activist arts organizations, now became involved in helping other young artists through the Minorities Arts Advisory Service. MAAS aimed to 'promote ethnic identity and preserve cultural traditions' (DeSouza, 2013: 201). Lloyd's contribution was to edit *Artrage*, the organization's journal which focused on the contributions to the British artistic scene that went largely ignored. Eddie Chambers, in 'The Emergence of the Black British Artist', argues that 'before 1980, major publicly funded galleries and museums took little or no interest in Black artists' work' (1997: 77), something Lloyd set out to change for the next generation. Although he continued to produce and comment on children's book art, Errol Lloyd's focus during the 1980s became the next generation of Black artists that a racist and oppressive Britain had produced. Lloyd would return to writing for children in the 1990s, producing (among other books) the novel *Many Rivers to Cross* (1995), which was nominated for the Carnegie Medal. In this book Lloyd returns to the theme of a unifying carnival, this time for older readers. Sandra, the main character, is born in Jamaica but migrates to England to join her parents several years after they do. Like Nini, Sandra feels she does not belong, but unlike Nini, not everyone tries to make her feel at home. She must get used to new siblings, tired parents and homesickness for her grandmother and brother she left behind in Jamaica. She suffers racism, called a 'golliwog' (Lloyd, 1995: 95) and a 'stupid monkey' (1995: 105) and told to 'go back to where you came from' (1995: 95) by white children in her school. The teachers not only seemingly fail to notice, they try to have Sandra placed in an ESN school, although her mother, armed with information from a teacher friend, forces the headmaster to prepare Sandra for the test, and then retest her.

During this period of the book, Sandra finds solace in music and art. The art teacher encourages her to paint a portrait of her grandmother, and when she 'painted Granny in a powdery shade of pink' (Lloyd, 1995: 100), Miss Rigby gently suggests she try to 'look at this burnt umber, and this gorgeous sienna brown. And here is a lovely vandyke brown! Mix them with yellow ochre, or with vermillion red ... you'd be surprised how many shades of brown you can get' (1995: 100). At first Sandra is ashamed that she denied her grandmother's – and her own – colour, but as she finds the right shade, she becomes 'excited' (1995: 100) and stays after school to get it right. At Christmas, Sandra's father brings out records of Black jazz artists, including 'Duke Ellington and Count Basie jazz standards, interspersed with ballads by Nat King Cole, Ella Fitzgerald, Ray Charles' (1995: 112); they then go to a post-Christmas house party where Sandra at first feels shy but is soon 'bopping away to the rhythms of calypso and reggae and soul music' (1995: 113–14) including the Melodians' 'Rivers of Babylon' and Motown songs by the Supremes and Aretha Franklin. Art and music allow her to feel connected and part of a community. Both art and music were critical means of bringing Black British people together for Lloyd, who got his start as an artist with the Caribbean Artists Movement (CAM), showing slides and discussing his work at the first 'Symposium of West Indian Artists' in June of 1967 (Walmsley, 1992: 80) alongside more experienced artists. CAM allowed Lloyd to find his identity as an artist, and network with other artists and writers. While art brought him together with an intellectual community, music was, for Lloyd, a way of connecting with the wider Caribbean community. For example, Notting Hill Carnival introduced him to Trinidadian forms of musical expression; he wrote that 'I grew up in Jamaica, and being a British colony where protestant churches dominated, there was no carnival more associated with catholic countries like Trinidad … it was quite new and exciting to me' (Lloyd, unpublished email 25 November 2020). Art and music situated Lloyd in Britain and in the world.

This is true for Sandra in *Many Rivers to Cross* as well. Artistic and musical expression unite in the book when a Trinidadian friend urges Sandra to join her family's steel band at Notting Hill Carnival. Throughout the book, Lloyd points out ways that not all West Indians are the same (Sandra's cabin-mate, on the ship coming to England, is a Trinidadian and they compare the different names they have for fruits) and Carnival is another instance of this. Sandra and her parents are uncertain about her participation at first, because 'the idea of carnival had never caught on in Jamaica' (Lloyd, 1995: 135–6). But Sandra joins, and becomes seduced by the making of costumes on the theme of 'Land of the Zulus', because 'she had never thought much about Africa and what she had seen in films or books was more likely to inspire shame than pride … she had never guessed at the beauty and magnificence of their dress and beadwork' (1995: 136). On the day of the carnival, she becomes 'somebody else, and that somebody else was one of her very own ancestors' (1995: 142). By the end of carnival 'Sandra lost the last of her inhibitions in a frenzy of dancing. For that moment she was a Zulu princess, proud and exuberant' (1995: 143). Carnival brings together her family, who come to watch, and the Black British community: 'Sandra had never seen so many black faces in one place in England' (1995: 141) and connects them all to each other and to their past, just as the carnival in *Nini at Carnival* had. Here, the police are present, but Lloyd reduces them to 'directing traffic' (1995: 141) and they disappear from the narrative. It is the Black community that matters, and the child's place within it.

Throughout his career, Lloyd used his art (painterly and narrative) to create what Rosemary Stones called 'positive dignified people whose domestic lives, families, neighbourhoods and festivals are worth recording' (Stones, 1979b: 3). Keen to ensure that the second generation knew they belonged in Britain, he presented them with ways of connecting their family background with their experience in Britain, blending the old and new. Like Nini with her African Kente cloth as carnival costume or Sandra with her layers of brown paint to recreate her grandmother's face, Lloyd allows the second generation to be Black *and* British in ways that promote their success, individually and as a community. Lloyd, unlike white activist-writers such as Chris Searle, did not set out to unite or produce literature for both white and Black British communities; his emphasis was firmly on the Black British child reader. Speaking to Ann Thompson, Lloyd argued that he did this because 'books, even though they can not solve these problems, can go some way towards giving the black child a positive image' (Thompson, 1980: 5). Lloyd was welcomed into a global Black community that encouraged his artistic and intellectual growth when he first arrived in London; his children's books recreated and reinforced community and identity for the next generation.

Taking it to the streets: Librarian activists in the 1970s and 1980s

Along with teachers, one of the most likely professionals to interact with the changing population of Britain were the librarians. Publicly funded libraries in Britain had altered considerably since the war, transformed from quiet places mostly for literary-minded adults to community hubs offering not just books, but services as well, to all ages and incomes. These changes came about in part due to the alterations in the education and public welfare systems after the war, and partly due to a new emphasis on children's librarianship that began with the introduction of the Carnegie (1936) and Kate Greenaway (1957) medals to honour quality children's books in Britain. Specialist courses in children's librarianship, common in America from the 1920s, only began in Britain in the 1950s; by 1975, librarians working with children – whether they had received specialist training or not – had several handbooks and booklists on children's and adolescent fiction to consult, including Colin and Sheila Ray's *Attitudes and Adventures* (1st edn 1965), Sheila Ray's *Children's Fiction: A Handbook for Librarians* (1970 [1972]), Janet Hill's *Children are People* (1973), and Margaret Marshall's *Libraries and Literature for Teenagers* (1975).

All of these books on children's libraries and librarianship included specialist sections or commentaries on books for the 'immigrant' reader, stressing the importance of considering their needs. Sheila Ray, who has an entire chapter on 'Fiction for Immigrants', opens it by saying, 'children's librarians working in areas where there are immigrant children can help by finding stories which are meaningful to these children. The same books will help the native-born English children to understand more readily' their new neighbours (Ray, 1970 [1972]: 177), although this apparently was not necessary in all-white areas. Margaret Marshall argues that 'where relevant the needs of particular sections of the teenage community are considered, as in the case of immigrants' (Marshall, 1975: 200). *Attitudes and Adventures*, a list of recommended titles for adolescents, includes nine titles about 'one of the most important contemporary social problems, with which all adolescents have to come to terms ... that of racial tolerance' (Colin and Sheila Ray, 1965 [1973]: 14). Although there was disagreement on who literature about New Commonwealth Immigrants was *for*, most librarians writing in the late 1960s or early 1970s felt it was an important consideration.

The Rays's *Attitudes and Adventures*, and other similar guides that followed, including Judith Elkin's *Multi-Racial Books for the Classroom* (1st edn 1971) and Grace Hallworth's and Julia Marriage's *Stories to Read and to Tell* (1978), all included recommended books for young people, and they were all published by some segment of the British library establishment (early ones listed the Library Association as publisher; later it was the Youth Libraries Group, the YLG). These guides suggested many books that might now be considered racist or at very least problematic, such as Claire Hutchet Bishop's *The Five Chinese Brothers* (recommended by Hallworth and Marriage), Harper Lee's *To Kill a Mockingbird* (recommended by the Rays) and Kipling's *Just So Stories* (recommended by Elkin and Hallworth and Marriage).

White librarian Janet Hill also tried to have a guide published by the YLG, her *Books for Children: The Homelands of Immigrants in Britain*. The YLG rejected the guide, not (according to Hill) because it was about new populations, but because Hill 'felt that we must do more than produce a list of recommended books; it was important to include those we thought mediocre or totally unacceptable ... they felt it would be better if our approach was less *negative*, and we omitted the bad titles' (Hill, 1973: 135). Later in the book, Hill praised Elkin's, and Hallworth and Marriage's lists as being 'of a much higher standard' than other YLG guides, although she noted that Elkin's was 'marred by the distressing but obviously unconscious insensitivity of listing novels which included black children among the characters under the general heading *Problems*' (1973: 143; Elkin removed the category in subsequent editions). But she felt strongly that 'many books are blatantly biased and prejudiced. Not surprisingly, this criticism applies most strongly to books about countries which have been closely connected with England' (Hill, 1971: 7) through the empire. Hill did eventually find a publisher who would allow her to speak her mind about these biased books: the Institute of Race Relations headed by A. Sivanandan. The library establishment was happy to celebrate multiculturalism in Britain, but was not keen to publish material critical of Britain's approach to race relations in children's books.

In providing systematic criticism of contemporary as well as classic children's literature, Hill became an activist librarian on the issue of race, as her criticism informed her actions as a Lambeth librarian and vice versa. She was a part of the movement for 'community librarianship', which Martin Walker in the *Guardian* argued was the idea 'that if the wider public, and particularly the working-class and the minorities, are not coming to the libraries of their own accord, then the libraries should go to them' (1982: 11). Hill, Walker noted, had amassed for Lambeth Library, 'the best collection of reggae tapes in the world' (1982: 11) and 'plenty of books that cater for Lambeth's ethnic minorities' (1982: 11). However, although Hill was an activist critic, she never authored any books for children to fill gaps in the market.

Other librarians, however, took community librarianship one step further and became authors for children and young people when they could not find books that told stories reflecting the lives of their Black and Asian British child book borrowers. This was most obvious during the early 1980s in the London borough of Brent, which had become a media target for what some newspapers called censorship. Nicholas Farrell, writing in the *Sunday Telegraph* quoted Alan Linfield, 'Brent librarian between 1980 and 1985' (1992: 7), who complained that 'Brent council allowed the inverted Nazism of radical librarianship free rein to withdraw, i.e. censor, anything that offended its sensibilities ... there was a witch-hunt for any books that could possibly be construed as sexist, racist or colonialist' (1992: 7). This included, as *Punch* cartoonist Kenneth Mahood noted, Hergé's *Tintin* comics – which Mahood 'redrew' in the 9th November 1983 edition of the magazine, colouring Tintin's dog black and renaming him Sooty, and charting the young reporter's immigrant journey through Britain (Mahood, 1983:18–19). Reports in the press suggested at least tens of thousands and possibly hundreds of thousands of books were removed from Brent Libraries in the period between 1979 and 1988. An article in the *TLS* by W. J. West, 'If In Doubt, Chuck It Out', for example, focuses on the complaint of Brent North conservative MP Richard Boyson. In the article, Boyson says that '105,070 books from Brent Library, removed for ideological reasons … had simply "lost out"' (West, 1991: 17) to the political left. This is likely an exaggeration on multiple levels, but represents the fears of many white British people that their history and heritage might be discarded.

Although several councils throughout Britain underwent changes in library stock during this period, Brent received such a high level of media attention because their programming also reflected the changing community population. 'Radical' librarianship extended to public lectures and exhibitions which responded to the interests of the community; in 1983, Baroness Cox complained about 'my own borough of Brent which recently allowed a CND [Campaign for Nuclear Disarmament] library exhibition. However … when the British Atlantic Committee asked permission to put on an exhibition showing the alternative position, this was refused' ('Educational Institutions: Information and Propaganda', 25 April 1983). Brent librarians were portrayed by the right wing media during this time period as performing 'social brainwashing' (Waterhouse, 1986: 8) on children who didn't want the books they were being offered; Simon Hoggart agreed, suggesting that 'our new Literary Guardians have a fairly scant knowledge of how children think and what children enjoy, but draw a considerable political satisfaction from making these decisions' (1984: 50). Unlike other 'radicals' operating during this period, such as Chris Searle or Rosemary Stones, the librarians of Brent and Lambeth did not label themselves radicals; they simply saw themselves, as Janet Hill put it, as 'starting to get out into the community and meet children where they are' (1973: 157).

In Brent, that meant addressing the Black and Asian populations who had been moving into the borough since the end of the Second World War. Although it is debatable whether the books from Brent Library were removed for 'ideological reasons', the library's supporters admitted that the alterations made to stock were in consideration of a changing community. Responding to W. J. West's article in the *TLS*, John Pateman, a librarian who worked in Hackney at the time, argued that the books 'were removed because they were no longer relevant to Brent Library users … The attempts, by Brent and others, to return libraries to their original purpose of empowering and educating the common man and woman are to be applauded' (1992: 13). The common man and woman (and child) of Brent was increasingly someone with a Caribbean or Indian background; Malcolm Barres-Baker, a local historian, notes that 'after the war many people came from the Caribbean, and later from the Indian subcontinent. In 1981 37% of Brent's population had been born outside the UK' (2007: 14). Librarian Ziggi Alexander, born in Dominica herself, wanted to do something positive for that 37 per cent and their children born in Britain.

Alexander had been 'talking with colleagues about Enoch Powell and the idea of repatriation' (Mackie, 1980: 2). When she told them Powell's idea was not new, but went back to Elizabeth I's 'edict about expelling blacks' (1980: 2), her colleagues were surprised. Alexander realized that Black participation in British history was unfamiliar to most Britons – no matter what their colour. Her job with Brent Library services 'was to try to attract people who would never normally go near a public library. She began to give lectures on black history and culture, illustrated with a few old photographs, and drew sizeable audiences' (Davie, 1984: 52). With her white British colleague from Ealing Council, Audrey Dewjee, who had become interested in British Asian history because of her marriage to a British Indian, Alexander began researching an exhibit; 'most people, [Alexander and Dewjee] say, have been under the vague impression – as they themselves were until not long ago – that the movement of blacks and Asians into Britain after World War Two is something new' (Davie, 1984: 52), Michael Davie commented. Alexander and Dewjee, working together, found something altogether different: a visible history of Black and Asian Britons dating back to the Tudor period. Alexander told an ITV interviewer, 'we went to all the museums and galleries in London and just went to the photographic departments and looked through absolutely everything' ('Roots in Britain', 1981: 3.40). Additionally, they had access to a few published resources available about Black British history, including Nigel File and Chris Power's *Black Settlers in Britain 1555–1958* (1981) – but this and other Black history resources were not widely available in schools and libraries.

Alexander and Dewjee revealed what was hiding in plain sight. With the information they found, they mounted (literally – it was mostly photocopied material with typed descriptions attached to folding moveable library display boards) an exhibition entitled 'Roots in Britain' which first opened in 1980.

'Roots in Britain' began by touring the libraries in Brent, and then, along with a specially produced pamphlet, was made 'available for loan to institutions and organisations' (Alexander and Dewjee, 1981: 1). The exhibition was designed for a general audience, but attracted many young people. Alexander commented that 'we've had very young children, in fact ... teachers, educationalists in general' ('ITV Roots in Britain', 1981: 6.30) attending the exhibition. That it was particularly important for young people to experience the exhibition was explained by Alexander when she said, 'I think it's important to realize that Britain has had a multiracial society for centuries and that Black people made a positive contribution to those societies in the past, particularly as we've had a lot of negative media input, Blacks are always associated with problems' ('ITV Roots in Britain', 1981: 4.30). The ITV interview with Alexander was produced in August 1981, just a few months after uprisings in Brixton, Handsworth, the St Paul's area of Bristol, Moss Side (Manchester), Chapeltown (Leeds) and Toxteth (Liverpool). Black youths, who had for years been targeted by the police, rose up in protest between April and July of 1981. Alexander and Dewjee also published some of their work in further pamphlets, including one on *Mary Seacole* (Dewjee and Alexander, 1982) and as a series of articles for Dorothy Kuya's journal *Dragon's Teeth* in the late 1980s, later collected in *Their Contribution Ignored* (NCRCB, 1988) with support from the World Council of Churches.

Yet despite Alexander's hard work, most libraries did not change substantially. She followed up her material on Black Britons with a book for the Association of Assistant Librarians, but it was treated differently from one written by a white librarian. John Vincent, a white librarian who first learned about community librarianship working with Janet Hill in Lambeth, published *An Introduction to Community Librarianship* in 1986. In it he argued that librarians had been hampered by the 'mixed messages' (Vincent, 1986: 18) with regard to the role of the library service. His *Introduction* was an example of these mixed messages. Published by the same group, the Association of Assistant Librarians, as Alexander's pamphlet, Vincent's is subtly endorsed in ways that Alexander's work is not. Vincent's work is copyrighted to the Association of Assistant Librarians, while Alexander's is copyrighted to herself, and there is a note which follows Alexander's copyright that states the standard disclaimer: 'The opinions expressed in this book are those of the author and do not represent the official view of the Association of Assistant Librarians' (Alexander, 1982: copyright page). Vincent's work has no such disclaimer, and is in fact part of a series called *AAL Pointers*. This series, which began with David Liddle's *What the Public Library Boss Does* (1985), was designed to give general advice for librarians on common questions. Vincent's contribution to the series covers the community librarian and a variety of different communities (twelve, to be exact, one of which includes 'prisoner's wives'), and it makes assumptions about those communities and about the librarians who serve them. Although Vincent's discussion is generally benevolent, and he recommends Alexander's pamphlet in his list of resources, he presumes a white librarianship who is both in charge and already anti-racist. He would not, for example, have to tell Ziggi Alexander that she should 'remember that the black community needs access to the widest range of materials' (Vincent, 1986: 18). He also suggests that librarians "be prepared to deal firmly with issues of racism that occur, for example comments from members of the public to black staff' (1986: 19). He does not seem to think that racism might exist within the library staff itself, despite arguing that 'the UK is an inherently racist society, and that ... racism shows itself in its institutions (of which libraries are an example) and in its products (which, of course, include library materials' (1986: 17). In his section on 'Serving Young People', nearly all the resources he lists are by white authors, despite Vincent's argument that the 'major area to investigate is the presentation of images in children's books, for example the treatment of black characters' (1986: 27) and suggesting that librarians have 'an active role in combatting racism' (1986: 27). For Vincent, it is the institution and its materials that are racist, but he gives the agents of the institution, the librarians themselves, a pass.

Alexander does not, on the contrary, pull any punches, writing that a 'disregard for racist attitudes and prejudices among staff members has sometimes resulted in unsuitable selection of individuals in racially sensitive areas' (Alexander, 1982: 27). The Association of Assistant Librarians may have published Alexander's work, but they were not ready to endorse it fully, much like the Youth Library Group did not want to publish Janet Hill's work because it was too "negative" or the governors at Chris Searle's school refused to publish children's poetry because it was too grim. Being anti-racist was fine for librarians (and others), as long as they were pleasant about it and not too critical of authorities. Alexander would publish one more significant work before she left librarianship for the field of health and social care, a co-edited (with Trevor Knight) book on *The Whole Library Movement: Changing Practice in Multicultural Librarianship* (1992). This book, which was also published by the Association of Assistant Librarians, shows how much had – and had not – changed during the 1980s. Alexander, in her introduction to the collection, grimly comments that 'there are strong indications that, at the present time, local authorities are trying to redefine the Equal Opportunities framework for both employment and service delivery. Notions of equity rather than equality seem to be gaining ground' (Alexander and Knight, 1992: 1). Although she believed that the emphasis on multiculturalism throughout the 1980s meant that the library community 'no longer excuses professional ignorance, and points to the UK black and minority ethnic communities in the eighteenth and nineteenth centuries, as well as more recent settlers' (1992: 6) in their collections focus, Alexander rightly feared that the tide was turning against the public library. Like the Inner London Education Authority (ILEA), public library funding was slashed in the 1990s and demands were made for accountability and cost-sharing. John Helling notes that 'between 1984 and 1994, public library expenditures per capita fell more than 9 percent' (Helling, 2012). This led to a drop in full-time librarian positions, and activist librarians like Alexander found other ways of channelling their activism. The Brent library pamphlets Alexander had produced all but disappeared.

Pushing back: Anti-racism, the IRR and the British government

The conservative policies of the 1980s had effects on other activists as well, including those working in public policy. The organization that published Janet Hill's recommendations for serving new communities of children in British libraries was the Institute of Race Relations, in the year that A. Sivanandan took over the organization. Sivanandan would go on to write and publish books for children himself. Writing about racism in Britain, his books were welcomed warmly at first, and purchased by several education authorities including the ILEA, partly through the suggestion of ACER founder Len Garrison (who

I discuss in Chapter 4). However, when Sivanandan became directly critical of the British government, and of white Britons in general, the British media and parliament took notice, and this had a direct effect on the saleability of the books.

Native to Sri Lanka, Sivanandan came to Britain in the late 1950s, at the same time as many Caribbean migrants who formed the Windrush generation were arriving. Sivanandan, who had left his home nation due to ethnic riots, arrived in Britain in time to see the Notting Hill Riots of 1958, and the racism directed at Britain's 'new immigrants'. He retrained as a librarian, and by 1964 he was chief librarian at the government advisory agency, the Institute of Race Relations (IRR).

The IRR had been founded in the 1950s to produce research – mostly funded by global corporations such as the Ford Foundation – into race relations in Britain and throughout the world. In its early decades, its research maintained colonial hierarchies, most notably E. J. B. Rose's *Colour and Citizenship*. Rose's massive tome (nearly 800 pages of text, plus appendices) appealed to 'British ideals of fair play' (Rose, 1969: 4) in treatment of the new commonwealth immigrants, and expected that 'coloured people … [would] become familiar with British norms of behaviour and adopt them' (Rose, 1969: 5). But many Britons – Black and white – had other ideas about race relations in Britain, and in 1972, a group led by Sivanandan forced most of the board of the IRR out because, as Sivanandan said, 'much of the knowledge produced by the Institute served the interests of the ruling elite' (Sivanandan, 1974: 20). The new board planned to take the organization in a different direction, one that would benefit the victims of racism rather than the government. The IRR's journal *Race*, under Sivanandan's leadership, became *Race and Class: A Journal on Racism, Empire and Globalisation*. To say that Sivanandan entirely altered the IRR is no exaggeration, but his mission went beyond that. Increasingly, he became interested in the plight of the second generation Black and Asian Britons and their treatment by governmental institutions.

By the mid-1970s, British governmental policy suggested that white Britons bore the burden of the immigrant 'problem'. Edward Short, secretary of state for education and science in 1969, argued at a conference on 'Education and the Immigrants' that the 'educational problem is clearly just a part of a very much wider social problem … it will also demand an attitude of mind among the British people, an attitude which accepts the equal worth of all races' (Short, 1969: 21). Short's use of the phrase 'British people' clearly referenced white British people. By the 1970s, this framing of the 'problem' had developed into multicultural and multiracial education, a move which seemed progressive because it argued, not for assimilation but for celebration of others' (by which was usually meant the formerly problematic immigrants') cultures. However, as Philip Cohen and Harwant S. Bains point out, 'the multicultural illusion is that dominant and subordinate can somehow swap places and learn how the other half lives, whilst leaving the structures of power intact' (Cohen and Bains, 1988: 12–13). Or, as Maureen Stone argues in *The Education of the Black Child in Britain*, 'the aims of multiracial education are tied in with the cultural deprivation theory which aims to compensate ... black children for not being white' (1981: 102). The concern that Bullock and others had about children stemmed in part from fear of racial divisions within the country. Demands for educational reform were coupled with an increase in police presence within Black communities. Often, this increased presence was explained as resulting from concern over radical Black militants such as the recently executed Black Liberation Army founder Michael X; but Sivanandan, as editor of *Race and Class*, opined 'the anxiety of the state about rebellious black youth stems not from the rhetoric of professional black militants (whose dissidence it can accommodate and legitimize within the system) but from the fear of mass politics that it may generate in the black under-class' (Sivanandan, 1976: 366–7). Multiculturalism as a response to that fear, argued Sivanandan, would do nothing to counter the systemic racism that Black youth experienced.

Britain has long been known for its polarized press, but attitudes found in right-wing newspapers about Black and Asian 'immigrants' were also mirrored in the schools, including in school textbooks. Gillian Klein, in *Reading into Racism*, complained about history and geography books that posited that '"civilization" in Africa began only with the arrival of the white man' (1985: 60) – or texts that completely left Africans and Asians out of history. But a bigger problem in the early 1980s were texts about British history that either failed to address the changing racial composition of Britain or did so in a problematic fashion. Philip Sauvain's *History of Britain Book 4: Modern Times*, for example, published by Macmillan in 1982, presents Britain as entirely made up of white people. On the very last page, in a section entitled

'Britain and the World', Sauvain did suggest that there might be something – and someone – beyond Britain's borders. After a discussion of the post-war political situation, Sauvain notes,

> Many Third World Countries were former colonies of the British Empire. In 1947 the old Indian empire was divided in two, between the Moslems [sic] in Pakistan and the Hindus in India. In the next thirty years many other former colonies gained their freedom, such as Kenya, Nigeria, Ghana and Malawi in Africa.
>
> Most of these new countries kept in touch with Britain by agreeing to stay in the commonwealth – a group of nations which all spoke English and saw the Queen as their head. (Sauvain, 1982: 75)

This passage typifies superior white British attitudes towards the former empire – some parts of which, like the Caribbean, apparently didn't exist, and some of which, like an old but impoverished ('third world') friend, happily switched to English from their native language and kept in touch with the queen, hoping to be invited to tea. Britain itself in this passage has no responsibility (either now or in the past) for the economic standing of 'Third World' countries and can therefore smile over them beneficently. Sauvain's book was published in the year following the Brixton Uprising, where mostly second generation Black Britons protested excessive policing of the Black community and when tensions between white Britons and Black and Asian Britons were at a high point, so Sauvain's paternalistic text is particularly jarring.

In the wake of the Brixton, Handsworth and Toxteth uprisings in 1981, and the Thatcher government's increased policing of Black and Asian communities, Sivanandan reached out to the liberal (and mostly white) educationalists in London, particularly in the Greater London Council (GLC) and the ILEA. Under the benign leadership of 'Red' Ken Livingstone, the GLC began to institute policies designed to eradicate racism and celebrate multiculturalism in London schools. Sivanandan was invited to speak at the GLC in March of 1983, and he made a plea for schools to focus on anti-racism rather than multiculturalism:

> Our concern ... was not with multicultural, multi-ethnic education, but with anti-racist education, which by its very nature would include the study of other cultures. Just to learn about other people's cultures is not to learn

about the racism of one's own ... But multiculturalism has become the vogue; it gives the 'ethnic' teachers a leg up and it exculpates the whites: they now know about my culture so they don't have to question their own. (Sivanandan, 1983: 5)

He went on to suggest that anti-racism 'involves not just the examination of existing literature for racist bias (and their elimination) but the provision of anti-racist texts' (1983: 9). As a start, he suggested two books that IRR had recently published: *Roots of Racism* (1982b) and *Patterns of Racism* (1982a).

Roots of Racism and *Patterns of Racism* are history books, but not like those typically found in British classrooms. Indeed, they offer a direct contradiction to the views presented in books like Souvain's *History of Britain*. The text in *Patterns of Racism*, for example, points out,

So ingrained has the sense of racial superiority among white people become that even the formal granting of independence to the colonies after the Second World War did not shift these attitudes ... Though these former colonies may now have their own governments, their economies are still tied to buying and selling the crops – tea, coffee, rubber – that cannot feed their own people, at prices that are fixed by powerful multinational companies based in the rich, white nations ... By and large, the Third World countries are still locked into the poverty that was forced on them in colonial times. (Sivanandan, 1982a: 40)

These two texts, unlike other British history texts of the time, focus on the profit motives underpinning the growth of imperialism and colonialism, and the ways that the white British (and other Europeans) used skin colour to establish their 'right' to gain those profits for themselves. For example, in *Patterns of Racism*, Sivanandan writes, 'while the culture of colonialism attempted to make colonised people feel inferior in every way, so that they would submit more easily to colonial rule, it also had the effect on white people of making them think they really were racially superior' (1982a: 37). He goes on to suggest that by the time the Windrush generation began arriving in Britain, 'it had ... come to seem "natural" for white people to feel racially superior' (1982a: 40). Sivanandan's texts are antiracist rather than multicultural because, as Mike Cole argues, 'antiracist education starts from the premise that the society is institutionally racist, and that, in the area of "race" and culture, the purpose of education is to challenge and undermine that racism' (2017: 114) rather than 'celebrating' (and thereby highlighting) difference, as multiculturalism does.

Despite the clear critique of British imperialism found in *Roots* and *Patterns*, the books were a success. Jenny Bourne notes that '*Roots* and *Patterns* appeared indeed to meet a need and there was then a whole host of anti-racist and socialist groups of teachers eager to use them. They were glowingly reviewed in over twenty papers and magazines, and especially those aimed at educationalists and teachers during 1982–3' ('Anti-Racist Witchcraft', 2015). These included specifically anti-racist publications like *Dragon's Teeth* (edited by the Black British activist Dorothy Kuya who had criticized the attempts of communists to speak on behalf of Black people) and more mainstream publications like the *Times Educational Supplement*. Bourne adds that 'because they were published at a time when there were progressives in local education authorities, these were widely purchased for use in schools and colleges – not least by the Inner London Education Authority – which sent them out to many institutions' (unpublished email 22 July 2019). The success of these books can be related to the fact that, in many educational circles (particularly in London), racism and imperialism were both connected with fascism rather than mainstream contemporary British policies. White teachers who supported anti-racist policies were often members of the Anti-Nazi League (the ANL), protesting the 'Keep Britain White' manifesto of groups such as the National Front. The ANL supported curricular changes that explained the origins of racism, such as Sivanandan's books.

But by arguing that racists were 'Nazis', white teachers were also denying the continuing presence of structural racism, as Paul Gilroy and Errol Lawrence point out in 'Two-Tone Britain': 'Being "Anti-Nazi" located the political problem of British racism almost exclusively in the activities of a small, though dangerous, band of lunatics' (Gilroy and Lawrence, 1988: 148). Racism may once, during colonialism, have been a systemic problem, but the results of that racism could now be rooted out within Britain by destroying the power of racist individuals. Although *Roots* and *Patterns* do call for a change in attitudes of all Britons, they still locate the problem largely in the past and even outside of Britain. For example, the conclusion of *Patterns of Racism* talks about how 'any civilized and just society should seek not to continue [inequalities], but to end them' (Sivanandan, 1982a: 40); it places the continuing problem of white racial superiority on 'multinational companies' (1982a: 40) and calls on Third World countries 'to redress the balance of power and regain control over their own resources and societies' (1982a: 41). None of these statements directly challenge the British government or its institutions, or highlight Black experiences of racism within Britain, and thus white teachers and local educational authorities could comfortably embrace the books.

However, in 1985 – a year in which Black Britons were again involved in violently protesting governmental, and particularly police, oppression, in places like Handsworth, Brixton and Bradford – the IRR published a third book in the series which was to prove extremely controversial. *How Racism Came to Britain* (1985) told the story of Britain's colonial and imperialist history and how it resulted, ultimately, in a racist British society. Sivanandan said in his preface that 'this book attempts to restore the study of racism to its proper perspective and, in relating British racism to its particular history in slave and colonial oppression and exploitation, make clear its growth and prevalence within British society today' (Sivanandan, 1985: iv). Unlike the first two books, *How Racism Came to Britain* used a 'cartoon' format in the hopes that it would be 'accessible to a wider range of readers' (1985: iv). Although the book was in cartoon format, it was not meant to amuse; it implicates the monarchy, judiciary, police, media, church and politicians in spreading racist attitudes (1985: 26) and in passing (1985: 36) and enforcing (1985: 35) racist legislation. *How Racism Came to Britain* also implicates teachers; in the section on education, the book comments, 'today the racism in schooling continues. New phrases and words for the same ideas …'(1985: 34). Sivanandan's book justifies Black resistance as a response to institutional racism, but many groups of white people, including politicians and teachers, felt that they as individuals were being attacked. Groups such as the All London Teachers against Racism and Fascism (ALTARF) continued to support the books, but many teachers did not. ALTARF blamed the ILEA for not supporting Sivanandan's books enough. In their newsletter, they described the controversy:

> Kenneth Baker has called on ILEA to assure him that [*How Racism*] will be removed from its schools, and called the book 'ideological, aggressive, and simplistic'. ILEA has retorted that its heads decide which books to stock, but

in a fairly typical ILEA back-stepping, went on to say that it was not on its approved list. (*ALTARF Newsletter* 27/28, 1987: 16)

For the government, the question was one of funding and ideology. As Baroness Cox put it, using Sivanandan's book as case in point, 'teenagers, particularly black teenagers, have been brainwashed to hate the police – and in many cases you, the ratepayer, are actually funding this form of hatred' (Cox, 1985a: 6). When Sivanandan had been focused on colonialism as a historical cause of racism, something in the past, his books were embraced. But when he began criticizing contemporary white Britons, he was increasingly ostracized.

The right-wing politicians and educationalists struck back, specifically attacking not only the book but the IRR, Sivanandan himself and the ILEA who had purchased the books for schools. In 'Racial Mischief: The Case of Dr Sivanandan', David Dale responded to the controversy about *How Racism Came to Britain*, arguing, 'for Sivanandan, exploitation is the plot of history' (Dale, 1985: 88). He complains that Sivanandan's book leaves out the 'fact' that, 'for centuries the institution of slavery aroused little moral concern anywhere in the world, and it was only at the insistence of a group of Englishmen that the trade was abolished' (1985: 92). And Baroness Cox added that *How Racism Came to Britain* 'is a strikingly biased account of Britain's record of colonialism where all is evil, cruel and avaricious. There is no mention whatever of some of the advantages associated with British involvement abroad, in health care, education, law and order, administration or economic advancement' (Cox, 1985b: 79). Then-secretary Kenneth Baker heard of the controversial books, and, according to Sivanandan, 'was particularly enraged … because the Inner London Education Authority bought these in bulk, I think it became a public thing … Baker said something in the media, so we had adverse publicity from the government' (Brodie, 'Interview with Ambalavener Sivanandan', 20 October 2010). Sivanandan concludes this discussion by saying, with a laugh, that the adverse publicity meant that 'we sold more copies' (2010). But in truth, the row over *How Racism Came to Britain* had far-reaching effects.

Baroness Cox brought up both the ILEA and Sivanandan's book in a House of Lords debate on 'Education: Avoidance of Politicisation' in February 1986, and Baroness Hooper, speaking for the government, concluded this debate by saying, 'the concern expressed in this debate is that there is a serious danger in some schools and colleges of a type of creeping politicisation of what goes on in the classroom in an attempt to influence the minds of pupils and students by biased teaching and distortion of the facts. The Government share that concern' ('Education: Avoidance of Politicisation' House of Lords Debate, 6 February 1986). Hooper would, the next year, become the under-secretary of education, working with Kenneth Baker to bring a National Curriculum to Britain and to begin the process of abolishing the ILEA. In the National Curriculum, the teaching of history became increasingly prescribed; while the history recommendations in 1988 gave a nod to 'multi-ethnic Britain', it was largely in terms of 'the kinds of skills, concepts, attitudes and substantive knowledge which are likely to counter ethnic stereotyping' (Department for Education and Science, 1988: 26) it also specifically discussed how 'a well-conceived course of history should not only pay scrupulous attention to objectivity and avoid political bias – it will, by its very nature, give young people the means to identify and resist indoctrination' (: 25). In short, students should learn to be tolerant of other people but resist the 'indoctrination' of anti-racism. The century or more of indoctrination about empire was not, of course, an issue for the government.

The swing to an 'objective' history curriculum was reinforced by many white teachers' opposition to ILEA's antiracist policies. Sarah Olowe notes that even among left-leaning teachers, the ILEA's antiracist curriculum was seen as 'too doctrinaire' (1990: 16) and there was a feeling that 'teaching was a profession and teachers should therefore be trusted to treat each child as an individual irrespective of colour' (1990: 16). The shift in emphasis from student to teacher's rights, according to Solomos, 'served to rationalise a conception of an embattled white majority culture' (Solomos, 1988: 229–30) that further led away from anti-racism and back towards multiculturalism, an especially easy move since the Swann Report, *Education for All* (1985) and mainstream publishers portrayed multiculturalism as addressing and celebrating the white child as much as the Black child. Swann writes, 'much of the task in countering and overcoming racism is concerned with attitude change and with encouraging youngsters to develop positive attitudes towards the multi-racial nature of society, free from the influence of inaccurate myths and stereotypes about other ethnic groups' (Swann, 1988: 321). Rather than examine the ways that historical racism continues to influence policy and educational decisions, students were encouraged to develop 'positive attitudes' about other people's cultures without digging too deeply below the surface of the 'multi-racial society'. Multiculturalism made it difficult to teach about historical events such as the enslavement of Black Africans by white Britons, or for classrooms to discuss recent uprisings of Black British and British Asian communities, as these were the opposite of celebratory for all British communities.

Sivanandan, through the IRR, continued to disagree with the ideas of multiculturalism and push for an antiracist curriculum. In the preface to his fourth book, *The Fight Against Racism*[1] (1986), he writes that 'multicultural studies ... allow racism to pass unchallenged' (Sivanandan, 1986: iv) because according to multiculturalism, racism is individual rather than institutional. *The Fight Against Racism* was based on an exhibition that the IRR had created and which it lent out to schools, entitled 'From Resistance to Rebellion'. The book used photographs and reproductions of media articles to demonstrate the individual and institutional racism in Britain, and the ways that Black and Asian communities fought against it. It included a list of 'Black deaths in police custody and prison' between 1971 and 1985 (1986: 28), and ends with a double-page spread showing, on the left-hand side, photographs from the Brixton Uprising of 1981; on the right-hand side is a poem, written by Leroy Cooper. The poet points out that uprisings are inevitable when the Black community is politically silenced, economically crippled, and the youth, particularly, are 'criminalised' (1986: 30). Cooper, who was from Liverpool 8, the district where a Black community has existed since the 1800s, was arrested in 1981 for challenging the police over an arrest of another Black young man. Interviewed in the *Liverpool Echo* in 2011, Cooper said, 'they don't like it when you challenge them. They were saying it was nothing to do with us but it was something to do with us, this was our community, these were our streets' (Waddington, Mark, 2011). Cooper's arrest sparked what would become known as the Toxteth Riots, Toxteth being the city government's name for Liverpool 8. Sivanandan published Cooper's poem because he believed that the silencing of antiracist thought would lead to further racial tension and violence.

---

[1] Sivanandan's first three books are still available and the covers can be viewed on the IRR's website: Materials on racism for teachers - Institute of Race Relations (irr.org.uk).

But this was not the view of the government, and Sivanandan's vision lost out to 'Education for All' and the conservative National Curriculum. The ILEA, including its Afro-Caribbean Education Resource library where teachers could borrow books like Sivanandan's, was completely shut down by 1990 (the ACER collection went to the Institute of Education's library, now part of the UCL system). Mainstream textbooks began to respond to racism in ways that acknowledged it but equated it with other forms of prejudice towards white people (such as the Irish and Jewish people), and placed racism in the past, as in Heinemann's 1989 history text by Paul Shuter and John Child, *The Changing Face of Britain*: 'first the Irish, then the Jews and since then the New Commonwealth immigrants all suffered initial hostility. But non-white skins and non-Western languages and cultures made the problems of mixing into the community harder' (Shuter and Child, 1989: 119). The passage goes on to use a passive voice to discuss white British reaction, arguing that 'racial tensions emerged' and 'there were fears that there wouldn't be enough jobs and housing' (1989: 119). Black Britons, on the other hand, were depicted negatively: 'immigrants complained of discrimination' (1989: 119). Nonetheless, fears and complaints, according to Shuter and Child, are all in the past: 'prejudice and discrimination have declined gradually since the 1950s, and British society has been enriched rather than damaged by its newest members' (1989: 119). Shuter and Child's text could exist where Sivanandan's couldn't, because they kept racism in the past and refrained from direct criticism of white Britons.

At the end of the day, the government allowed anti-racism as long as it was historical and any criticism was aimed outside of Britain. As I say elsewhere, 'criticizing the historical roots of racism was acceptable; criticizing the police and other contemporary British institutions was not' (Sands-O'Connor, 2017: 99). Although the first three books of the IRR series can be purchased on their website, Sivanandan's fourth book, detailing specific cases of police brutality and Black resistance, is now unavailable. Jenny Bourne indicates that, 'the last booklet, "The Fight Against Racism" was actually based on an exhibition which we were commissioned to do for the Greater London Council and at this point, funding was quite scarce. So it is possible that we only printed 5,000 of this one which explains why it is out of print' (unpublished email 22 July 2019). The funding which had been available when progressive white teachers were part of the Anti-Nazi League was less readily available when Black and Asian Britons were fighting their own battles in the streets of Britain.

In the 1970s and 1980s, Britain was a difficult place to be for the generation of Black Britons either born in the country or too young to remember any place else. Their parents often urged them to remember their Caribbean roots and assimilate into Britain – but their British experience made the Caribbean seem foreign and their Blackness made assimilation an impossibility. The excessive policing that targeted young Black (mostly male) Britons more than any other group only exacerbated their confusion over identity. Black activists during this period turned their focus to helping young Black Britons and creating literature for them that embraced a permanent and long-term place for Black people in Britain. Acknowledging the historical and cultural contributions of Black Britons, making space in the real and the book world for them, and advocating for equal treatment and the right to protest oppression, writers like Errol Lloyd, Ziggi Alexander and A. Sivanandan gave readers new ways of belonging in Britain. But while Lloyd's fictional texts were generally celebrated by the white British community with award nominations, Alexander's and Sivanandan's non-fiction received more hostile receptions. These authors' attempts to bring wider attention to Black British and British Asian history caused some commentators to fear that white British history would be 'chucked out' – or worse, 'revised' in a way that highlighted negative aspects of British history and society. The backlash against books such as *How Racism Came to Britain* led in part to the Swann Report's embrace of a less-controversial policy of multiculturalism over anti-racism. But the fight over Britishness and British history would continue to be played out in children's books into the twenty-first century.

4

'Good' Britishness: Black identity, white racism and children's publishing 1965–95

The construction of young blacks as an 'alien' element within the polity also involved a reassertion of the attributes of a national identity of the majority population – ranging from shared language, customs, religion, family ties, sport etc. Such culturally sanctioned attributes were constructed in such a way as culturally to exclude from the category of 'British' those who were of a different culture, religion, lifestyle.

John Solomos, *Black Youth, Racism and the State:*
The Politics of Ideology and Policy 1988: 229

Britishness discourses can normalise and privilege Whiteness, pitting White Britons against those who are Othered … Often the voices of ethnic minority communities are invisible and marginalised in political and policy conversations on Britishness.

Sadia Habib, *Learning and Teaching British Values:*
Policies and Perspectives on British Identities 2018: 11

Being Black and British should not be a radical idea. There have been people of African descent in Britain since at least the Roman Empire. And yet, as seen from the quotations above written thirty years apart, the two concepts have frequently been viewed as irreconcilable by individuals and government policymakers. The inability of some white Britons, including those in government, to see people of colour as British or espousing British values often led to the formation of radical organizations uniting Black and Asian Britons as they tried to define themselves and be heard in British society. These organizations were sometimes supported by white radicals and activists who drew parallels between British society and other, more openly racist, societies such as South Africa under apartheid. Black Power and other Black radical activists tried to improve the lives of Black people in Britain, primarily through intensive community building. Building up the Black community, however, could (either deliberately or by default) isolate Black Britons from their white counterparts, including those white activists who wanted to help. Additionally, predominantly white British institutions, including the British government, the education system and mainstream publishing were wary of Black radical organizations, and frequently ignored their efforts or actively worked to shut them down. Mainstream publishing, particularly, favoured authors who took a less radical approach and who praised the work of white activists. Yet, as Julia Mickenberg points out in *Learning from the Left*, children's books are uniquely able 'to challenge the most oppressive elements of the status quo' (2006: 282), and radical ideas did find their way into children's books. This chapter will examine radical activists for Black empowerment, and how those activists turned their ideals into literature for children.

Black power, anti-racism and the policing of Blackness 1965–80

The British population began changing radically in the late 1940s, with the now-iconic 1948 arrival of the Empire Windrush bringing Caribbean workers and writers to Britain and the partition of India in 1947 causing many South Asians to relocate to Britain as well. Those arriving in Britain at this time and throughout the 1950s struggled against racism and the push for them to 'assimilate' into British culture, but a desire to succeed in their new homeland and provide better educational opportunities for their children kept many in this generation from organized resistance. By the mid-1960s, this reticence around organizing had disappeared *because* of that second generation. While many Caribbean and South Asian parents had come to Britain for better educations and futures for their children, they discovered that Britain was not always open to providing those opportunities. Protest movements solidified around two issues: education, and the treatment of Black and Asian youth by police. The activists and radicals involved in these movements in many cases would go on to create literature specifically for Black British children.

In the mid-1970s and early 1980s, Black and Asian Britons confronted an institutionally racist society. More likely to be subject to police surveillance and less likely to be afforded educational and employment opportunities, Black and Asian Britons banded together to demand their rights through community groups such as the Black Parents' Movement and through uprisings and protests such as the 1981 Black People's Day of Action over the New Cross Fire. British children's history books, however, continued to ignore Black and Asian contributions to British history. Even though the Rampton Report, *West Indian Children in our Schools* (1981), argued that 'public and school librarians should attempt to ensure their stocks represent in a balanced manner the range of cultures present in British society, by including books which reflect the culture and achievement of West Indians' (1981: 79), few such books were available. And often, those that were continued to reproduce stereotypes or misinformation about former colonies and their relationship with Britain.

The Windrush generation is now an acknowledged part of British history, although this is partly due to the Home Office scandal in which Black commonwealth Britons who came during the period of legal migration (not immigration) were facing deportation in 2017 as 'illegals' in the country (see Chapter 5). And while prime ministers can speak of the Windrush generation's contribution to British society, it is undeniable that for most of their history in the country, Black Britons from the Caribbean and Africa, as well as Asian Britons from the Caribbean, India, Pakistan and Uganda, were seen as a problem – by which I mean a problem for white Britons. In the British press, Black and Asian Britons were depicted as failing at school, taking white jobs and housing (not to mention demanding union and governmental protections), and as potential criminals.

Some of the earliest literature for Black British children was in fact produced by radical activists involved in the development of organizations to support the Black community and counter the image they had in the British press. I have written at length elsewhere (most notably in *Children's Publishing and Black Britain, 1965–2015*) about the work of Black British publishers John La Rose, who founded New Beacon Press, and Jessica Huntley, who founded Bogle L'Ouverture. John La Rose was never a militant activist, although he actively participated in protests and campaigns for

Black justice throughout his career as an independent publisher with New Beacon. However, Ruth Bush suggests that intellectual aspects of Black Power appealed to him:

> La Rose was consistently opposed to exclusive forms of black nationalism and saw New Beacon's work as part of a fundamental (that is, *radical*) change in the organization of society and culture. Black consciousness movements, such as Black Power and Rastafarianism, together with Marxist ideas fed into his thinking. (*Beacon of Hope*, 2016: 22; italics in original)

The connection with Black Power ideals, in La Rose's case, signalled an emphasis on sustaining and improving Black self-image and forging ancestral connections with the Caribbean and Africa. Jessica Huntley came from Guyana, where she had been active in labour movements and socialist politics (Andrews, 2014: 29–31, 50–60), and in Britain helped to found a West Indian branch of the local communist party. She met the writer Andrew Salkey, who helped her set up Bogle L'Ouverture and became one of its earliest editors, at a Black Power seminar in 1968 (Walmsley, 1992: 156). Both La Rose and Huntley began their publishing careers with adult literature, but through the influence of Andrew Salkey, who had written for Oxford University Press's children's division in the 1960s, and Bernard Coard, an education doctoral student who descried the placing of Black children in Educationally Sub Normal (ESN) classrooms and schools, both Huntley and La Rose became interested in literature specifically designed for Black British children.

The most significant publications from La Rose and Huntley regarding children were by Coard and his wife Phyllis. New Beacon published *How the West Indian Child is Made Educationally Sub Normal in the British School System* (1971), Bernard Coard's exposé of the British schools' inability to see Black British children, especially boys, as teachable. The proceeds from this work were then used to fund Jessica Huntley's publication of Phyllis and Bernard Coard's *Getting to Know Ourselves* (1972), an introduction to reading that 'also taught the history of people of African descent' (Sands-O'Connor 2017: 64) to very young children. The book focused on Pan-Africanism, that is, the idea that all people of African descent are connected through ancestry in the continent, despite the movement of Black people throughout the globe due to colonialism and slavery. It was a way to bring the Black communities in Britain, African and Caribbean together while at the same time instilling a sense of pride in young Black readers.

Jessica Huntley intended *Getting to Know Ourselves* to be followed by sequels, but the Coards left soon after its publication to return to the Caribbean. Bernard Coard later participated in a revolutionary coup in Granada. While Coard's speech about British education has been reprinted and widely influential, particularly on Black British educational theory, the children's book that he wrote with his wife is largely unknown. This may partly be because of its low production values – *Getting to Know Ourselves* had paperboard covers, handwritten text, and was stapled together; few copies remain. But additionally, as Barry Troyna points out, 'historically it has been the case that criticisms by parents, particularly black and working-class parents, about the educational opportunities offered to their children have rarely stimulated major policy appraisals and change' (1992: 76). Huntley and John La Rose continued to publish literature for a Black British audience, and provide community spaces for Black organizations, but their brand of activism was more about community-building than government-toppling. Although their bookshops faced racist attacks, ultimately the reach of their children's books was limited to the Afro-Caribbean community, particularly in London. Additionally, the pan-Africanism they embraced did not always speak to a generation who had never known anything but life in Britain. In many ways, it was left to the second generation of Black Britons to radicalize in British spaces, and produce literature for children that had an impact on the wider society.

By the 1970s, the children of the Windrush Generation were beginning to come of age, and for them, looking back to the Caribbean or Africa was ultimately problematic. As Stuart Hall wrote in 'What is this "Black" in Black Popular Culture?',

> Blacks in the British diaspora must … refuse the binary black or British. They must refuse it because the 'or' remains the site of *constant contestation* when the aim of the struggle must be, instead, to replace the 'or' with the potentiality or the possibility of an 'and'. (2018: 91; italics in original)

In any discussion of Black radicalism, the Black Panthers are often the first group to come to mind. Originating in the United States in the late 1960s, the

Black Panthers had as one of their goals the education (and often re-education) of the Black child away from the ideas of white superiority and towards a sense of Black pride and strong self-worth. The British Black Panthers (BBP), active between 1968 and around 1973, were inspired by but not affiliated with the US Black Panthers, and there were some significant differences between British and American Panthers. Although the BBP concerned themselves with many of the same issues, including education and the treatment of Black people by police, they were a broader-based organization which included British Asians (most notably with regard to children's literature, the writer Farrukh Dhondy) as well as Black Britons such as poet Linton Kwesi Johnson and photographer Neil Kenlock. Kenlock argues that the BBP's interest in education stemmed from the fact that,

> In school, there was no black history. We did every form of English history, but learnt nothing about our own. If you asked the teachers where black people came from, they would say: 'Somewhere in Africa, up a tree', and that's it. So with the Black Panther movement we had educational classes, public meetings and lectures. (Hazelann Williams, 2012)

However, most educational classes were aimed at adults rather than children. Additionally, unlike the American Black Panther/Black Power movement that had the parallel cultural movement of Black Arts, the BBP did not always embrace its writers and artists. Farrukh Dhondy, in 'The Black Writer in Britain', describes his and other writers' experiences in the BBP as non-nurturing:

> There were several young West Indians in the [BBP] Movement who wanted to write and actually did. Most of them kept it a secret, because the leadership of the Movement had never seen the political growth of which we were all a part, as the establishment of blacks, culturally and politically in Britain. (1979: 67)

Dhondy, who initially wrote for the BBP newspaper but ultimately found it too stifling, suggests that the BBP movement was short-lived in Britain 'because of the attitude it took to black creativity … A community does not live by rhetoric alone' (Dhondy, 1979: 68). For Dhondy, radical action could not be achieved solely by leaders making policy that the masses followed blindly. He understood that radical action could only be achieved if Black Britons understood the forces against them, not as uniformly resistant to Black peoples' progress, but as primarily made up of indifference and self-interest on the part of white people. Many of his works for British teenage readers criticize the kind of white anti-racism espoused by people like Chris Searle and Rosemary Stones, well-meaning liberals who did not experience the day-to-day oppression of being Black in Britain.

Dhondy's stories show the way that those white British institutions, particularly educationalists, did not understand the communities they served. Bhupinder, the main character in 'Dear Manju', the first story in *East End at Your Feet*, is given a book by 'White Man's Burden' author Rudyard Kipling for a prize (Dhondy, 1976: 15); succeeding at school clearly required at least tacit and unironic acceptance of the given version of Britishness. However, even when Dhondy presents anti-racist white British characters, they ultimately put their own self-interest before that of the Black British community. In 'KBW', the narrator's father is a working-class, communist union leader, and he tells the narrator, 'don't have no truck with racialist swine' (Dhondy, 1976: 74). It takes radical thinking to counter the standard narrative about immigrants; when typhoid breaks out, most of the narrator's community complains that 'the foreigners have brought it in, that's for sure, from Istanbul and Pakistan and now from that Ugandan Asians' place' (Dhondy, 1976: 81). The narrator's father responds, 'it used to be the Jews in the thirties, now it's bleedin' Indians and Pakistanis' (Dhondy, 1976: 82). But despite his radical stance, in the face of violence, the narrator's father stays inside his flat and does not help the neighbours under threat. 'He had wanted to help Tahir's dad, I am sure, but he felt helpless', the narrator explains, 'there were too many of the others, he couldn't have said nothing' (Dhondy, 1976: 85). Dhondy leaves it to the reader to decide whether the narrator is stating a fact about the forces his father would face, or covering up for the fact that his father was not quite as committed to the anti-racist cause as he proclaimed.

Dhondy's depiction of white middle-class Britons is considerably sharper. In *Come to Mecca*, his second book of short stories, he includes several middle-class white people who put their own interests ahead of Black and Asian communities, even when they seem to be liberal. In the title story, a young white woman named Betty tries to bring attention to a factory strike by Bengali workers for better pay. Shahid, a factory worker, and his friend the narrator, are curious about Betty, but they also mistrust her. 'Betty was a decent girl too, she had a good accent, but like other white girls she didn't know how to behave, where to go and where not to go' (Dhondy, 1978a: 17). Betty uses Shahid's sexual interest in her to get him to come to socialist party meetings, and then tries to get him to sell party papers to 'Asians' (Dhondy, 1978a: 25). 'When she talked to us she said "Bengalis", but when she made speeches she said "Asians"' (1978a: 23), the narrator comments. Betty is not interested in racism, but in class struggle – she tells Shahid he 'should forget about being Bengalis only' (1978a: 20). The overthrow of the system must, for white Britons, start with what will benefit them.

In 'Two Kinda Truth', a sympathetic white teacher encourages a young Black boy with his poetry, but tries to get him to follow white British poetry conventions, citing Auden, T. S. Eliot and Gerard Manley Hopkins. The teacher, nicknamed Wordsy, criticizes Bonny's poetic efforts, saying, 'the poem is too much of a slogan; to be poetry it has to have the sound, not of propaganda but of, well, how shall I put it, of *truth*' (Dhondy, 1978a: 39). Bonny, however, becomes wildly popular in the community and gets an Arts Council grant to be poet in residence at the Lambeth Library. He tells Wordsy, 'truth is what the masses like' (1978a: 42). Dhondy highlights the conflict between white and Black Britons' ideas about education and values; the white British teacher wants his students to conform to convention and assimilate, with the implication that it is for their own good to do so; but the Black British students reject the white teacher's definition of success in British society.

Nonetheless, in these stories the Black people are not ultimately harmed by sympathetic white characters. Bonny succeeds with his poetry and gets the grant to be poet in residence in Lambeth without compromising his poetic style. Shahid dumps the socialist papers Betty wants him to sell in the Thames and goes back to his Bengali community. And even Tahir's family in 'KBW' simply moves away once they find that their 'sympathetic' neighbours are of no use. Rashid Mufti notes that Dhondy creates characters who 'do not reveal their identities simply as a consequence of responding passively to racism' ('Review: *Come to Mecca*', 1979: 9) and that white and Black characters are all subject to a racist society. But in Dhondy's most radical work, *The Siege of Babylon* (1978b), he argues that white Britons will never understand racism or be interested in eradicating it, and this made the book extremely controversial.

Dhondy's *The Siege of Babylon* depicts radical Black youths in a siege against the police. Although part of Dhondy's point was the failure of Black radical organizations such as the British Black Panthers to create real and meaningful change, his novel is sympathetic to the struggles of Black British youth, and critical of the police as well as white Britons who attach themselves to anti-racist activity without being prepared to truly commit to the cause or suffer any consequences. Bobbie Whitcombe, in 'East–West: The Divided Worlds of Farrukh Dhondy' comments about Dhondy's treatment of Edwina, a liberal white drama group leader who becomes involved (sexually and politically) with the main Black characters:

> Edwina enjoys both the excitement and the danger in flirting with the blacks' world, but she thinks that she can withdraw when she is ready, even though she admits to herself a certain irresponsibility in her actions. But the blacks cannot escape their situation. (1983: 42)

Unlike Shahid in *Come to Mecca*, the Black British characters in *Siege of Babylon* are very clear in their understanding of Edwina's actions; one of them tells her, 'I know how you play. It's kicks for you and bullets for us' (Dhondy, 1978b: 42). Dhondy's depiction of Edwina was widely criticized, particularly when reviewers were writing after the death, in April 1979, of the New Zealand-born teacher and anti-racism advocate, Blair Peach. Whereas Dhondy's short stories had been prize-winning, and praised for their depiction of the difficulties of growing up in a racist society, *The Siege of Babylon* was either ignored by reviewers or treated cautiously, even by formerly sympathetic sources, because his book suggested that white people were not entirely helpful to the anti-racist cause. Dhondy trusted his readers to understand what he was trying to do; writing about white Britons fighting racism, he said, 'any assessment of the effect on racism … must ask blacks for their experience, and any force that begins to counter it must understand what blacks have been doing to fight it. You can't be for blacks without knowing what they are doing' (Dhondy, Beese and Hassan, 1982: 16–17). Too many white Britons, Dhondy suggested, had their own interests (or even amusement) ahead of the needs of the Black community.

White critics who did review the book, focused less on the depiction of Black struggle and more on the negative way white Britons were seen by

Black Britons. Rosemary Stones called *Come to Mecca* a work of 'outstanding achievement of committed socialist writing for young people … not to be missed' (Stones, 1979b: 23) but *The Siege of Babylon* 'marred by its sexist perception of the white women' (1979b: 23). Maggie Hewitt, reviewing *Siege* in the *Children's Book Bulletin*, expressed concern that 'in a book riddled with racist and sexist views in its characters, the author fails to take any standpoint himself' (Hewitt, 1979: 25) and adds that teachers should read it before giving it to students. But Dhondy's 'standpoint' was clear, even if it was one that white British people didn't like: Black people were being treated poorly by Britain, leading them to radicalize; white British people who purported to help were often out for their own gain first, if not solely. Mainstream Britain was not yet ready for such a message, and Dhondy's books went out of print by the early 1980s.

Beyond Babylon: Len Garrison and the voice of young Black Britain

Responding to the sense of alienation that the second-generation Black Britons felt required the creation of a new kind of community, one that paid attention to the voices of that generation. Len Garrison came from Jamaica to reap the benefits of a British education at the age of eleven with his parents, and attended grammar school in Chelsea. He experienced 'daily racism' (Waters, 2019: 151) there, and it influenced his desire to improve the experience of young Black children, particularly Black boys to whom he taught supplementary Black history classes in 1960s Brixton. His work with Black youth in Brixton led him to make a major study of Rastafarianism as it manifested in Britain, and to the establishment, in cooperation with the Inner London Education Authority (ILEA) of the Afro-Caribbean Educational Resource (ACER) project.

Like earlier book creators for Black children, Garrison was particularly interested in understanding and supporting the Black child growing up in Britain. Whereas the Huntleys and John LaRose had looked backward to the Caribbean, and Dhondy offered fairly bleak possibilities for a generation growing up in a racist society, Garrison's work highlighted the voice of Black youth and empowerment who more successfully rejected white British institutions. In his study on *Black Youth, Rastafarianism, and the Identity Crisis in Britain*, Garrison argues that many Black British youth 'openly reject all forms of symbols of white domination' (1979: 35) and embrace Rastafarianism because it 'provided an historical awareness and a basis on which Black youngsters are attempting to routinize their social and cultural existence in British society' (1979: 34). It is important to understand the version of Rastafarianism that young Black Britons embraced; Robert Miles hypothesized that 'Rastafarianism could become the vehicle for a political organization in black communities, as opposed to being a more diffuse cultural expression of protest or a "church"' (1978: 23). In other words, whereas their parents may, like the Huntleys and John LaRose, have embraced communism, many young people turned to Rastafarianism as a political statement against the police and other authorities. Peter Clarke adds that 'the Rastafarian movement ... is creating something new, especially for those young black people in, for example, London, who feel neither British nor West Indian. To these people in particular the movement gives strength and a sense of identity' (1986: 98).

But there was a danger that by associating themselves with the Rastafarian community, Black youth could permanently alienate themselves from mainstream society. In order to prevent further alienation, Garrison argued that the educational system had to include all its students; he argued there is a 'need for a shift from the Euro-centric curricula activities to a more culturally plural approach to allow the cultural experiences of all children of different ethnic backgrounds to be broadened and shared' (1979: 36). Garrison recognized that attachment to Rastafarianism was in part an attempt by Black youth at forming an identity; he did not want them to give up that identity, but rather wanted the rest of society, particularly white British people, to understand and accept it.

It was because of this that Garrison, after two years of running an Afro-Caribbean Resource Centre on his own, decided to link more directly with white institutional Britain. Garrison, like Chris Searle, made youth voices central to his publishing efforts; yet unlike Searle, he chose a somewhat more mainstream route to publication, partnering with the ILEA rather than an independent publisher. While this increased the number of young people who were reached by ACER and its materials, the ILEA was far from apolitical, which proved to be both a blessing and a curse for ACER.

The ILEA had been organized under the 1963 Local Government Act, and in its first decade it acted as general overseer to the expansion of comprehensive and progressive school education. Beginning in the 1970s, however, it began to be more directly involved in the curriculum of the London schools, and this included creating and commissioning its own materials and media. The ability of the ILEA to produce and distribute print and audio-visual materials across London's schools is almost universally agreed to be one of its biggest successes. Tim Brighouse writes that the 'rich flow of curriculum materials, books and resources grounded in the best practice of London's schools' (Brighouse, 1992: 55) was something that 'had more effect on curriculum … than all the other initiatives, ranging from Nuffield to the Schools' Council, put together' (1992: 55). And David Mallen adds that the ILEA's efforts made London school libraries 'better stocked than anywhere else … The quality of its materials was outstanding' (Mallen, 1992: 70). They had a television centre from 1969, a publishing centre and a lending library of learning materials, all of which functioned in tandem. So, for example, ILEA television produced the programme *Sing a Song* in 1975; in 1976 they produced a *Sing a Song Bumper Book One* of some of the songs used in the programme; and the lending library could deliver both book and programme to classroom teachers in the London area it covered.

Unlike many of the mainstream television programmes and publishers, the ILEA embraced and celebrated the multiracial nature of London's schools; *Sing a Song* had in its television and book incarnations children of many racial groups and ethnic origins depicted. The book includes illustrations of interracial friendship (including an interracial kiss on page 31) and songs representative of the multi-ethnic backgrounds of London children, including a Christmas calypso (ILEA, 1976: 33) and a West Indian song and story about dumplings (1976: 39). The work that the ILEA did in producing literature that represented Black and Asian children at this time was perhaps greater than any other publisher in the country at the time, and had a very broad reach as many of the books and materials were sold to schools and libraries outside the London area. This reach, commitment to representative depiction, and educational focus all appealed to Len Garrison as he began to think about allying the Afro-Caribbean Education Resource centre with the ILEA.

However, like many mainstream publishers at the time, the ILEA focused almost exclusively on positive interactions between children of different racial and ethnic groups. In the mid-1970s, British educationalists were embracing a policy of multiculturalism, at least in multiracial areas. The Bullock Report, *A Language for Life* (1975), followed reports in the 1960s (particularly the Plowden Report of 1967) that worried about the education of so-called immigrant children (this referent stuck throughout the 1970s, even though many of the 'immigrant' children were born in Britain) and the books to which they had access in schools. Bullock asked the questions, 'if the school serves a multiracial society, does it have books about the homelands of its immigrant families, about their religions and cultures and their experiences in this country?' and 'has the school removed from its shelves books which have a strong ethnocentric bias and contain outdated or insulting views of people of other cultures?' (Bullock, 1975: 286). Although he gave a nod to the idea that the books chosen for schools had 'implications here for the education of all children, not just those of families of overseas origin' (1975: 286), the primary focus of Bullock's attention was achieving multicultural books for multicultural classrooms. The ILEA produced books such as the wordless Phototalk series that depicted Black and Asian children in British urban settings, but without any hint of poverty, unemployment or police surveillance, all of which were common to the experience of Black and Asian Britons, and which affected young children.

The ILEA's *Going to the Park* (1984), for example, differs from Errol Lloyd's *Nini at Carnival* in significant ways. While both books remove the threat of the police, Lloyd's book depicts children under their own authority organizing and enjoying a carnival. Lloyd has given children ownership and control of the carnival which had in real life come under heavy surveillance by the police. *Going to the Park*, on the other hand, starts and ends with a photo of a family. In the cover photo, all three children are under physical control of the parents. There are no other people in the book, so unlike *Nini at Carnival*, there are no interactions with the community. The children participate in only two activities which are not supervised by the parents, playing a game of tennis and smelling some flowers. The rest of the photos have adults (the parents) firmly in control. This is the case in most of the ILEA Phototalk books; the grounding in the realism of photography does not allow for children to have autonomy outside of the family unit. While some saw the lack of conflict and multiracial nature of the Phototalk books as positive depictions of what these communities could and did achieve in Britain, others saw it as failing to represent the day-to-day experience of institutional racism and its effects on Black and Asian children. As Mike Mulvaney suggested about primary schools embracing multiculturalism, 'the "minority" parents turn out to provide food costumes, artefacts, etc., and appear to be eternally grateful. At the end of all such events staff and parents say "namaste" to each other, and the school reverts to its celebration of white, male, middle-class experience' (Mulvaney, 1984: 27). Multiculturalism, for many white teachers under the ILEA, was a part-time concern.

Garrison and Boateng argued that, even when 'well-intentioned' (Garrison and Boateng, 1980: 22), white liberal efforts often resulted in limited success because 'instead of accepting that the fault lay in the nature of the school system itself, it was automatically assumed that it was the children and their parents who were deficient' (1980: 22). Garrison blamed the 'inheritance of colonialism and imperialism' (Garrison, 1982: introduction) for Black alienation *and* white inability to confront racism. When Garrison initially set up the ACER centre in 1976, it was as an independent organization. But 1976 was also the year that the Race Relations Act banning discrimination in education (among other things) was passed, and this 'provided the mainstream support' (Olowe, 1990: 13) to focus on multi-ethnic education within the ILEA. The leadership of the ILEA's new Multi-Ethnic Inspectorate was eager to form a partnership with Garrison's ACER centre.

For Garrison, the partnership had benefits as well. In addition to its own publishing arm, the ILEA had both funds and the ability to reach all students in the City of London and the twelve innermost boroughs directly. Half of these students were from Black and ethnic minority backgrounds. Working with the ILEA allowed Garrison to force the school system to acknowledge its Black students in a way they hadn't before. 'Our philosophy was that schools should be made to work for all pupils', Garrison wrote, 'Black children should not have to go outside the mainstream schools to seek recognition and gain confidence in being themselves. White pupils should also learn about being black in a white society' (Garrison, 1990: 175). For Garrison, it was not just about interracial harmony – in fact, in some ways, it was not about harmony at all. Rather, the ACER project aimed to assert the identity of the

Afro-Caribbean student and teach both Black and white children about the effects of continuing institutional racism.

This meant not shying away from uncomfortable topics, and the educational materials that ACER produced for teachers included discussions of police oppression, educational disadvantage and casual racism in children's books. Garrison knew that as part of an educational institution like the ILEA he would have to tread carefully. His friend Ansel Wong, who had opened the first Black supplementary school to partner with the ILEA, the Ahfiwe school, in 1974, had recently seen it close, partly due to 'a move toward a specific Black Studies curriculum' (Sands-O'Connor, 2021: 25). But Garrison felt that by focusing on the voices of young people themselves, rather than using radical Black reading material from America as Wong had, he could avoid the negative attention that the Ahfiwe school had received.

Additionally, Garrison felt that too often, adults had spoken for and about children's experiences. Like Chris Searle, Garrison was part of a trend towards publication of young people's writing. Themed contests, writers' groups and classroom activities during the 1970s often led to the publication of anthologies. While many of these were general – W H Smith and *The Daily Mirror* had been running a competition for young writers since 1959, for example – others were specific to the voices of young people from underrepresented British communities. Small community presses such as Centerprise in Hackney had begun publishing young writers in the early 1970s with surprising success. Black British teenager Vivien Usherwood's collection of poems, for example, published by Centerprise in 1972, sold over 6,500 copies in five years (Worpole, *Local Publishing*, 1977: 21) and led to the community centre publishing more work from teenagers. Ken Worpole, who brought Usherwood's poems to Centerprise's attention, writes that Usherwood's poems were 'mostly about feeling rejected at school and in the children's home where he was in care' (Worpole, 1977: 3). Worpole believed that 'access to books, both to be able to buy them easily, and to be involved in producing them, we regard as a right' (1977: 3) and a way of belonging in society. Centerprise's success with Usherwood's poems led to their willingness and ability to publish Chris Searle's *Stepney Words* as well.

In the late 1970s, both the ILEA and ACER published books of poetry written by London school children. Alasdair Aston, head of English for ILEA, invited 'contributions to the Authority's first published collection of poetry. Written by pupils of all ages, the book was intended to be part of the exhibition "The Richer Heritage", reflecting the variety of cultural traditions within inner London schools' (Aston, 1978: 5). The poems were on any subject, and while a few dealt with racism or prejudice, most did not. Garrison also wanted children to belong to the world of books, but the young people's writing he published had a very specific focus. Kate Douglas and Anna Poletti suggest that 'life narrative practices can be a means for young writers and artists to increase their participation within their respective cultures … the production of life writing for a public is a means for asserting agency for many young people' (Douglas and Poletti, 2016: 6) and "life writing often provides a way for young people to negotiate and assert their citizenship" (2016: 7). The balance between cultural participation and citizenship assertion was more difficult for those outside the dominant culture, however, as participation in minority cultures often called into question the assertion of Britishness. As a historian, Garrison felt it was crucial for children to speak for themselves about the racism they experienced, and in 1978 he set up the first Black Youth Penmanship Competition. This competition was not as much about penmanship as about ideology; young writers were given prompts or topics to discuss in essay, fiction, or poetry format. The winners each year were 'published' in a spiral-bound book, but on two occasions, ACER collected the winners into book form: in 1987, the winning essays and creative pieces from the early years (1979–84) were published as *Black Voices: An Anthology of ACER's Black Young Writers Competition* (edited by Paul McGilchrist), and in 1990, the winners of a competition focused on Martin Luther King's most famous speech were published in *I Have a Dream: ACER's Black Young Writers Winning Essays 1989*. Although Garrison's name is not in or on these books (*Black Voices* was edited by a postgraduate student), his philosophy of encouraging radical youth voices runs through the early collection especially. Essay prompts such as 'Let the Pen Speak for I', 'What Rastafarianism Means To Me' and 'Reggae Music Is a Source of Strength Because …' all connect to Garrison's earlier research into Rastafarianism and identity.

Garrison also more directly influenced the contest by teaching creative writing to young people in London. Nicola Williams, whose essays 'A Black British Childhood' and 'Black Achievement in Sport is not enough because

'...' won first and second prize and were later published in *Black Voices*, wrote that in his creative writing classes, 'Len challenged the stereotypes of what the mainstream thought black culture was supposed to be' (Pears, 2013). Williams took this message to heart, writing in her second essay that 'Black people are portrayed as one-sided, not multi-faceted, individuals. The worrying thing is that this is so subtly done, particularly in the media, that some Black people have begun to believe them and thus such myths become self-perpetuating' (Williams, 1985a: 272). Williams, who went on to become a successful barrister and crime novelist, was more measured than some of the essayists in the collection. C. Brown, aged seventeen, wrote in an essay on 'Should We Protect, Share or Lose Our Culture and Lifestyle in Britain?" that 'The first benefit I get from maintaining my culture is that I know I am not a part of a nation of oppressors who travel the globe exercising brute force and violence' (Brown, 1985: 80). Yet Michael Beckles (who became a leading lung cancer specialist) argued that belonging was important: 'the next thing that must be done by the school authorities is to make Black pupils feel as though they belong to society' (Beckles, 1985: 278). These views are varied, but all point to the necessary roles that identity and society play in the success of Black youth in Britain.

ACER's second collection of essays, *I Have a Dream*, reflect changes in British society and London's educational system occurring between 1985 and 1989. In ACER's early days, anti-racism was, if not universally accepted, at least understood as a possibly useful response to the oppression of the police under Thatcher's government and the prevalent racism throughout white British society. However, after areas like Brixton, Handsworth and Toxteth experienced a second wave of uprisings in 1985, the UK government began coming down harder on left-leaning anti-racist efforts. The ILEA and the Greater London Council (GLC), who had organized a Year of Anti-Racism in 1984, were dismantled by the late 1980s. According to Patrick Vernon and Angelina Osborne, 'With ACER's funding greatly diminished, Garrison moved to Nottingham, where he established East Midlands and African Caribbean Arts' in 1988 (Vernon and Osborne, 2020: 175). Although he continued to be involved in another major London project, the establishment of the Black Cultural Archives, he stepped back from his role at ACER.

Garrison's lack of involvement is obvious in the collection of essays published in honour of Martin Luther King. First, the emphasis is no longer on the young Black Briton's identity, but on the wider, even global, Black community (similar to the move made by Chris Searle from *Stepney Words* to *The World in a Classroom*). Essay prompts for this collection include 'The Role of the Black Church', 'The Politics of Aid and Famine' and, of course, 'King's Dream Speech' itself. Many of the essays in this collection do not consider Black Britons at all, instead considering the position of Black people globally, especially in America and South Africa. Dena Lawrence's poem, 'I Saw it Happen', for example, considers the experiences of Black people in Egypt, Mississippi and Soweto (Dena Lawrence, 1990: 85–6), but not Britain. Lynette Charles' first place essay, 'Has Martin Luther King's Dream Been Fulfilled?' argues that 'In Britain today Martin's dream has partly been fulfilled because we can now find Black people in important jobs' (Charles, 1990: 2), but in South Africa, 'it is obvious that no attempts have been made to fulfil any aspect of King's dream there' (1990: 3–4). Victor Amokeodo's essay on 'The Politics of Aid and Famine' (Amokeodo, 1990: 37–44) discusses Africa and foreign aid, but although the essay criticizes France, the Soviet Union, the United Nations and the United States, it never even mentions Britain.

Garrison's decreased involvement in the penmanship competition may also have been because of his understanding of Black history and community. In 1985, following the uprisings in Brixton and the death under mysterious circumstances of fifteen-year-old anti-racist campaigner Elaine Clair (sometimes spelled Claire), Garrison published a book of poems, *Beyond Babylon*, aimed at the Black British youth he served in the community. Ansel Wong, Garrison's fellow community activist and educator, wrote that in the book 'Len has succeeded in fusing photographic images with his creative talents to capture in meaningful words the feelings and contradictions of Afro-Caribbean peoples 'in Babylon' (Wong, 1985: 4). Stuart Hall, who wrote the book's introduction, suggests that although Garrison's poems are 'defined by a highly distinctive, individual "voice", [they] also contain the "voices" of a whole generation' (Hall, 1985: 15). This is the generation of Rastafarian youth. Rastafarian ideas – from the obvious Babylon in the title and in poems, to images and poems about dreadlocks and their significance to Jah and Ethiopia – filter throughout the collection. In the book's title (and final) poem, Garrison calls for the young to create a 'new life' (Garrison, 1985: 58) beyond Babylon that will embrace and demand recognition of

Black culture, history, rights and dignity (1985: 58), just as he had through his penmanship competition.

One of the poems in *Beyond Babylon*, 'For Thelma B. Moore', celebrates underacknowledged Black history, particularly the contribution of Marcus Garvey (Garrison, 1985: 39–41). In 1987, the centenary of Garvey's birth, Garrison's ACER project mounted an exhibition based on *The Life and Times of Marcus Garvey 1887–1940*, accompanied by an educational resource of the same name by Lottie Betts-Priddy (ACER, 1988). Betts-Priddy's introduction shows the way that ACER put the emphasis on the Black experience while targeting the white learner as well. Garvey was important because of 'his philosophy of Black pride, unity and economic self reliance for the Black race' (Betts-Priddy, 1988: 1); but because the 'true history of Britain is intricately entwined with the history of its former colonies and their peoples' (1987: 1), it should 'be taught from a perspective that encompasses the whole' (1987: 1). For Garrison, Black history was of primary importance for the identity of the Black child, but it had broader benefits as well. Writing in 1990, he suggested that

> Schools which had been hesitant and even resistant began to see positive results as black children began to accept unapologetically their colour before their friends and teachers. White pupils, encouraged by ACER materials, began to accept difference in a positive way, and teachers bean to feel less threatened by being asked to treat race-related issues positively (Garrison, 1990: 178).

But Garrison was concerned for the ACER following the demise of the ILEA; he felt that (as had happened with public library funding), ACER would be expected 'to place the primary focus of the funding of ACER onto its commercial viability' (Garrison, 1990: 179) in order to receive funding from public sources. No longer able to demand rights and dignity now, as Garrison did in *Beyond Babylon*, Black British youth would have to settle for Martin Luther King's dream in some far-off future. Increasingly, the culture of education began to downplay British racism and highlight racism outside of its borders. This was particularly the case with two African campaigns, one concerning Biafra and the other South African apartheid, which became acceptable causes for anti-racists.

Beverley Naidoo, Buchi Emecheta and Africa in Britain

At the same time that the British government was trying to deny the long history of British racism, its colonial past came back to haunt it in the form of two campaigns in aid of Black Africans: in Nigeria's breakaway region of Biafra and in South Africa. In both cases, British people were urged to become involved in 'helping' Africa and Africans. The Biafran Relief campaign and the Anti-Apartheid Movement (AAM) in Britain were in many ways similar to the abolitionist movement, because as Graham Harrison notes, 'campaign representations of Africa are principally evoking notions of Britishness – or more specifically *good* Britishness – over and above their efforts to represent Africa' (Harrison, 2013: 534). Harrison goes on to argue that the opposition that British campaigns set up is as much between good British citizens and 'the "remote" them of Africa/Africans' (2013: 534) as it is about British people putting pressure on the UK government to end involvement (in slavery, in apartheid). The remoteness of Africa/Africans is critical to understanding the different responses to two activist authors from Africa who had emigrated to Britain, white South African Beverley Naidoo and Black Nigerian Buchi Emecheta.

While both Nigeria and South Africa were, by the 1960s, independent nations, they were both part of the Commonwealth and (more importantly) Britain had critical economic interests in both and was therefore interested in maintaining political stability as far in as was possible. In Nigeria, ethnic tensions between the Igbo and the Hausa people led to coups, reprisal killings, and eventually, millions of Igbo refugees from the north of the country moving to the southern region of Biafra. The Biafran region attempted to secede and form its own government in 1967, leading to a two-year civil war. Ilkka Taipale notes that while other colonial powers and some of the former British colonies in Africa (including South Africa) supported the Biafrans, 'Great Britain, which had significant financial interests in the area … supported Nigerian unity. Nigeria produced 10% of the UK's oil, and it came from Biafra' (Taipale, 2017: 208). Similarly, the British government's economic interest in South Africa meant that it was ambivalent about apartheid; Ron Nixon points out that 'Britain was the biggest foreign investor in and principal trading partner of the country' (Nixon, 2016: 90) and because of this the Thatcher government opposed sanctions against South Africa. As with the abolition campaigns of the eighteenth and early nineteenth centuries, Britons participated through activism *against* the British government and *for* African people in both Biafran Relief and anti-apartheid protests, but the methods were different.

In the Biafran crisis, Britons were urged to aid the country through charity; with South Africa, boycott and protest were both used as means of helping. Biafra was the first post-imperial depiction of the 'starving African' in the media. Suzanne Franks writes that 'the media account of the crisis focused upon a terrible famine. There were shocking pictures which caused outrage in the West and prompted calls for support' (Franks, 2010: 80). The media not only depicted Africans as starving and helpless (an image which was reintroduced in other famines, such as Somalia and Ethiopia), the British who offered help were depicted as 'angels of mercy' (2010: 80). Anti-apartheid efforts, on the other hand, targeted activism towards the governmental system of oppression rather than the effects of that system (e.g. poverty, segregation, lack of access to education and employment). While charitable aid was undoubtedly a part of the anti-apartheid movement, consumer boycotts were a bigger focus. These boycotts were aimed at putting pressure on the British government to sanction South Africa and the South African government to end apartheid. However, as Johann de Jager points out, 'while the overall aim of these campaigns may have been seen as placing economic pressure on South Africa, it also had the purpose of creating public consciousness of apartheid and establishing a culture of activism against it' (De Jager, 2018: 62). Thus, boycotts allowed British people to feel good about themselves through their consumer activity; participation in a boycott function more as virtue signalling than as a direct factor in change. In both the case of Biafran charity and South African boycott, the benefit to British self-image is as much as, if not more than, the benefit to actual African people. These images, of Black Africans as helpless and of (often, though not always, white) British as 'angels of mercy' had an impact on the reception of two African-born children's writers, Beverley Naidoo and Buchi Emecheta, in the 1970s and 1980s.

Naidoo, a white teacher and exile from South Africa, became involved in British opposition to apartheid through the Defence and Aid Fund for Southern Africa, an organization started by John Collins, the canon of London's St Paul's cathedral. By the time she joined, the group had shifted their efforts from legal defence to encouraging a 'hearts and minds' campaign. Naidoo recalls, 'I still remember an early meeting when the group was discussing how young people could find out about South Africa. Everyone thought that what was needed was a work of fiction – something that could reach the heart' (Naidoo, 1985 [1995]: viii). At that point, Naidoo had not written fiction, but she volunteered to give it a try because 'there was a story I really wanted to write' (1985 [1995]: viii). *Journey to Jo'Burg*, the resulting book, was published in 1985 to great acclaim; it won several awards, including the 1985 Other Award in the UK, and was adopted across the country in both primary and secondary schools.

The story of *Journey to Jo'Burg*, about two Black children who must walk 300 kilometres to find their mother who works in Johannesburg, is not Naidoo's story. Although an exile from South Africa, Naidoo was born into relative privilege, a white South African who had a nanny. She based her story on (and dedicated it to) her nanny, who she called Mary although that was not her name. Mary's two young children died of diphtheria hundreds of miles away from her while she cared for young Beverley. Naidoo writes about that experience, indicating the way that apartheid's racism affected her own world view:

> If you had spoken to me at the time, I am sure I would have said that I was sad that her daughters had died but I would probably have added that 'Mary' was lucky to have a job with our family and that we sent her children presents at Christmas. Now looking back on it all, I still feel very angry about how the racism of the white society stopped me and other white children from really seeing and understanding what was going on. Racism damages everyone in the society. (Naidoo, 1985 [1995]: vii)

Years later, at university in South Africa, Naidoo became politically active in the anti-apartheid movement. She was arrested and detained for 90 days in solitary confinement in 1964; following this experience she decided to continue her education in England. She married another exile, a South African of colour, and her 'visit' to England became permanent (because apartheid laws made their marriage a crime and their children illegitimate). Writing *Journey to Jo'Burg* was not just an act of rebellion against the apartheid laws, but a 'journey' of her own: 'the journey is more than a physical one. It is a psychological one, too – for my characters, for me the author, and, hopefully, for my readers' (Gallo, 1990: 145). Naidoo's writing was born out of activism, but she was not an activist for or even speaking to her own community.

Journey to Jo'Burg does not show a complex picture of racism. The book contains few white people; only the children's mother's employer and the police. 'Madam', as the mother's employer is called, is annoyed with Mma and allows her to go to her sick child only after a 'very important dinner party' (Naidoo, 1995: 23). Madam adds, 'if you are not back in a week, I shall just have to look for another maid, you understand?' (1995: 23). White police are universally threatening; the children learn of the crackdown in 1976 when 'the police aimed their guns and began to shoot with real bullets, killing whoever was in the way' (1995: 34). They shoot indiscriminately, and even children die. Naidoo attempts to highlight the dehumanizing effect of racism by making all white people bad and all Black people good.

She had the opportunity to complicate the picture by depicting the racial background of the doctor who treats the children's baby sister; but because the book is focalized through the children, Naledi and Tiro, and only Mma goes into the hospital, it is not even clear whether the doctor treating the baby is Black or white. This may have been in part because Naidoo was not sure herself whether they would have had Black doctors in the townships; she wrote a letter asking questions about the health care system at the behest of Liz Finkelstein, telling the addressee (identified only as 'Rachel'), 'my deadline is very near and I've still got to work through the scene in the hospital' (Naidoo, 1983); her final question was to ask 'about what proportion of doctors in bantustan [sic] hospitals would now be black?' (1983). It is unclear whether Naidoo ever received a reply, so perhaps her vagueness was because she herself did not know.

However, whatever the reason for keeping the hospital scene hidden from the reader's view, Naidoo's failure to show any positive white characters helps strengthen her case that racism 'damages everyone'. *Journey to Jo'Burg* does an excellent job of introducing the damage done to Black Africans under apartheid, but distances white racism and apartheid from her expected readership of mostly white British children. Naidoo wrote that she 'hoped that empathizing with Naledi on her psychological as well as physical journey would encourage all children to explore and help strengthen their responses to the injustice of racism' (Naidoo, 1987: 43). Although she acknowledged that Britain was 'a society in which racist ideas flourished' (1987: 43), Naidoo's book raises awareness of and sympathy for Black South Africans suffering under apartheid through a comfortable distance that does not require readers to question the racism in their own surroundings or themselves.[1]

This lack of questioning about racism closer to home is reinforced by *Journey to Jo'Burg*'s original cover. Naidoo writes in a letter, 'we were fortunate to find two young South Africans willing to pose for Longman's 1st edition cover of J to J' (Naidoo, 'Unpublished description'). Naidoo discusses the set-up for the photograph, the photographer brought an orange tree and 'the children were asked to dress in their oldest clothes' ('Unpublished description'). There is no indication why they were asked this, but in an era of high-profile charity efforts (1985, the year the book was published, was also the year that both 'We are the World' and 'Do They Know it's Christmas?', pop songs that raised funds to help famine victim in Africa, were on the music charts), the decision to use photographs of real children in old clothes certainly implies a need to engender sympathy in the reader. To have a book cover which focuses on real South African children, in combination with the newspaper clippings and introductory material, suggests a desire to portray Naidoo's story as 'true' or 'real'; but taking photographs of children in their oldest clothes problematizes this 'truth'. At least two photographs were taken; the one chosen was the one Naidoo felt was the 'saddest' one. All of these choices complicate Naidoo's desire to give agency to Black South Africans – despite the book being about children taking the initiative to go find their mother 300 kilometres away, the message of the book embodied in the 'sad' picture is that the (mostly white) readers should feel sorry for and help South African Black people. There is no mention of Britain's historical culpability in the creation of a racially divided South Africa in the novel. Naidoo herself acknowledges that 'in a paradoxical way, J to J's association with the anti-apartheid movement (conceived as a moral movement against the immorality of apartheid, racism, colonialism)

---

[1] Naidoo does more to encourage British readers to think about racism in their own country in later books; for example, her novel *The Other Side of Truth* (2000) discusses the effect on Black African children of going through Britain's refugee and asylum system.

assisted it [British ideas of superiority]' (Naidoo, 2021). Naidoo's book takes an anti-racist stance, but it is one that (perhaps inadvertently) discourages readers from considering their own racism or that of their government. This contrasts sharply with Anthony Delius's contribution to *The Young Travellers* series 40 years earlier (Figure 2).

The financial success of *Journey to Jo'burg* enabled Naidoo to turn to writing full time, a luxury few Black anti-racist writers were ever to achieve. Naidoo succeeded in bringing awareness of South African apartheid to British children, but through the (then common) method of engendering sympathy which maintained national and racial hierarchies between Britain and Africa. Despite this, however, Naidoo's book – unlike Phyllis and Bernard Coard's, Farrukh Dhondy's and Sivanandan's – remains in print and is used in schools, even now that the system of apartheid has become historical memory.

Naidoo's success in writing about racism outside Britain can also be set against the work of another African writer, one who also exposed grim realities of life for Black Africans. But Nigerian-born Buchi Emecheta was not writing about the realities of life in Africa. She wrote about the experience of being an African woman in London – an experience very different from Naidoo's because of British racism. In books such as *In the Ditch* (1972) and *Second Class Citizen* (1974), Emecheta described life for Black African women and children in London. *In the Ditch*, according to Janice Ho, 'was praised as an insightful sociological depiction of poverty ... but critics also expressed disbelief that [main character] Adah, an educated Nigerian, could ever find herself in such a situation' (Ho, 2015: 139). Black Nigerians *in Africa* could be victims of destitution, as the Biafran media images demonstrated, but not in London. *Second Class Citizen*, which Emecheta wrote partly to respond to these criticisms, made it plain that the main reason for Adah's second-class status was British racism. 'only first-class citizens lived with their children, not the blacks ... The children had no amusements and their parents would not let them out for fear they would break their necks on the steep stairs' (Emecheta,1974 [1994]: 46). Race defined what Black African immigrants could expect from Britain: poor housing and lack of job opportunities. Being denied access to basic needs and employment had a direct effect on identity: 'could she be black and proud of it when she had so little of which to be proud *except* her race and her children?' (Emecheta, 1972 [1988]: 90).

Figure 2 The first front cover of Naidoo's book is designed for a white audience taught to feel sympathy for distant Africans through charity appeals.

The Black Africans that Emecheta describes in her novels of the 1970s have experiences of British racism in housing, education and employment similar to Afro-Caribbeans, Indians and Pakistanis who came to Britain in the decades of the 1950s and 1960s. The difference for Emecheta's characters, however, is that they do not have a community of fellow Africans facing similar struggles to support them.

Concerns about poverty and British racism are also reflected in Emecheta's children's books. While Charlotte Bruner says that Emecheta 'includes only a small section of the social protest so typical of her adult novels' (Bruner, 1986: 135), the books are highly critical of systemic and individual British racism. In *Titch the Cat* (1979), Emecheta's characters are discussing an acquaintance who got rid of her cats because ginger cats were 'unlucky' (Emecheta, 1979: 31); upon hearing this, one of the children responds, 'it's like being born black and people blaming you for it' (1979: 31). Racism is manifested in poor housing from the council; *Titch the Cat*'s family lives in a rodent-infested house that 'had been left empty for a long time before we moved in' (1979: 44). In *Nowhere to Play* (1980), the main character struggles because 'there was no safe place for a nine-year-old girl like me to play' (Emecheta, 1980: 8). The Black African children have each other, so they have more of a community than Adah in Emecheta's earlier novels, but they still face racism from the same quarters. When they try to play at the 'Crown Flats which belonged to the Queen' (1980: 26), they are chased off by the white residents. When they try to go to church, the children are told by a white woman that they aren't dressed 'smart' enough (1980: 66), and June says that 'even the church doesn't want us' (1980: 68). They do not get to enjoy the summer, but are eager for school to begin again because 'the teachers are paid to keep us there, so the school's bound to have us' (1980: 69). The people chasing the children away from potential sites of play are ordinary white Britons representing institutions (the 'Crown', the church). The only institution that will accept them (education) is one where they will have to work, not play. Emecheta argues that systemic and individual racism in Britain robs Black children of their fundamental right to play and to enjoy childhood.

Emecheta's children's books did not enjoy the publishing success of her adult fiction. While Penguin has recently republished *Second Class Citizen* (1974 [2021]) as a Penguin Modern Classic, *Nowhere to Play* and *Titch the*

Cat have never been reprinted. In contrast, Naidoo's *Journey to Jo'Burg* went on to win the Other Award, for 'progressive books of literary merit' ('Other Award Exhibition Catalogue', 1985: 2), has never been out of print and is still frequently used in schools to teach about anti-racism and apartheid. Emecheta's and Naidoo's relative success in the children's market can be put down in part to their presentation of racism. In Naidoo's book, racism is perpetrated by white South Africans against Black South Africans, while the (white) British reader is positioned to sympathize from afar. In Emecheta's books, the Black Nigerian experiences exclusion and discrimination from white British people in Britain. While, as Tom Buchanan writes, 'white minority rule in South Africa was frequently and readily presented in Britain as a deeply moral cause and an affront to fundamental human rights' (Buchanan, 2020: 71), Black African poverty and racism *in Britain* did not allow the white reader to feel morally beneficent in the way that literature about Africans in Africa did.

What does it mean to be Black and British?

Fundamentally, radical Black and Asian narratives with an antiracist message written by activists of colour for child readers of colour have been seen by (some) white Britons as potentially dangerous. Madan Sarup argues that many teachers and educationalists reject anti-racism 'as something "negative". It does not give a balanced view, it is illiberal – a form of indoctrination. They feel frightened that a militant anti-racist stance may provoke a counter-productive reaction' (Sarup, 1991: 41). Black and Asian British empowerment suggested to many readers a white British *disempowerment*, and literature written to boost the self-image of children of colour and connect them with their history often faced difficulty finding mainstream acceptance because they did not encourage Black and Asian British people to embrace white British traditions and history. The works published by radicals such as La Rose and Huntley had a restricted audience and limited marketing, but even so their bookshops were vandalized and threatened while police refused to intervene. Radicals who criticized white anti-racists or the British government and its institutions, such as Dhondy, Sivanandan and Emecheta suffered criticism, indifference or even direct censorship. In order to stay in print and find a sustained and widespread readership, radicals and activists for Black and Asian empowerment had to package their children's books to be acceptable to white readers. Many refused to do so, but those who did, like Beverley Naidoo, have remained in print to this day.

5

Hostile environments for history and publishing: Activists addressing children of colour 2012–21

In the decade from 2012 to 2021, British activism around issues of race had been on the increase. The implementation by the British government of the Hostile Environment policy in 2012 and the murder in the United States of African-American George Floyd in 2020 galvanized anti-racist activity. Some of that activity has been focused on producing literature specifically for a Black British child audience, addressing issues of racism and belonging in Britain. In this period, activist historians, including Corrine Fowler, David Olusoga and Jeffrey Boakye, placed particular emphasis on the radical revision of British history in children's literature. Writers of historical fiction like Catherine Johnson, Benjamin Zephaniah and Alex Wheatle use naïve Black narrators to counter stereotypes that both Black and white readers might hold. And activist literacy organizations, such as the Centre for Literacy in Primary Education and Booktrust, began interventions into the children's book industry by publishing annual statistics, beginning in 2018, to record the representation of racial diversity in children's books and the experiences of children's book authors and illustrators of colour. As with similar efforts in the past, all of these activists have experienced negative reactions to their work; however, their literary activism has also resulted in visible changes in the children's book market, potentially marking a more long-term or permanent change.

This chapter begins in 2012 because several events of that year highlighted the participation of Black people in Britain and Britishness. The summer Olympics were held in London in 2012, and the opening ceremony, designed by a team that included film director Danny Boyle and novelist Frank Cottrell Boyce, was an effort to produce, according to Catherine Baker, 'a deliberate and distinctive historical narrative, developed and negotiated at a time of major political contestation in the UK regarding the nature of the citizenship ties between the people and the state' (Baker, 2015: 412). The narrative included, as Baker further points out, an emphasis on Britain as a multicultural nation by depicting 'black immigrants arriving on the Empire Windrush from the Caribbean' (2015: 414). Both Baker (2015: 417) and Aaron Winter note that the 'multiculturalism' on display in the London opening ceremony revises history through what it *doesn't* include; Winter, for example, writes, that the Windrush segment of the ceremony was 'the only notable reference to colonialism' (Winter, 2013: 4). This surface-level multiculturalism led to the opening ceremony being criticized by both the left and the right (2013: 4).

History was a battlefield in other arenas in 2012. Efforts to stop a statue of Crimean War-era nurse Mary Seacole being built near the St Thomas hospital in London and an effort to remove her from the national curriculum intensified in 2012 (see *Children's Publishing and Black Britain 1965–2015*, Chapter 6). The statue and inclusion of Mary Seacole caused consternation from conservative critics such as members of the Nightingale Society, who argued that 'Mrs Seacole was a businesswoman who never nursed at all! She sold fine wines and meals to officers, while Nightingale nursed and got the filthy hospitals cleaned up, laundries and kitchens established for the benefit of British soldiers' (Nightingale Society, 2016). Finally, the year 2012 was the year when then-Home Secretary Theresa May announced the Hostile Environment policy on illegal immigration – a policy that would directly affect the Windrush generation when children who came over on their parents' passports faced deportation as adults.

The Windrush scandal became a flashpoint for ways of thinking about who belonged in Britain because the idea of Windrush itself encapsulates the history and experiences of colonialism and its aftermath. The triumphal image of the model of the *Empire Windrush* in the London Olympics Opening Ceremony was soon belied by the Hostile Environment policy. By 2017, reports were beginning to surface that the Home Office was arresting and attempting to deport Black Britons who had come to the country legally under the British Nationality Act of 1948 as children and – because they often came on their parents' passports – had no proof that they arrived before 1973 when the law changed. Maya Goodfellow pointed out in *Hostile Environment* that 'landing cards, the only proof of when they arrived in the UK, were destroyed by the Home Office in 2010. This made it near impossible for them to show they were in this country legally' (Goodfellow, 2020: 4). The very office that was demanding proof had already destroyed the only proof many of them had. Amelia Gentleman, who was one of the reporters who broke the story in the mainstream press, wrote that 'this vision of the British state, in a final shrug of post-colonial nonchalance, trying to flick citizens back to the same Caribbean islands where centuries earlier their ancestors had been brought from Africa by British colonisers as slaves, was painful to witness' (Gentleman, 2019: 9). Home Secretary Priti Patel called the scandal 'an ugly stain' ('Statement on Windrush Lessons Learned Review', 2020) on British history, but deportations continued and some who had been deported died before being exonerated[1].

The Windrush Scandal, in tandem with the murder by police in the United States of George Floyd and the pulling down of the statue of slave-trader Edward Colston in Bristol in summer of 2020 has led to further youth protest in the form of Black Lives Matter demonstrations and a reinvigorated movement to promote and understand Black British and British Asian history. But some white British people saw a focus on Black and Asian British history as a threat. The issue of who belonged in and to Britain became (again) an issue for Westminster; the land itself became a site of Britishness battles when the National Trust announced it would partner with Corinne Fowler and the *Colonial Countryside Project* to investigate links to colonization and the enslavement of Black people at their properties. Racial representation in children's literature became part of the national conversation when the *Reflecting Realities* project led by the Centre for Literacy in Primary Education exposed just how white children's books had always been when it published the first of its reports in 2017. This chapter will examine the ways in which Britain became an increasingly hostile environment for Black people after 2012, and how activists writing for children responded. As in past activist periods, the contestation of history, promotion of children's and Black people's voices, and freedom from institutional oppression were all important elements

---

[1] In 2013, Theresa May – architect of the Hostile Environment policy – said that citizenship was 'a privilege and not a right', a justification that Patel relied on in her 2021 Nationality and Borders Bill that allows the UK government to strip someone of their British citizenship without prior notice.

of activist efforts to make space for Black child readers in the British children's book world.

The Empire, turned inside out: Britain and people of colour in history

One of the common responses to Black Britons who criticize hostile governmental policies is to be told they should 'go back to their own country'. This refrain implies that skin colour determines who belongs where – and that whiteness is a determining feature of Britishness. Historians have long noted the presence of Black and Asian Britons, and books such as Peter Fryer's *Staying Power* (1984), Sukhdev Sandhu's *London Calling* (2003), Rosina Visram's *Asians in Britain: 400 Years of History* (2002), Gretchen Holbrook Gerzina's *Black London* (1995), Jeffrey Green's *Black Edwardians* (1998), more recently Miranda Kaufmann's *Black Tudors* (2017) and David Olusoga's *Black and British: A Forgotten History* (2016), provided constant corrective to the idea that Britain was exclusively white. However, thanks to the persistence of 'tourist Britain' which markets a Downton Abbey-esque version of Britain's rural past, the countryside of England has continued to be envisaged as a place that people of colour do not belong[2].

This idea of the British countryside as a protected haven for white people is critical in a country that extols its rural sections as a kind of utopia embodied in William Blake's accidental hymn 'Jerusalem'. Corinne Fowler, a literature professor at the University of Leicester, writes about the 'unspoken' presence of people of colour in British country houses in much the same way that Edward Said did in his chapter on 'Jane Austen and Empire' in *Culture and Imperialism* in 1993. In fact, in 2017, Fowler responded to Said's chapter in her own essay, 'Revisiting Mansfield Park' where she wrote, 'historians increasingly see colonialism's cultural, economic, and material

---

[2] Anita Sethi's *I Belong Here: A Journey Along the Backbone of Britain* (2021) and the row over a Muslim hikers' group (McLean, Sloper and Mullen, 'Muslim Hiking Group Set Up by Coventry Man Faces Racist Abuse After Christmas Day Walk', *Coventry Telegraph Online*, 5 January 2022) are two recent attempts by people of colour to open up the British countryside despite negative reaction from some white Britons.

legacies as more formative of modern Britain than even Said suggested' (Fowler, 2017: 363). But while historians (including literary historians like Fowler) may have seen colonialism as formative, this history needed to be uncovered for the general public, something Fowler had already begun to do. Fowler's project to make plain the presence of Black and Asian people in Britain's country houses was crucial, she felt, because 'despite country houses' material connection with empire, they have been instrumental to depicting rural England as a white preserve which valiantly resists foreign influence' (Fowler, 2016: 400). Fowler wrote these words in 2016, about the time she started to conceive a larger project to investigate those links between country houses and empire. The project would involve Fowler's academic research into National Trust properties to make plain the links between Britain's wealth and prosperity, embodied in country houses, and its history of enslavement and colonialism. Along with three National Trust curators, Fowler authored the Trust's *Interim Report on the Connections between Colonialism and Properties Now In the Care of the National Trust, Including Links with Historic Slavery* (Huxtable et al., 2020). The report found that about a third of the properties managed by the National Trust have direct links to colonial histories, and

> challenge the familiar, received histories, which both exclude the vital role that people of colour have played in our national story and overlook the central role that the oppression and violence of the slave trade and the legacies of colonialism have played in the making of modern Britain. (Huxtable et al., 2020: 6)

The backlash against the Trust's investigations was severe, and began even before the report was published. In June of 2020, Victoria Baillon wrote an article for *The Conservative Woman* entitled 'Woke virus infects the National Trust'. In it, she calls Fowler 'menacing' and argues that 'the Trust has plumbed new depths by its committed support for the Black Lives Matter campaign' (Baillon, 2020). The criticism of the National Trust was not confined to online or media discussions, but extended to Parliament; the leader of the House of Commons, Jacob Rees-Mogg, attacked the report in a parliamentary speech, saying that the National Trust should remember that 'its properties were given to it by people who expected them to be custodians of our history, proud of our history and to think well of our great nation' (Kaonga, 2020). Similar to previous governments that preferred only positive representations of race in contemporary depictions, and little or none at all in the past, Rees-Mogg defined historical properties as beneficial only if they celebrated Britain's past. Coming only months after a similar backlash against (mostly young, mostly Black) protestors who toppled the statue of slave-trader Edward Colston in Bristol, Rees-Mogg's comments about history and national pride were further volleys in a war over Britain's representation of history.

In *Green Unpleasant Land* (2021), Fowler demonstrates how the backlash against the National Trust's report on colonial links to its properties was part of a long tradition of idealizing the English countryside as a place untouched by Empire's darker side. The resistance 'reflects precisely the same sentiments of the builders and purchasers of many country houses, whose wealth derived from empire's human and material exploitation' (Fowler, 2021: 126), she wrote, adding, 'the rural location of houses and garden estates placed them at a remove from the port cities and commercial centres and further still from the wider unease about aspects of colonial activity that were believed to threaten national virtue' (2021: 126). The controversy over the *Colonial Countryside Project* mirrored the earlier debates over the use of Mary Seacole in the classroom. Fowler was rewriting history, revising history, or even 'perpetuating "cultural Marxist dogma"' (Sophie Yeo, 2021), just as those who wanted to bring Seacole into the curriculum were trying to 'bolster Seacole's achievements at the expense of [Florence] Nightingale for reasons of "political correctness"' (Furness, 2014). Fowler, in *Green Unpleasant Land*, argues that 'the determined opposition to an anti-colonial history suggests a nation at a crossroads: either prone to comforting nationalist myths, or a country ready to embrace its fuller histories and the global connections of its people' (Fowler, 2021: 11). The idea that Britain has reached that crossroads is possibly optimistic, but Fowler, like many activists before her, places her hope in the next generation.

The controversy over Fowler's work might have soon disappeared and gone largely unnoticed by the general public if she had not, as part of the Colonial Countryside programme, encouraged British schoolchildren to investigate these links at National Trust properties, and then to express their feelings and observations about these links in writing. Mitchell and Sobers argue that 'audiences often look for themselves in the work with which they are engaged. Participatory media therefore offers the opportunity ... to blur the distinction between the researcher (investigator), the researched (site of investigation) and the audience' (2013: 152). By allowing children to research and then respond to historical sites, Fowler's project raised objections similar to that raised by Chris Searle's Board of Governors when he wanted to publish children's work: that it was too negative. But the criticism of Fowler's involvement of children also recalls objections to Mary Seacole as a heroic British nurse, in that both were seen as revisionist history. Restore Trust, an organization set up to counter the National Trust's 'agenda', 'warned the poetry project appeared to encourage youngsters to lament the country's past' (Simon Osborne, 2021). The criticism is, up to now, only based on minimal evidence; the *Colonial Countryside Project* is planning to publish a book based on children's work in 2022 with Peepal Tree press, but some conclusions can be drawn from the few poems and essays are available on the Colonial Countryside website, based on children's experiences at Charlecote Park, a sixteenth-century country house and gardens.

The written responses came from primary school children 'most of whom are of African, Caribbean and South Asian heritage' (Fowler, 2018: 2) who spent time examining and discussing objects at National Trust properties with creative writers and historians. The children are encouraged to respond creatively to the objects through poetry and short essays. One of these objects at Charlecote Park is the painting of Thomas Lucy, the house's owner, from 1680. The painting shows Lucy, his horse, and in the corner, an unidentified Black boy. The children's poetry is often descriptive, but the descriptions are poignant. 'He wears a silver collar', Lana Habeel writes, adding in the next line, 'like a pet' (Habeel, 2018: 4). Other poems comment on his isolation, his use as a nameless object in the painting rather than a named subject like Captain Thomas Lucy. The essays focus on the weather compared to Jamaica, and the beauty of the house. None of them suggest that Thomas Lucy was violent towards the boy. The mere facts of ownership, namelessness and placement in the background of the painting are what the children focus on – but these are symbolic of a hierarchical system that, as a young writer named Theo wrote, 'thought that I, a black majestic war horse, was far more important than an enslaved boy' (2018: 5). These poems and essays are not so much about lamenting the past as about recognizing the past that is hidden in plain sight. Through *the Colonial Countryside Project*, Fowler gives voice to the Black British and British Asian child writers on the project, encouraging them to find their history in the British colonial past.

But helping children to connect with and think about history has consequences. Madge Dresser and Andrew Hann, in their introduction to *Slavery and the Country House* (2013), argue that making a 'personalized connection has an impact beyond those who count themselves among the descendants of the enslaved and the colonized to reach into our very notions of who "belongs" to Britain' (Dresser and Hann, 2013: xiv). Historian Caroline Bressey acknowledges that 'challenging the whiteness of British country houses requires a reconfiguration of British history' but adds 'this does not mean British history should be reinvented, but that its dominant discourses should recognize the complexities and legacies of slavery, colonial expansion and empire' (Bressey, 2013: 130). The National Trust's decision to publish its report on its properties' historic links with slavery led to accusations of wrongdoing by the charity, and an investigation by the charity commission. Even though the commission concluded that 'the charity acted in line with its charitable purposes, and the trustees fulfilled their legal duties and responsibilities' (Charity Commission, 2021) some media outlets seized on the resignation of its chairman, Tim Parker, who faced 'political opposition from government ministers over the trust's examination of historical links between its properties and the UK's legacy of slavery and colonialism' (Kevin Rawlinson, 2021) as evidence that (white) British people opposed the Trust's investigations. This despite the fact that in April 2021 alone, the National Trust signed up 50,000 new members ('National Trust Seeks New Chair', 2021). Fowler's project is contentious for many of the same reasons that earlier activist literature was: it is about British history and whose voice matters in it. By encouraging Black British and British Asian child participation in her activist project, Fowler suggests it is their voices that matter. As with earlier activist initiatives, including Chris Searles' publication of working-class child poetry, this has led to charges that Fowler is telling children how to think. Unlike Searle, however, Fowler has been careful to make her project a partnership, not just with the children, but with Peepal Tree Press and with the National Trust, both of whom publicly underscore the careful research of the work. The National Trust's website, for example, argues that the Trust will ensure the 'robustly researched stories of empire are communicated accurately' (*Colonial Countryside Project*, 2021). By making the *Colonial Countryside Project* a collaboration between academics, the heritage sector, publishing and children, Fowler emphasizes that producing an accurate understanding of history is everyone's concern.

Ghost town or Electric Avenue? History from Black British perspectives

Fowler examined spaces traditionally coded as white for evidence of Black British and British Asian presence in history. David Olusoga's *Black and British: A Short, Essential History* (2020) is a children's version of his *Black and British: A Forgotten History* (2016). Like Fowler, Olusoga is searching for the Black presence in Britain, but he does it from the perspective of someone who grew up Black in Britain. Historian Jeffrey Boakye has looked at everyday aspects of being Black *as history*. Boakye's *Musical Truth* (2021) examines Black music to demonstrate how it connects to larger British (and global) histories.

David Olusoga's *Black and British: A Short, Essential History* (2020), the young people's version of his *Black and British: A Forgotten History* (2016), attempts to achieve the balance between the audiences who buy and those who consume his book. It is produced in a standard children's paperback size, in order to make it look less like an educational book, and although it contains picture credits for the many photographs, maps and illustrations, and a glossary of more difficult words, there is no reference list (or recommended further reading) and no index. But the book also focuses heavily on the periods that are prescribed in the National Curriculum for KS2 – in fact, one commentator on a review of the book, Michael Bowyer, complains that Olusoga 'skips from the Romans to the Tudors' (Bowyer, 2020) even though there is evidence of Black people in medieval times as well. The reality of writing history for children, however, is that publishers want material keyed to the history curriculum. Authors might change what is covered in those time periods, but it is unlikely that they will change the curriculum.

And yet, David Olusoga's book does not ignore other time periods. In fact, he spends more than a quarter of *Black and British* on the Georgian period. In the two chapters that he devotes to Early and Late Georgians, it becomes clear why this period is significant for Olusoga. By skipping from the Tudors to the Victorians in the KS2 curriculum, schools can effectively ignore the history of the trade in enslaved people. While he does not directly criticize the National Curriculum in the book, in his introduction he writes about the importance of learning about 'Black people like Dido Elizabeth Belle and Olaudah Equiano who lived in Britain in the eighteenth century. I also learned about the Black children who lived as slaves in the houses of rich people in London, Bristol, Liverpool and other cities' (Olusoga, 2020: 2). The immorality of white Britons enslaving Black children and the presence of both wealthy Black people and Black abolitionist campaigners remain unknown to young people if the curriculum does not expand beyond particular periods. On CBBC's Newsround, Olusoga spoke more directly to this point: 'without these stories about slavery and the empire, it's very difficult to make sense of the country that we live in today' ('Newsround', 2020). That 'country that we live in today' includes 'the "hostile environment" [where] thousands of British people of West Indian heritage ... had been stripped of their British citizenship' (Olusoga, 2020: 209) in the Windrush Scandal, and 'young protestors who were aware of [Bristol's] historical role in the Atlantic Slave Trade pulled down a statue of Edward Colston, a seventeenth-century slave trader' (2020: 210). Olusoga's activism is insistent but indirect; he demonstrates the anti-racist acts of people who know and understand their history, history which he does not shy away from reporting and defending. Olusoga recently testified in the trial of the 'Colston Four' who helped topple the statue of Colston, arguing 'having a statue of someone of that calibre in the middle of the city I believe is an insult' to British people (De La Mare, 2021).

He also links his book with The Black Curriculum, a charity that advocates for 'changing the national curriculum and building a sense of identity in every young person in the UK' ('Mission Statement', 2020). In the report the group produced on *The Black Curriculum: Black British History in the National Curriculum* (2021), author Jason Arday suggests that 'the need for a more critical engagement with issues around Empire and slavery is essential in understanding Britain's troubled and oppressive history, in its absolute unfiltered entirety' (2021: 11). The charity provides teacher resources as well as podcasts aimed at younger people (they begin with definitions of words such as 'colonialism'), and they produce a zine on topics such as Black hair and Notting Hill Carnival. They also offer courses for teachers on how to integrate Black history into the curriculum, and supplementary education classes for teens and tweens on Black history through the use of music. This multimedia approach is one way they hope to achieve their aims 'to provide a sense of belonging and identity to young people across the UK' and 'to teach an accessible educational Black British history curriculum that raises attainment for young people' ('Mission Statement', 2020). It also extends the way that a traditional academic historian like Olusoga can reach out to a media-savvy generation.

The use of music to teach Black history is also the approach utilized by Jeffrey Boakye in his book *Musical Truth* (2021a). Boakye, a London teacher and journalist has long been interested in the intersections between music, Blackness and masculinity. His first book, *Hold Tight: Black Masculinity, Millenials, and the Meaning of Grime* (Boakye, 2017) considers all of these things from a teacher's perspective talking (at least some of the time) to other teachers with suggestions of how to use grime in the classroom. He followed this book up with another book for adults, *Black, Listed* (Boakye, 2019) which investigates the different terminology used for and by Black people about the Black community. He describes this exercise as 'terrifying' (Boakye, 2019: 393) adding that the linguistic 'landscape I'm picking through is a war-torn disaster zone' (2019: 393). Despite this fearful description, David Lammy called Boakye's book 'emancipatory, particularly when the black community takes ownership of the terms of prose' (Lammy, 2019). The terms we use and how we define them is, for Boakye, a political act.

This is true for his writing for children as well. His book on *What is Masculinity? Why Does It Matter? And Other Big Questions* (Boakye and Chetty, 2019), co-authored with Darren Chetty, urges readers to think about 'the entertainment industry, full of movies, video games and music that promote hypermasculinity; tough guys doing tough things' (2019: 19). But with *Musical Truth*, Boakye explores Black British history through the lens of music – and that history is often the history of racism. In much the same way that Linton Kwesi Johnson's dub poetry addressed Black oppression in the 1970s (and Johnson's 'Sonny's Lettah' is one of the musical selections in Boakye's book), Boakye appeals to young readers' interest in music to teach them both positive and negative aspects of being Black and British.

While scholars have long acknowledged that Black music 'is driven by and permeated with the memory of things from the cultural past' (Floyd, 1995: 10), Boakye uses music to teach a specifically Black British history. In 'Sonic Settlements: Jamaican Music, Dancing, and Black Migrant Communities In Postwar Britain', Jason McGraw argues that 'contextualizing Jamaican music in postwar Britain as an audience-centered art form, then, offers new ways to think about immigrants' experiences and their creation of social life in the face of changing and often repressive legal regimes' (2018: 355). Boakye begins his book, not with music, but with a description of Operation Legacy, in which the British Foreign Office, worried about the country's image as Empire declined after the Second World War, 'destroyed the evidence. Files that revealed the crimes of empire were burned, buried, even dumped at sea' (Boakye, 2021a: 11). The book continues to point out 'the legacy of the British empire' (2021a: 12) in Black British history, including riots; housing, education and employment discrimination; white appropriation of Black music; police oppression and the Windrush scandal – all through songs which had an impact on the British music charts. In this way, Boakye can discuss the racist history of the British government while reminding his readers how much Black people brought to British culture.

Boakye does not describe himself as an activist, but he does acknowledge that his work is political. 'Writers who are not white find ourselves, whether we like it or not, politically positioned as infantry in the fight for diversity. Our stories become odes to persecution and prejudice, our words become incendiary and intense' (Boakye, 2021b). David Olusoga also denies that his work is activist: 'I don't want to be the "angry black guy" on television', he says. 'I'm interested in telling these histories, just trying to make them amazing … not trying to tell them always with a political edge, because I don't think people listen to that' (Mukherjee, 2017). Yet, like earlier activists, they both speak up for the voiceless and use their speech to actively promote change. Their work treats activism as a normal, everyday activity in which children can participate through familiar media – suggesting new pathways for activist writing for children of colour (and all children, for that matter) into the future.

Free to rebel: Catherine Johnson's, Benjamin Zephaniah's and Alex Wheatle's British historical fiction

While Olusoga and Boakye were introducing Black history through nonfiction, other writers for children used historical fiction as a mode of introducing readers to 'forgotten' Black Britons. The idea of introducing 'forgotten' communities into history was far from new; white writers like Bob Leeson were doing this in the 1970s, and Black writers – most notably Catherine Johnson – had made their career out of writing Black people into historical fiction for children. Johnson said it was necessary for Black writers to write their own histories, but that it was often more comfortable for publishers and readers to have white people writing these stories: 'the words of a white author are a comfortable buffer, a reassurance that nothing in the story will be too shocking, too hard to understand; the author is like you, and you can trust him or her to tell you this story in familiar terms' (Johnson, 2011). Johnson found that many publishers did not want books from her about eighteenth-century Black British children having adventures, but they did want books about enslavement of Black people. Johnson did not want to tell Black history in familiar terms, she wanted stories 'in which people like me, mixed race, not white, get to wear frocks and have adventures. It's important for someone like me to say that we've been here for a very long time. People of colour are part of the warp and weft of the UK' (Johnson and Bold, 2020: 131), a part of British history and not just Black British history.

When Scholastic asked Johnson to write a novel about enslavement, she did not follow the brief: 'rather than setting the story around abolition acts as suggested, she chose instead to write about the massacre on board the slave ship the Zong and the subsequent court case, all seen through the eyes of slaves and former slaves themselves' (Andrea Reece, 2020: 9). This book became *Freedom*, which in 2018 won the Little Rebels Children's Book Award for radical fiction. The Little Rebels award was set up in 2013 to honour fiction that was

> informed by *any* of the following: anti-discriminatory, environmental, socialist, anarchist, feminist concerns OR promotes social equality or challenges stereotypes and/or the status quo or builds children's awareness

of issues in society OR promotes social justice and a more peaceful and fairer world. (littlerebels.org)

The award was a way for Letterbox Library, who administer the award, to promote activist and radical ideas, similar to the Other Award in the 1970s.

For Johnson, the recognition was a long time coming. Although she had published historical fiction as early as 2001, with her novel about a Black female boxer in *Hero*, her books became increasingly more insistent on telling historical stories about Black people who spoke out about oppression. *Freedom* not only exposes the racist actions of some white Britons, describing the Zong trial as 'not simply about whether some rich white folk get richer, this is about whether we are human beings' (Johnson, 2018: 95); it also showcases a Black community living in London and working for justice. Nathaniel, the main character, is introduced to the Sons of Africa, the real-life group of activists working for abolition alongside white campaigners like Wilberforce. Among them is Olaudah Equiano. Upon meeting him, Nathaniel 'was astonished – a black man, writing his own story! I thought books were for white people' (Johnson, 2018: 97). In *Freedom*, Johnson sums up much of what Black activists have advocated for in their books for children: freedom from oppression, recognition in society, community and voice. Catherine Butler and Hallie O'Donovan, in *Reading History* (2012), argue that historical fiction for children frequently functions as a way of 'projecting contemporary concerns on the past, or understanding the present in terms of historical precedent' (Butler and O'Donovan, 2012: 184) and Johnson's *Freedom* does both. It is part of a larger movement to make Black Britons visible in history, but since the book's plot is concerned with activism, it allows readers to consider activism within the safe space of a book.

Benjamin Zephaniah's *Windrush Child* (2020) also goes beyond highlighting a 'forgotten' community. In fact, because Zephaniah's book was written in the wake of the Windrush scandal, the Black community he describes is not really forgotten in the same way that Black Tudors or Black Victorians might be for young readers. However, Zephaniah's book shows them as forgotten in different ways. The Windrush generation in children's books is often celebrated as bringing new foods or musical styles to Britain; while casual racism may be depicted in these books, it is rare to see British colonialism implicated in the splitting up of families – even though adult books about the Windrush generation, including Andrea Levy's *Small Island* (2004) or Alex Wheatle's *Brixton Rock* (1999), show this clearly. Zephaniah's main character, Leonard, and his mother only join Leonard's father in England after a decade of him working there to make enough money to bring them over. By this time, not only is Leonard's father a stranger to him, but he has formed a romantic attachment to a white woman named Shirley. This relationship, when it is revealed, breaks up Leonard's family for a time.

Zephaniah parallels Leonard's family breakup with what many saw as the British government's breaking of trust with its Windrush citizens. By integrating the Windrush Scandal into the novel, Zephaniah brings attention to the way that the government was eager to forget its colonial past. Many of the Windrush deportations (attempted and actual) were of pensioners, and were carried out in violent fashion; as David Matthews writes, people were 'denied status, healthcare, pensions, sacked from work, jailed, separated from kith and kin, deported, humiliated' (Matthews, 2020: 4). Zephaniah ends his fictional story with the hero, Leonard, retired and wanting to take his own daughter to Jamaica to learn about her heritage. Zephaniah describes Leonard's attempt to get the necessary travel documents:

> I applied for my passport, but when we arrived at the passport office, the border and immigration officer behind the screen beckoned over two police officers. They threw me against a wall and detained me in front of my screaming wife and daughter. Do you know how bad that feels? It was humiliating. (Zephaniah, 2020: 189)

Violence, both physical violence and the emotional and psychological violence of separation from loved ones and from society, is exposed as a deliberate policy of imperialism. Zephaniah's exposition of this violence in modern times is part of a tradition of activist children's literature that goes back to works such as Amelia Opie's 'Black Man's Lament'. Although the British Empire no longer exists, its effects are still real, and Zephaniah, long an anti-racist campaigner, is interested in ensuring that British readers do not forget the ways that racism operates at an institutional level. In 2015, he commented that, 'I no longer have to run away from skinhead thugs, but I still get stopped by the police. On the whole, society *is* more accepting, but we still have institutional racism'

(Zephaniah, 2015: 3.45–4.02). He directly linked British racism to the British Empire when he famously, and publicly, refused an OBE, writing,

> It is because of this concept of empire that my British education led me to believe that the history of black people started with slavery and that we were born slaves, and should therefore be grateful that we were given freedom by our caring white masters. It is because of this idea of empire that black people like myself don't even know our true names or our true historical culture. (Zephaniah, 2003)

Zephaniah's book asks readers to question the celebratory narrative of Windrush as depicted in public arenas (such as, the Olympic Opening Ceremonies).

The book also pushes the reader beyond questioning and towards action by its concluding remarks from Amnesty International, which endorsed the book. After giving a history of the Windrush Scandal, the Amnesty afterword states, 'many people still have to register their citizenship, including thousands of children who have grown up feeling as British as their friends' (Zephaniah, 2020: 197). The afterword suggests several possible actions before concluding 'every action you take, no matter how small, makes a difference' (2020: 197). In this way, Zephaniah's book moves from the individual activism of correcting the historic record to the collective activism of redressing injustice.

Another author who links British Empire injustices with post-imperial racism is Alex Wheatle. Wheatle's *Cane Warriors* (2020) like Catherine Johnson's *Freedom* and Benjamin Zephaniah's *Windrush Child* is a piece of historical fiction from the point of view of those with less power. It tells the story of Tacky's War against the British in 1760 from the perspective of a fourteen-year-old boy who participated in it. In many ways, the book's structure mirrors that of nineteenth-century historical fiction such as that written by G. A. Henty, where a young boy in the British colonies becomes involved in historic events, along the way meeting a famous person who compliments the young boy on his bravery – only Wheatle's boy is Black, not white, and his hero is the leader of a rebellion against the British Empire. Wheatle's story, unlike Henty's, cannot end in glorious triumph (the rebellion was brutally put down by the British) but neither does it end without hope. The main character Moa, and his friend Hamaya, speak about their potential future children. Hamaya says she will make sure that her children will remember Tacky and what he and his rebels did; Moa responds that not only will they remember, 'they will back de evil against de wall' (Wheatle, 2020: 180). That evil is the oppressive force of the British military and the system of enslavement that caused Black people in the Caribbean to rise and take up arms. The book is violent, not for the sake of violence, but because oppression leads to a violent response.

Because Wheatle, in *Cane Warriors*, is writing about the historical violence of the British enslavement of African people, now recognized by the British as well as (most of) the rest of the world to be wrong, the violence is seen as justified, and allowable in a children's book (albeit one marketed at an older age group). However, Wheatle came to writing in part because of his participation in another rebellion against an oppressive British force. As a young man living in Brixton, having been brought there knowing nothing of Black culture after years of living in a notorious care home in Kent, Wheatle experienced the sus laws and hyper-surveillance of the British police under Margaret Thatcher. In 1981, the combination of the police's rush to criminalize Black youths with their failure to investigate potential crimes perpetrated against Black people (the New Cross Fire was a flashpoint), led to an uprising that the media quickly labelled a riot. During the Brixton uprising, Wheatle threw a brick at police. He was arrested and imprisoned. Wheatle's Brixton uprising story is the story of how Wheatle became an activist, not because he participated in riots, but because in prison he began to read revolutionary Black literature. Just as Black Power literature inspired writers like Linton Kwesi Johnson in the 1960s and 1970s, Wheatle was motivated to become an activist when his Rastafarian cellmate introduced him to C. L. R. James's *The Black Jacobins*. Wheatle talks about this experience in *Uprising* (2017):

> That same morning, after breakfast, the dread took me to the prison library. He got out a book for me to read. It was called *The Black Jacobins* and it was by C. L. R. James. It was about slaves in Haiti who had fought for freedom from their French rulers. I found it exciting and inspiring. Nobody taught me this kind of history in school. (Wheatle, 2017: 29)

Learning about Black history may have inspired Wheatle to write *Cane Warriors*, but his own story of the Brixton uprising was not published by a children's publisher or marketed towards young people. Diffusion Books, who published *Uprising*, is a division of SPCK, the Society for the Promotion of

Christian Knowledge – the third oldest publishing house in Britain, having been established in 1698.

During the nineteenth century, the SPCK changed its model to include much more children's literature. As I write elsewhere, 'The SPCK published hundreds of volumes for children, some obviously religious in tone, and others much more popular in nature … These books received wide circulation because they were often given as Sunday School prizes' (Sands-O'Connor, 2008: 53). Today, their children's range consists primarily of picture book retellings of Bible stories designed to make 'learning and understanding faith easily more fun' ('Children's Christian Picture Books'). However, they have another division – in which Wheatle's *Uprising* falls – designed for prisoners. These books are commissioned to 'help improve reading skills while emphasising the importance of making good life choices and fostering positive relationships. We resource prison reading groups with the books they need to improve literacy in prisons' ('Diffusion Books'). Wheatle's story is written in simple language, and has considerably less description of violence than *Cane Warriors*. Compare, for example, the description of Tacky's fight with the British in *Cane Warriors* to the description of the clash with police in *Uprising*. The violence in *Cane Warriors* results in 'broken cheeks, shattered noses, smashed skulls and stomachs spilling whatever was inside of them' (Wheatle, 2020: 153–4). It is immediate and sensory. In *Uprising*, however, Wheatle employs narrative distance in describing events. Sometimes this is through his use of passive voice: 'before I knew it, a police van was rocked over and its windows were kicked in' (Wheatle, 2017: 19). At other times, Wheatle simply reports events without additional description: 'I spent most of my time fighting with the police. They had arrested me and beaten me up a number of times before' (2017: 19). The most detailed descriptions of violence are attributed to the authorities in *Uprising*; the staff at the care home where Wheatle grew up beat him 'almost every day with whatever the staff had to hand – wooden hair brushes, belts, shoes and, once, with an iron fire poker. Then there were two times when a child psychiatrist sexually abused me' (2017: 4). Although the events are listed, the beatings and abuse are not reported graphically, as the events are in *Cane Warriors*. Similarly, the initiating event of the Brixton Uprising is reported rather than vividly described: 'This young black guy ran in and shouted that the police had stabbed a black youth to death in broad daylight!' (2017: 18). Although *Uprising* is considerably less violent than *Cane Warriors*, the Brixton Uprising had almost never appeared in children's literature when Wheatle was writing his memoir in 2017. On the rare occasion, such as A. Sivanandan's *The Fight Against Racism*, where there is a discussion of the events of April 1981, books have faced censorship. However, David Olusoga's *Black and British: A Short, Essential History* includes several pages on the uprisings of 1981, defining them as spreading across the country because 'young Black people, the children of the Windrush generation, were marginalized and persecuted by the police' (Olusoga, 2020: 198). Olusoga not only mentions the Windrush generation and the Windrush Scandal in his book, he links these events with the killing of African-American George Floyd in 2020. Hassan and Noack point out that the murder of George Floyd in 2020 sparked 'demonstrations that forced countries to grapple with their own histories of police brutality, racism, inequality and colonial transgressions' (Hassan and Noack, 2021). This was a reckoning that had already begun in the publishing industry.

Children's publishing and the (new) historical record: Reflecting realities

In the late-eighteenth century when Hannah More did not like the children's books she saw, she began publishing for herself. Amit Chaudhuri, detailing the different forms of literary activism, argues that there is

> A mode of intervention that can only be approximated by the term 'market activism'. The bolder agents and publishers abandoned the traditional forms of valuation by which novelists were estimated, published, and fêted, and embraced a dramatic, frontiersman style of functioning that involved the expectation of a reward more literal than any form of cultural capital. (Chaudhuri, 2004: 11)

Focusing on publishing, rather than writing, is not unique to More; other activists started publishing for themselves when they could not find the books that they wanted for children, including Una Marson, Chris Searle, Jessica Huntley and Verna Wilkins. In 2017, David Stevens and Aimée Fellone left Scholastic to form their own publishing house, Knights Of, for reasons similar to many of their predecessors. Fellone told Caroline Carpenter that 'Knights Of was born out of a frustration with the lack of representative voices and narratives in children's fiction. With Knights Of we can publish uniquely, putting our differences first and celebrating them, making it central to our business' (Carpenter, 2017). While many earlier publishers had made political writing (e.g. economic justice or racial justice) their emphasis, Knights Of focuses instead on consumer justice for readers of colour. Their books, which include the *Knights and Bikes* series (beginning in 2018) by Gabrielle Kent, Sharna Jackson's *High Rise Mystery* (2020) and *Happy Here* (2021) offer readers genre choices that they generally did not have previously.

In fact, *Happy Here*, a collection of short stories by different Black British and British Asian authors, is a market intervention in several ways. It intervenes by bypassing the market altogether: thanks to a collaboration with two literacy charities, Booktrust and CLPE, a copy of the book was donated in autumn of 2021 to every primary school in Britain. But it also responds to findings by Booktrust and CLPE that Black British writers do not get to write and Black British readers do not get to read genre fiction, such as mysteries, science fiction or comedy. The story by Patrice Lawrence, 'The After Ever After Bureau', for example, is about a family business in which 'Marla and her Mum connect the jaded folk from fairytales, myths and legends with unique and unparalleled experiences in the real world' (Patrice Lawrence, 2021: 240). The 'jaded folk' include European fairy tale princesses (Sleeping Beauty), English legendary characters (Robin Hood) and Greek mythological figures (Sisyphus). But Lawrence's main characters are soucouyants, Trinidadian witch figures who can remove their skin, and Anansi also plays a role. Marla and her mum live in Peckham, but Marla's grandmother is from the Caroni Swamp in Trinidad. Lawrence creates a story that anyone who likes fantasy and folklore can enjoy – but Black British readers from a Caribbean background can feel like they are, not just part of that world, but active participants and main characters. By putting the book in every primary school, not just schools with a significant Black population, Knights Of, Booktrust and CLPE indicate their commitment to the idea that Black British children's literature is for all children.

Booktrust and CLPE have both, as organizations, initiated activist research urging intervention in the children's book market to improve representation in the industry. The Booktrust research, *Representation of People of Colour among Children's Book Creators In the UK* (2019 and 2020) is by Melanie Ramdarshan Bold, a children's publishing scholar whose work highlights needed changes in the publishing industry. In 2018, Ramdarshan Bold wrote that a lack of diversity in children's books is an industry-wide problem: 'in addition to the pressure to be a spokesperson for their particular community, many authors of colour felt tokenized or fetishized by the publishing industry' (Ramdarshan Bold, 2018: 387). Her research for Booktrust focuses on authors and illustrators of colour producing literature for children, including how many of these book creators are British. Statistics over time show only slight gains in the number of British authors and illustrators of colour, from less than 1 per cent in 2007 to 2.86 per cent in 2019 (Ramdarshan Bold, 2020: 10). In the 2019 report, Ramdarshan Bold makes the argument that the industry needs to take 'collective action to break down the systemic barriers to representation of creators of colour' (Ramdarshan Bold, 2019: 15).

The CLPE research, *Reflecting Realities*, is an annual report (the first one appeared in 2018) on ethnic diversity in publishing. The reports are authored by Farrah Serroukh, the Learning Programme leader at CLPE, and were modelled upon work done by the Cooperative Children's Book Centre (CCBC) in the United States. Serroukh wrote in the 2020 report that

> The lack of quality, inclusive, representative books that reflect the realities of the children in our classrooms has been a longstanding issue in the UK. Positive change requires collective and consistent efforts and many people have been advocating and active in this field for many years. Our charity was keen to contribute to these efforts by providing the metrics to measure and monitor the extent of the issue, keeping the importance of a commitment to inclusive quality literature in the collective consciousness. (Serroukh, 2020: 4)

The reports are based on material sent upon CLPE's request by individual publishers that the publisher feels includes ethnic representation. The emphasis in the first year was on the statistical representation, stark figures which showed that only '4% of children's books published in 2017 featured BAME characters' (Serroukh, 2018: 6) despite the fact that roughly a third of students of compulsory school age are from a minority ethnic background.

Serroukh wanted to ensure that the reports 'contribute to an ongoing conversation that supports the producers of literature to be critically reflective and considered about the choices that are made in the book making process' (Serroukh, 2019: 4), so in 2019, the report included models of good practice, including examples like Anna McQuinn's *Zeki Gets a Check Up* (2018) and Sita Brahmachari and Jane Ray's *Corey's Rock* (2018). Melanie Ramdarshan Bold, who is also part of the CLPE steering group, added that in 2019 the CLPE report 'introduced a new lexicon to help us identify some of the problematic depictions of these characters (or lack thereof)' (Ramdarshan Bold, 2020: 4). This included a list of terms that describe 'Degrees of Erasure' (Serroukh, 2019: 18–19), ways of including people of colour in children's books without giving them full presence. For example, some of the books that CLPE received in 2019 had 'Cover Short Change' in which 'BAME characters were only featured on front covers, conveying the promise of presence within the body of the narrative, only for the reader to open the book and find that the cover is the only place where the character is visible' (Serroukh 2019: 18). Because Serroukh wants Reflecting Realities to be an industry-supported effort, the books with lower quality representation (and their publishers) are never named, and the publishing statistics are for the whole industry, not for individual publishers. However, if the publishers request it, CLPE will meet with them and discuss their submissions and offer suggestions for future publishing strategies to better reflect the experiences of all readers. The market activism of literacy organizations like CLPE and Booktrust is significant because it emphasizes collective action, not just of a single part of the children's book world, but of every stakeholder. Providing quality children's literature that is representative of its readership is not the work of one book, one author, or even one organization – it is, these organizations suggest, everyone's responsibility.

A collective sense of Britishness

Darren Chetty, in 'You Can't Say That! Stories Have To Be About White People', argues that the British children's book world is stacked against the British reader of colour:

> We learn so many things from reading stories, including the conventions of stories such as good versus evil ... The problem is that, when one of these conventions is that children in stories are white, English and middle-class,

then you may come to learn that your own life does not qualify as subject material. (Chetty, 2016: 99)

Literary activism of the type that I discuss in this book is about challenging those conventions so that all children can see themselves and their histories in books. Abolitionists who wrote in the voice of enslaved people, anti-colonialists and anti-racists who formed their own publishing companies, activists who rejected adult definitions of literature in favour of child writing, historians who used Black experiences to retell standard histories, all present challenges to conventional definitions of British (who counts as British?) children (what role do children play in the books they read?) and literature (what makes something worth publishing?). Activism is about challenging existing power structures that provide pre-existing answers to those questions (Britishness is whiteness; children learn the lessons of the books they read but don't get to decide what gets published; literature is about formal qualities and not politics). Paradoxically, however, most of the activist literature I discuss here has not been included in standard children's literature histories because they reject those power structures and try to replace them with something else. Abolitionists like Opie and anti-apartheid activists like Naidoo have succeeded in part because they had the backing of religious groups and criticized white people outside of Britain; but additionally, they fit into the definition of people who belong in the British book world: white and middle-class. Since the end of the Second World War, Black British and British Asian writers and activists have tried to change the definition of Britishness to make it more inclusive, but it has – until recently – been too easy to marginalize individual voices such as Farrukh Dhondy's or Buchi Emecheta's as being not representative of Britishness. The collective action taken by activists, particularly since 2012, has been an attempt to make British people see that they have a role to play in producing children's books that represent a wider definition of Britishness, one that hears the stories – and histories – of all children in Britain.

Bibliography

Aberbach, Jesse. '"Here in India": Nineteenth-Century British Women Navigating Their Position in the Empire through Children's Literature'. *International Research in Children's Literature* 11, no. 2 (December 2018): 173–85.

'Abolition of ILEA'. *House of Commons Debate,* 28 March 1988: Volume 130, Column 734. Available online: Abolition Of Ilea – Monday 28 March 1988 – Hansard – UK Parliament (accessed 28 May 2021).

Abrams, Mark. 'The £900m. Teenage Market'. *Financial Times,* 11 February 1959: 6.

ACER Centre. *I Have a Dream: ACER's Black Young Writers Winning Essays 1989.* London: ACER, 1988.

Akpan, Paula. 'Black Students Will Suffer Most From A-Level Cancellations'. *The Independent,* 23 March 2020. Available online: Black students will suffer most from A-level cancellations – they routinely outperform their predicted grades | The Independent | The Independent (accessed 31 May 2021).

Alderson, Brian. 'Capitalizing on the Comprehensives'. *The Times,* 5 February 1982: 10.

Alderson, Brian and Pat Garrett. *The Religious Tract Society as a Publisher of Children's Books.* Hoddesdon: The Children's Books History Society, 1999.

Alexander, Ziggi. *Library Service and Afro-Caribbean Communities.* London: Association of Assistant Librarians, 1982.

Alexander, Ziggi and Audrey Dewjee. *Mary Seacole: Jamaican National Heroine and 'Doctress' in the Crimean War.* London: Brent Library Service, 1982.

Alexander, Ziggi and Audrey Dewjee. *Roots in Britain: Black and Asian Citizens from Elizabeth I to Elizabeth II.* London: Brent Library Service, 1981.

Alexander, Ziggi and Trevor Knight (eds). *The Whole Library Movement: Changing Practice in Multicultural Librarianship.* London: Association of Assistant Librarians, 1992.

Alleyne, Alvona. 'Literary Publishing in the English-Speaking Caribbean'. In *Twenty Years of Latin American Librarianship,* 222–48. Austin: SACALM Secretariat, 1978.

ALTARF. 'Baker Attempts Book Ban'. *ALTARF Special Double Issue Newsletter* 27/28 (September/November 1987): 16–17.

Alves, Alicia. ' "Let Them See Your Face, My Child, and Thus Know the Meaning of All Things": Unity, the Child, and the Natural World in Rabindranath Tagore's *The Crescent Moon*'. *Southeast Asian Review of English* 55, no. 2 (2018): 41–56.

Amokeodo, Victor. 'The Politics of Aid and Famine'. In *I Have a Dream: ACER's Black Young Writers Winning Essays 1989*, 37–44. London: ACER, 1990.

Andrews, Margaret. *Doing Nothing Is Not an Option: The Radical Lives of Eric and Jessica Huntley*. Middlesex: Krik Krak, 2014.

Appiah, Kwame Anthony. 'Racial Identity and Racial Identification'. In *Theories of Race and Racism: A Reader*, edited by Les Back and John Solomos, 669–77. London: Routledge, 2009.

Arday, Jason. 'The Black Curriculum: Black British History in the National Curriculum'. *The Black Curriculum*, 2021. Available online: TBC+2021++Report.pdf (squarespace.com) (accessed 28 May 2021).

'Asian Women's Writers Collective'. *South Asian Diaspora Arts Archive*. n.d. Available online: Asian Women Writers Collective | SADAA (accessed 28 May 2021).

Ashley, Bernard. *The Trouble with Donovan Croft*. Oxford: Oxford University Press, 1974.

Aston, Alasdair. *Hey Mister Butterfly and Other Poems Written and Illustrated By Pupils of All Ages at Inner London Schools*. London: ILEA, 1978.

August, Thomas. *The Selling of the Empire: British and French Imperialist Propaganda, 1890-1940*. Westport: Greenwood, 1985.

Back, Les. 'The Fact of Hybridity: Youth, Ethnicity and Racism'. In *Companion to Racial and Ethnic Studies*, edited by John Solomos and David Theo Goldberg, 439–54. London: Blackwell, 2001.

Baillon, Victoria. 'Woke Virus Invades the National Trust'. *Conservative Woman*, June 2020. Available online: Woke virus infects the National Trust | The Conservative Woman (accessed 28 May 2021).

Ballin, Ruth. Unpublished note to Beverley Naidoo, with accompanying memo from BBC Schools Broadcasting Service, *Seven Stories Collection*, 11 April 1985.

Baker, Catherine. 'Beyond the Island Story?: The Opening Ceremony of the London 2012 Olympic Games as Public History'. *Rethinking History*, 19, no. 3 (2015): 409–28.

Barbauld, Anna Letitia. 'Master and Slave'. *Evenings at Home; or, the Juvenile Bidget Opened*, edited by John Aikin, 1–6. London: J. Johnson, 1792–6, 81–8.

Barr, Mark L. 'Prophecy, the Law of Insanity, and *The [First] Book of Urizen*'. *Studies in English Literature 1500–1900* 46, no.4 (Autumn 2006): 739–62.

Barres-Baker, Malcolm. *A Brief History of the London Borough of Brent*. London: Brent Heritage Services, 2007.

Barrie, J. M. *Peter Pan; or, The Boy Who Wouldn't Grow Up*. 1904. London: Hodder and Stoughton, 1928.

Barrie, J. M. *Peter and Wendy*. London: Hodder and Stoughton, 1911.

Batty, C. D. 'Librarianship by Degrees'. *Library World* 68, no. 6 (December 1966): 155–60.

Beauchamp, Kay. 'Application to Commission for Racial Equality for Grant Aid, 1985–86'. *School of Oriental and African Studies, Liberation Archives Racism Education Project Materials*, Box 23 Folder 139. 1985.

Beauchamp, Kay. *Black Citizens*. London: British Communist Party, 1973.

Beauchamp, Kay. *One Race, the Human Race*. London: Liberation, 1979.

Beauchamp, Kay. Unpublished letter to Greater London Council's cultural committee, 10 February 1984. *School of Oriental and African Studies Archives,* Box 21 Folder 120.

Beckles, Michael. 'How Can Schools Serve the Interest of the Black Community?' In *Black Voices: An Anthology of ACER's Black Young Writers Competition*, edited by Paul McGilchrist, 278–80. London: ACER, 1985.

Bennett, Louise. *Anancy and Miss Lou*. Kingston: Sangsters, 1979.

Bennett, Louise. *Anancy Stories and Dialect Verse*. Kingston: Pioneer, 1950.

Berg, Leila. 'The Five-Year Gap'. *Manchester Guardian*, 20 November 1967. Available Online: The 5-Year Gap (Manchester Guardian 20/11/67) | Leila Berg, author & story-teller (accessed 28 May 2021).

Berg, Leila. 'Moving Toward Self-Government'. *Children's Rights*, edited by Paul Adams, Leila Berg, Nan Berger, Michael Duane, A. S. Neill and Robert Ollendorff, 9–53. London: Granada, 1972.

Berg, Leila. 'Such Enchanted Children'. *Manchester Guardian,* 20 October 1964. Available Online: Such Enchanted Children (Manchester Guardian, 20/10/64) | Leila Berg, author & story-teller (accessed 28 May 2021).

Bernstein, Robin. *Racial Innocence: Performing Childhood and Race from Slavery to Civil Rights*. New York: New York University Press, 2011.

Betts-Priddy, Lottie. *The Life and Times of Marcus Garvey 1887–1940*. London: ACER, 1988.

'Black Curriculum'. *Website*. 2021. Available online: The Black Curriculum (accessed 29 May 2021).

'Black People and the Police Cont'd'. *The Times,* 3 April 1973: 14.

Blake, William. *The Book of Urizen*. 1794. New York: Dover, 1998.

Blake, William. 'The Little Black Boy'. In *Songs of Innocence*. 1789. New York: Dover, 1971: 40.

Boakye, Jeffrey. *Black, Listed*. London: Dialogue, 2019.

Boakye, Jeffrey. *Hold Tight: Black Masculinity, Millenials, and the Meaning of Grime*. London: Influx, 2017.

Boakye, Jeffrey. *Musical Truth*. London: Faber, 2021a.

Boakye, Jeffrey. 'On Being a Black Writer and a Writer Who Is Black'. *GQ UK online*, 30 April 2021b. Available online: Black writers and authors who are black | British GQ (gq-magazine.co.uk) (accessed 28 May 2021).

Boakye, Jeffrey and Darren Chetty. *What Is Masculinity? Why Does It Matter? And Other Big Questions*. Londond: Wayland, 2019.

Boehmer, Elleke. *Empire, the National, and the Postcolonial 1890–1920: Resistance in Interaction*. Oxford: Oxford University Press, 2005.

'Born to Fail?'. *Man Alive*, 9 January 1974. BBC Television.

Bourne, Jenny. 'Anti-racist Witchcraft'. *IRR* website, 15 January 2015. Available online: Anti-racist witchcraft – Institute of Race Relations (irr.org.uk) (accessed 13 December 2019).

Bourne, Jenny. Unpublished email to Karen Sands-O'Connor, 22 July 2019.

Bowyer, Michael. 'Comment on "David Olusoga: We Need to Normalize Black British History"'. *Voice Online,* 4 October 2020. Available at: David Olusoga: 'We need to normalise Black British history' – Voice Online (voice-online.co.uk) (accessed 28 May 2021).

Brahmachari, Sita and Ray, Jane. *Corey's Rock*. London: Otter-Barry, 2018.

Breinburg, Petronella. *Doctor Sean*. London: Bodley Head, 1974.

Breinburg, Petronella. *My Brother Sean*. London: Bodley Head, 1973.

Breinburg, Petronella. *Sean's Red Bike*. London: Bodley Head, 1975.

Bressey, Caroline. 'Contesting the Political Legacy of Slavery in England's Country Houses: A Case Study of Kenwood House and Osborne House'. In *Slavery and the British Country House*, edited by Madge Dresser and Andrew Hann, 121–31. Swindon: English Heritage, 2013.

Brighouse, Tim. 'The ILEA Balance: Credit or Debit?' In *Education in the Capital*, edited by Michael Barber, 50–63. London: Cassell, 1992.

Brodie, Louise. 'Interview with Ambavalener Sivanandan'. *BBC Sounds Part 8*, 20 October 2010. Available online: Sivanandan, Ambalavaner (8 of 10). National Life Stories: General – Charity and social welfare – Oral history | British Library – Sounds (bl.uk) (accessed 28 May 2021).

Brown, C. 'Should We Protect, Share or Lose Our Culture and Lifestyle in Britain?' In *Black Voices: An Anthology of ACER's Black Young Writers Competition*, edited by Paul McGilchrist, 80–1. London: ACER, 1985.

Bruner, Charlotte. 'The Other Audience: Children and the Example of Buchi Emecheta'. *African Studies Review* 29, no. 3 (September 1986): 129–40.

Bryan, Beverley, Stella Dadzie and Suzanne Scafe. *The Heart of the Race: Black Women's Lives in Britain*. London: Virago, 1986.

Buchanan, Tom. *Amnesty International and Human Rights Activism in Post-War Britain, 1945–1977*. Cambridge: Cambridge University Press, 2020.

Bullock, Alan. *A Language for Life*. HMSO, 1975.

Bunkle, Phillida. 'The 1944 Education Act and Second Wave Feminism'. *Women's History Review* 25, no. 5 (2016): 791–811.

Burnett, Frances Hodgson. *The Secret Garden*. London: Heinemann, 1911.

Bush, Ruth. *Beacon of Hope: New Beacon in Poetry and Prose*. London: New Beacon, 2016.

Butler, Catherine and Hallie O'Donavan. *Reading History in Children's Books*. New York: Palgrave, 2012.

Calder-Marshall, Arthur. 'West Indian Writers'. *Times Literary Supplement,* 23 May 1952: 348.

Campbell, Alexander. *It's Your Empire*. London: Left Book Club, 1945.

Carby, Hazel. 'White Woman Listen! Black Feminism and the Boundaries of Sisterhood'. In *Theories of Race and Racism: A Reader,* 2nd edition, edited by Les Back and John Solomos, 444–58. New York: Routledge, 2009.

Carpenter, Caroline. 'Inclusive Children's Publisher Knights Of Launches'. *The Bookseller Online*, 27 October 2017. Available online: Inclusive children's publisher Knights Of launches | The Bookseller (accessed 17 October 2021).

Castle, Kathryn. *Britannia's Children: Reading Colonialism through Children's Books and Magazines*. Manchester: Manchester University Press, 1996.

Chambers, Eddie. 'The Emergence of the Black British Artist'. In *Transforming the Crown: African, Asian and Caribbean Artists in Britain 1966–1996*, edited by M. Franklin Sirmans, 77–9. London: Franklin H. Williams Caribbean Cultural Center/African Diaspora Institute, 1997.

Chambers, Eddie. *Roots and Culture: Cultural Politics in the Making of Black Britain*. London: I. B. Taurus, 2017.

Charity Commission (UK). 'Press Release'. *Charity Commission Finds National Trust Did Not Breach Charity Law – GOV.UK*, 11 March 2021. Available online: (www.gov.uk) (accessed 28 May 2021).

Chakravorty, Swapan. 'Literacy Surrogacy and Literary Activism: Instances from Bengal'. In *Literary Activism: A Symposium*, edited by Amit Chaudhuri, 279–306. Norwich: Boiler House Press, 2016.

Charles, Lynette. 'Has Martin Luther King's Dream Been Fulfilled?'. In *I Have a Dream: ACER's Black Young Writers Winning Essays 1989*, 1–6. London: ACER, 1990.

Chaudhuri, Rosinka. '*The Flute, Gerontion*, and Subalternist Misreadings of Tagore'. *Social Text* 22, no. 1 (2004): 103–22.

Chetty, Darren. '"You Can't Do That! Stories Have to Be About White People"'. In *The Good Immigrant*, edited by Nikesh Shukla, 96–107. London: Unbound, 2016.

'Children's Books: Entertainment and Education, Tales of Many Lands'. *Times Literary Supplement,* 8 August 1942: 394.

'Children's Christian Picture Books'. *SPCK online*. 2021. Available online: Childrens Christian Picture Books – SPCK Publishing (accessed 28 May 2021).

'"Children's Librarianship Course." North-Western Polytechnic (London) Advertisement'. *Library Association Record* 57 (1955): 322.

Children's Rights Workshop Newsletter no. 1. London, 1974.

Clarke, Peter B. *Black Paradise: The Rastafarian Movement*. Wellingborough: Aquarian Press, 1986.

CLPE. 'Reflecting Realities Year 2 – FAQs'. *CLPE* website. Available online: CLPE REFLECTING REALITIES Q&A 2019.pdf (accessed on 24 February 2022).

Coard, Bernard. *How the West Indian Child Is Made Educationally Subnormal in the British School System*. London: New Beacon, 1971.

Coard, Bernard and Phyllis. *Getting to Know Ourselves*. London: Bogle L'Ouverture, 1972.

Cohen, Philip and Harwant S. Bains (eds). *Multi-Racist Britain*. Basingstoke: Macmillan, 1988.

Cole, Mike. *Critical Race Theory and Education: A Marxist Response*. Rev. 2nd edn. London: Palgrave Macmillan, 2017.

'Colonial Countryside Project'. *National Trust*. Available online: Colonial Countryside project | National Trust (accessed 18 October 2021).

Colwell, Eileen. 'At the Beginning'. *Signal* 13 (January 1974): 30–7.

Conrad, Rachel. '"My Sole Desire Is to Move Someone through My Poetry, and Allow For My Voice to be Heard": Young Poets and Children's Rights'. *Lion and the Unicorn* 40, no. 2 (April 2016): 196–214.

Conservative Commonwealth Council. *Colonial Rule: Enemies and Obligations*. London: Conservative Political Centre, 1955.

Cook, Dave. 'Charter of Demands'. In *Black and Blue: Racism and the Police*, edited by Dave Cook and Martin Rabstein, 28–32. London: British Communist Party, 1981.

Cook, Dave and Martin Rabstein (eds). *Black and Blue: Racism and the Police*. London: British Communist Party, 1981.

Cornelius, Paul. 'Interracial Books: Problems and Progress'. *The Library Quarterly* 41, no. 2 (April 1971): 106–27.

Cox, Caroline. 'Brainwashed to Hate the Police'. *Daily Mail,* 8 October 1985a: 6–7.

Cox, Caroline. 'From "Auschwitz – Yesterday's Racism" to GCHQ'. *Anti-Racism: An Assault on Education and Value*, edited by Frank Palmer, 74–81. London: Sherwood, 1985b.

Crenshaw, Kimberlé. 'Mapping the Margins: Intersectionality, Identity Politics, and Violence against Women of Colour'. *Stanford Law Review* 43, no. 6 (July 1991): 1241–99.

Crowther, Geoffrey. *The Crowther Report: Education 15 to 18.* London: HSMO, 1959.

Dahl, Roald. *Charlie and the Chocolate Factory.* London: George Allen and Unwin, 1964.

Dale, David. 'Racial Mischief: The Case of Dr Sivanandan'. In *Anti-Racism: An Assault on Education and Value*, edited by Frank Palmer, 82–94. London: Sherwood, 1985.

Darton, F. J. *Children's Books in England: Five Centuries of Social Life.* Cambridge: Cambridge University Press, 1982.

Davie, Michael. 'The Memoirs of a Black Florence Nightingale'. *Observer,* 11 March 1984: 52.

Day, Thomas. *The History of Sanford and Merton.* London: J. Stockdale, 1783.

De Jager, Johann Nicolaas Wilhelm. 'Political Consumerism in the South African and British Anti-Apartheid Movements: The Historical Role of Consumer Boycott Campaigns'. In *The Oxford Handbook of Political Consumerism*, edited by Magnus Boström, Michele Micheletti and Peter Oosterveer, 48–66. Oxford: Oxford University Press, 2018.

De La Mare, Tess. 'David Olusoga Defends Those Accused of Tearing Down Colston Statue'. *Independent Online,* 16 December 2021. Available online: David Olusoga defends those accused of tearing down Colston Statue | The Independent (accessed 2 January 2022).

Delius, Anthony. 'The Intellectual's Plight in South Africa'. *Africa Report* 8, no. 4 (April 1963): 23–4.

Delius, Anthony. 'The Struggle of the Tongues: The South African Literary Scene'. *Books Abroad* 29, no. 3 (Summer 1955): 261–9.

Delius, Anthony. *The Young Traveller in South Africa.* London: Phoenix House, 1947.

Delius, Anthony. *The Young Traveller in South Africa.* Revised edition. London: Phoenix House, 1959.

Department for Education and Science. *History from 5–16.* London: HMSO, 1988.

DeSouza, Pauline. 'Minorities' Arts Advisory Service'. In *Companion to Contemporary Black British Culture*, edited by Allison Donnell, 201. London: Routledge, 2013.

Dhondy, Farrukh. 'The Black Writer in Britain'. *Race Today*, May 1979: 66–9.

Dhondy, Farrukh. *Come to Mecca*. London: Collins, 1978a.

Dhondy, Farrukh. *East End at Your Feet*. London: Macmillan Topliners, 1976.

Dhondy, Farrukh. *The Siege of Babylon*. London: Macmillan, 1978b.

Dhondy, Farrukh, Barbara Beese and Leila Hassan. *The Black Explosion in British Schools*. London: Race Today, 1982.

Dickinson, Peter. *Tulku*. London: Gollancz, 1979.

'Diffusion Books'. *SPCK Publishing* website. 2021. Available online: Diffusion Books - SPCK Publishing (accessed 29 May 2021).

Dixon, Bob. *Catching Them Young 2: Political Ideas in Children's Fiction*. London: Pluto, 1977.

Donnell, Alison. 'Introduction'. *Una Marson: Selected Poems*, edited by Alison Donnell, 11–39. Leeds: Peepal Tree, 2011.

Donnelly, Seán. 'Ireland in the Imperial Imagination: British Nationalism and the Anglo- Irish Treaty'. *Irish Studies Review* 27, no. 4 (2019): 493–511.

Douglas, Kate and Anna Poletti. *Life Narratives and Youth Cultures: Representation, Agency and Participation*. London: Palgrave, 2016.

Dresser, Madge and Andrew Hann. 'Introduction'. *Slavery and the British Country House*, edited by Madge Dresser and Andrew Hann, xiii–xv. Swindon: English Heritage, 2013.

Eddo-Lodge, Reni. *Why I'm No Longer Talking to White People About Race*. London: Bloomsbury, 2017.

Edgeworth, Maria. 'The Grateful Negro'. *Popular Tales*. 1804. London: Macmillian, 1900. 419–41.

Edgeworth, Maria. 'The Good Aunt'. 1801. *Moral Tales*. Philadelphia: Appleton, 1848. 85–7.

Edgeworth, Maria and Frances Anne Beaufort Edgeworth. *A Memoir of Maria Edgeworth, with a Selection of Her Letters*, Volume 1. London: J. Masters, 1867.

'Education: Avoidance of Politicisation'. *House of Lords Debate*, 5 February 1986. Volume 140, Column 1169. Hansard UK Parliament website. Available online: Education: Avoidance Of Politicisation – Wednesday 5 February 1986 – Hansard – UK Parliament (accessed 13 December 2019).

'Educational Institutions: Information and Propaganda'. *House of Lords Debate*, 25 April 1983. Volume 441, Column 778. Hansard UK Parliament website. Available online: Educational Institutions: Information And Propaganda – Monday 25 April 1983 – Hansard – UK Parliament (accessed 29 May 2021).

Edwards, Dorothy. *Joe and Timothy Together*. 1971. Harmondsworth: Puffin, 1975.

Elkin, Judith. *Multi-Racial Books for the Classroom: A Select List of Children's Books*. 3rd edn. Towcester: Library Association Youth Libraries Group, 1980.

Elliott-Cooper, Adam. *Black Resistance to British Policing*. Manchester: Manchester University Press, 2021.

Emecheta, Buchi. *In the Ditch*. 1972. London: Fontana, 1988.

Emecheta, Buchi. *Nowhere to Play*. London: Allison & Busby, 1980.

Emecheta, Buchi. *Second Class Citizen*. 1974. London: Heinemann Educational, 2021.

Emecheta, Buchi. *Titch the Cat*. London: Allison & Busby, 1979.

'Existing Inequalities Have Made Mental Health of BAME Groups Worse During Pandemic, Says Mind'. *Mind* website, 15 July 2020. Available online: Existing inequalities have made mental health of BAME groups worse during pandemic, says Mind | Mind, the mental health charity – help for mental health problems (accessed 31 May 2021).

Farrell, Nicholas. 'Blyton Goes Missing in Brent'. *Sunday Telegraph*, 23 February 1992: 7.

Feldman, Paula R. 'Endurance and Forgetting: What the Evidence Suggests'. In *Romanticism and Women Poets: Opening the Door of Reception*, edited by Harriet Kramer Linkin and Stephen C. Behrendt, 15–22. Lexington: University Press of Kentucky, 1999.

Fenwick, I. G. K. *The Comprehensive School, 1944–1970*. London: Methuen, 1976.

Ferguson, Moira. 'Fictional Constructions of Liberated Africans: Mary Butt Sherwood'. In *Romanticism and Colonialism: Writing and Empire 1780–1830*, edited by Tim Fulford and Peter J. Kitson, 148–63. Cambridge: Cambridge University Press, 1998.

Fischer, Bob. 'Musty Books: The Third Class Genie (1975)'. *Haunted Generation* website, March 2020. Available online: The Third Class Genie – The Haunted Generation (accessed 28 May 2021).

File, Nigel and Chris Power. *Black Settlers in Britain, 1555–1958*. London: Heinemann, 1981.

Floyd, Samuel A. *The Power of Black Music: Interpreting Its History from Africa to the United States*. Oxford: Oxford University Press, 1995.

Ford, Richard. 'Ethnicity Labels Are Divisive, says Phillips'. *The Times Online*, 21 May 2015. Available online: Ethnicity labels are divisive, says Phillips | The Times (accessed 14 October 2021).

Foucault, Michel. *History of Madness*, ed. Jean Khalfa, trans. Jonathan Murphy and Jean Khalfa. London: Routledge, 2006.

Fowler, Corinne. 'Charlecote Park Reinterpreted: Poetry'. *Colonial Countryside Project* Website. Available online: CharlecoteParkReinterpreted. PoemsbyColmorePrimary.pdf (accessed 28 May 2021).

Fowler, Corinne. *Green Unpleasant Land: Creative Responses to Rural England's Colonial Connections*. Leeds: Peepal Tree, 2021.

Fowler, Corinne. 'Revisiting Mansfield Park: The Critical and Literary Legacies of Edward W. Said's Essay "Jane Austen and Empire" in *Culture and Imperialism* (1993)'. *The Cambridge Journal of Postcolonial Literary Inquiry* 4, no. 3 (2017): 362–81.

Fowler, Corinne. 'The Rural Turn in Contemporary Writing by Black and Asian Britons'. *Interventions* 19, no. 3 (2016): 395–415.

Frankenburg, Ruth. *White Women, Race Matters*. Minneapolis: University of Minnesota Press, 1993.

Franks, Suzanne. 'The Neglect of Africa and the Power of Aid'. *The International Communication Gazette* 72, no. 1 (2010): 71–84.

Fryer, Peter. *Staying Power: The History of Black People in Britain*. London: Pluto, 1984.

Furness, Hannah. 'CBBC Sketch "Inaccurately" Painted Florence Nightingale as Racist, BBC Trust Finds'. *Daily Telegraph*, 30 September 2014. Available online: CBBC sketch 'inaccurately' painted Florence Nightingale as racist, BBC Trust finds (telegraph.co.uk) (accessed 28 May 2021).

Fuscoe, Jan. 'Fighting Fascism, Art as Activism'. *Byline Times*, 17 November 2020. Available online: Fighting Fascism: Art As Activism – Byline Times (accessed 29 May 2021).

Gallo, Donald (ed). *Speaking for Ourselves, Too*. Champaign: National Council of Teachers of English, 1990.

Garrison, Len. 'The Afro-Caribbean Resource Project'. *Against the Tide: Black Experience in the ILEA*, edited by Sarah Olowe, 175–81. London: Hansib, 1990.

Garrison, Len. *Beyond Babylon*. London: Black Star, 1985.

Garrison, Len. *Black Youth, Rastafarianism, and the Identity Crisis in Britain*. London: ACER, 1979.

Garrison, Len. *Images and Reflections: Education and the Afro-Caribbean Child*. London: ACER, 1982.

Garrison, Len and Paul Boateng. *ACER 2nd Annual Project Report, 1979–80*. London: ACER, 1980.

Gentle Author. 'Dan Jones at Bethnal Green Library'. *Spitalfields Life*, 12 March 2012. Available online: Dan Jones at Bethnal Green Library | Spitalfields Life (accessed 29 May 2021).

Gentle Author. 'Dan Jones, Rhyme Collector'. *Spitalfields Life*, 17 April 2010. Available online: Dan Jones, Rhyme Collector | Spitalfields Life (accessed 29 May 2021).

Gentleman, Amelia. *The Windrush Betrayal: Exposing the Hostile Environment*. London: Guardian/Faber, 2019.

Gerzina, Gretchen Holbrook. *Black London: Life Before Emancipation*. Rutgers: Rutgers University Press, 1995.

Gilchrist, Alexander. *Gilchrist on Blake: Life of William Blake Pictor Ignotus*, edited and with an introduction by Richard Holmes. 1863. London: HarperPerennial, 2005.

Gilroy, Paul. 'Police and Thieves'. In *The Empire Strikes Back: Race and Racism in 70s Britain*, edited by the Centre for Contemporary Cultural Studies, 143–82. London: Hutchinson, 1982.

Gilroy, Paul. *There Ain't No Black in the Union Jack*. 1987. London: Routledge, 2005.

Gilroy, Paul and Errol Lawrence. 'Two-Tone Britain: White and Black Youth and the Politics of Anti-Racism'. In *Multi-Racist Britain*, edited by Philip Cohen and Harwant S. Bains, 121–55. Basingstoke: Macmillan, 1988.

Gleadle, Kathryn and Ryan Hanley. 'Children Against Slavery: Juvenile Agency and the Sugar Boycotts in Britain'. *Transactions of the RHS* 30 (2020): 97–117.

Goldworthy, Joanna. 'Letter to Ethel de Keyser'. Seven Stories archives, 13 June 1983.

Goodfellow, Maya. *Hostile Environment: How Immigrants Became Scapegoats*. 2nd edn. London: Verso, 2020.

Goswami, Supriya. *Colonial India in Children's Literature*. London: Routledge, 2012.

Green, Jeffery. *Black Edwardians: Black People in Britain 1910–1914*. London: Taylor and Francis, 1998.

Grenby, M. O. 'The Origins of Children's Literature'. In *The Cambridge Companion to Children's Literature*, edited by M. O. Grenby and Andrea Immel, 3–18. Cambridge: Cambridge University Press, 2009.

Habeel, Lana. 'The Little Boy'. *Colonial Countryside Project* website, 2018. Available online: CharlecoteParkReinterpreted.PoemsbyColmorePrimary.pdf (accessed 28 May 2021).

Habib, Sadia. *Learning and Teaching British Values: Policies and Perspectives on British Identities*. London: Palgrave, 2018.

Hall, S. C. and S. C. Hall. 'Memories of the Authors of the Age: A Series of Written Portraits (From Personal Acquaintance) of Great Men and Women of the Epoch'. *Art Journal, 1839–1912* 45 (1865): 285–8.

Hall, Stuart. 'Introduction'. In *Beyond Babylon*, edited by Len Garrison, 9–15. London: Black Star, 1985.

Hall, Stuart. 'Policing the Police'. In *Black and Blue: Racism and the Police*, edited by Dave Cook and Martin Rabstein, 7–10. London: British Communist Party, 1981.

Hall, Stuart. 'What Is This "Black" in Black Popular Culture?'. In *Essential Essays Volume 2: Identity and Diaspora*, edited by David Morley, 83–94. Durham, North Carolina: Duke University Press, 2018.

Hall, Stuart, Tony Jefferson, John Clarke, Chas Critcher and Brian Roberts. *Policing the Crisis*. London: Macmillan, 1978.

Hallworth, Grace and Julia Marriage. *Stories to Read and to Tell*, Pamphlet 13. Birmingham: Youth Libraries Group, 1978.

Harrison, Graham. 'Campaign Britain: Exploring the Representation of Africa and Its Role in British Identity'. *The British Journal of Politics and International Relations* 15 (2013): 528–47.

Hassan, Jennifer and Rick Noack. 'How George Floyd's Killing Sparked a Global Reckoning'. *Washington Post Online*, 25 May 2021. Available online: How George Floyd's killing sparked a global reckoning - The Washington Post (accessed on 24 February 2022).

Helling, John. *Public Libraries and Their National Policies*. Oxford: Chandos, 2012.

Henry, Lauren. ' "Sunshine and Shady Groves": What Blake's "Little Black Boy" Learned from African Writers'. In *Romanticism and Colonialism: Writing and Empire 1780–1830*, edited by Tim Fulford and Peter J. Kitson, 67–86. Cambridge: Cambridge University Press, 1998.

Hewitt, Maggie. 'Review: *The Siege of Babylon*'. *Children's Book Bulletin* 2 (Autumn 1979): 25.

Hewitt, Maggie, Neil Martinson and Jean Milloy. 'Young People's Writing in Print'. *Children's Book Bulletin* 2 (Autumn 1979): 8–10.

Hewlett, R. T. 'Review: *Cradle Tales of Hinduism*'. *Nature* 77, no. 2009 (30 April 1908): 605.

Hill, Janet. *Books for Children: The Homelands of Immigrants in Britain*. London: IRR, 1971.

Hill, Janet. *Children Are People: The Librarian in the Community*. London: Hamish Hamilton, 1973.

Hirsch, Afua. *Brit(ish): On Race, Identity and Belonging*. London: Jonathan Cape, 2018.

Ho, Janice. *Nation and Citizenship in the Twentieth-Century British Novel*. Cambridge: Cambridge University Press, 2015.

Hoffman, Mary. *Amazing Grace*. London: Frances Lincoln, 1991.

Hoggart, Simon. 'Rupert the Racist'. *Observer*, 22 January 1984: 50.

Howe, Darcus. 'Is a Police Carnival: *Race Today* September 1976'. In *Here to Stay Here to Fight: A Race Today Anthology*, edited by Paul Field, Robin Bunce, Leila Hassan and Margaret Peacock, 51–4. London: Pluto Press, 2019.

Huxtable, Sally, Corinne Fowler, Christo Kefalas and Emma Slocombe. *Interim Report on the Connections Between Colonialism and Properties Now In the Care of the National Trust, Including Links with Historic Slavery*. National Trust, 2020. Available online: Interim Report on the Connections between Colonialism and Properties now in the Care of the National Trust Including Links with Historic Slavery (accessed 28 May 2021).

Ibekwe, Stella. *Teenage Encounters*. London: Centerprise, 1978.

Ikoli, Tunde and Maggie Pinhorn, directors. 'Tunde's Film'. Basement Project Films, 1973.

ILEA. *Going to the Park*. London: ILEA Learning Resources Branch, 1984.

ILEA. *Sing a Song Bumper Book 1*. London: ILEA, 1976.

Iremonger, Lucille. *The Young Traveler in the West Indies*. New York: Dutton, 1955.

Iyer, M. Srinivasa. 'Sister Nivedita'. In *Eminent Orientalists: Indian, European, American*. 1922, New Composed Edition, edited by Rani Kapoor, 197–213. New Delhi, Cosmo, 2000.

Izbicki, John. 'Taught to Despair'. *Daily Telegraph*, 29 January 1976: 14.

Jackson, Nicole M. 'The Ties that Bind: Questions of Empire and Belonging in Black British Educational Activism'. In *Blackness in Britain*, edited by Kehinde Andrews and Lisa Amanda Palmer, 117–29. London: Routledge, 2019.

Jackson, Sharna (introducer). *Happy Here: 10 Stories from Black Authors and Illustrators*. London: Knights Of, 2021.

Jackson, Sharna. *High Rise Mystery*. London: Knights Of, 2020.

Jarrett-Macauley, Delia. *The Life of Una Marson, 1905–65*. Manchester: Manchester University Press, 1998.

Jekyll, Walter (collector). *I Have a News: Rhymes from the Caribbean*. New York: Lothrop Lee and Shepard, 1994.

Jekyll, Walter. *Jamaican Song and Story*. London: The Folklore Society, 1904.

Jelnikar, Ana. 'W. B. Yeats's (Mis)Reading of Tagore: Interpreting an Alien Culture'. *University of Toronto Quarterly* 77, no. 4 (Fall 2008): 1005–24.

Johnson, Catherine. *Freedom*. London: Scholastic, 2018.

Johnson, Catherine. 'Where Are Britain's Black Writers?' *Guardian Online*, 5 December 2011. Available online: Where are Britain's black writers? | Catherine Johnson | The Guardian (accessed 28 May 2021).

Johnson, Catherine and Melanie Ramdarshan Bold. 'Writing to Feel Rooted: An Interview with British Children's Literature Innovator Catherine Johnson'. *Lion and the Unicorn* 44, no. 2 (2020): 129–35.

Kaonga, Gerrard. 'Jacob Rees-Mogg Attacks "Shamefaced" National Trust in Fiery Winston Churchill Row'. *Daily Express Online*, 25 September 2020. Available online: Jacob Rees-Mogg attacks National Trust in fiery Winston Churchill row | UK | News | Express.co.uk (accessed 28 May 2021).

Kaufmann, Miranda. *Black Tudors*. London: Oneworld, 2017.

Keats, Ezra Jack. *The Snowy Day*. New York: Viking, 1962.

Kemp, Gene. *The Turbulent Term of Tyke Tiler*. London: Faber, 1977.

Kent, Gabrielle. *Knights and Bikes*. London: Knights Of, 2018.

Kipling, Rudyard. *The Jungle Book*. London: Macmillian, 1894.

Kipling, Rudyard. *Just-So Stories*. London: Macmillian, 1902.

Klar, Malte and Tim Kasser. 'Some Benefits of Being an Activist: Measuring Activism and Its Role in Well-Being'. *Political Psychology* 30, no. 5 (2009): 755–77.

Klein, Gillian. *Reading into Racism*. London: Routledge, 1985.

Kutzer, M. Daphne. *Empire's Children: Empire and Imperialism in Classic British Children's Books*. London: Routledge, 2000.

Kuya, Dorothy. '100 Years of Abuse'. In *Black and Blue: Racism and the Police*, edited by Dave Cook and Martin Rabstein, 17–18. London: British Communist Party, 1981.

Kynaston, David. *Family Britain, 1951–57*. London: Bloomsbury, 2009.

Lammy, David. '*Black, Listed* by Jeffrey Boakye Review: The Power of Words'. *Guardian*, 15 April 2019. Available online: Black, Listed by Jeffrey Boakye review – race and the power of words | Society books | The Guardian (accessed 30 May 2021).

Lang, Andrew. *The Blue Fairy Book*. 1889. New York: Dover, 1966.

Lang, Andrew. *The Brown Fairy Book*. 1904. New York: Dover, 1965.

Lawrence, Dena. 'I Saw It Happen'. In *I Have a Dream: ACER's Black Young Writers Winning Essays 1989*, 85–6. London: ACER, 1990.

Lawrence, Patrice. 'The After Ever After Bureau'. In *Happy Here*, edited by Sharna Jackson, 235–69. London: Knights Of, 2021.

Lennon, Joseph. *Irish Orientalism: A Literary and Intellectual History*. Syracuse: Syracuse University Press, 2008.

Leeson, Robert. *Children's Books and Class Society, Past and Present*. London: Children's Rights Workshop, 1977.

Leeson, Robert. *Grange Hill Rules OK?* London: Fontana, 1980.

Leeson, Robert. *Grange Hill for Sale*. London: Fontana, 1981.

Leeson, Robert. *Maroon Boy*. London: Collins, 1974b.

Leeson, Robert. 'Public No Longer a Sleeping Partner'. *Morning Star*, 12 September 1974a: 4.

Leeson, Robert. *Reading and Righting*. London: Collins, 1985.

Leeson, Robert. *Strike: A Live History 1887–1971*. London: George Allen and Unwin, 1973.

Leeson, Robert. *The Third Class Genie*. London: Collins, 1975.

Leeson, Robert. 'The Way Ahead'. *Children's Literature in Education* 17, no. 4 (1986): 253–60.

Lester, Julius. *To Be a Slave*. New York: Dial, 1968.

Levy, Andrea. *Small Island*. London: Review, 2004.

Liddle, David. *What the Public Library Boss Does*. London: Association of Assistant Librarians, 1985.

'Little Rebels Children's Book Award'. *About – The Little Rebels Children's Book Award*. Available online: littlerebels.org (accessed 18 October 2021).

Lloyd, Errol. *Many Rivers to Cross*. London: Methuen, 1995.

Lloyd, Errol. *Nini at Carnival*. 1978. New York: Thomas Y. Crowell, 1979.

Lloyd, Errol. *Nini on Time*. London: Bodley Head, 1981.

Lloyd, Errol. Unpublished email to Karen Sands-O'Connor, 25 November 2020.

Lloyd Jones, Linda. 'Fifty Years of Penguin Books'. In *Fifty Penguin Years*, 11–103. Harmondsworth: Penguin, 1985.

Lofting, Hugh. *The Adventures of Doctor Dolittle*. New York: Frederick Stokes, 1920.

Lovett, Verney. *History of the Indian Nationalist Movement*. London: John Murray, 1920.

'Lucille Iremonger'. *Daily Telegraph*, 18 January 1989: 19.

MacGibbon, Jean. *Hal*. London: Heinermann, 1974.

Mackay, David, Brian Thompson and Pamela Schaub. *Breakthrough to Literacy: Teacher's Manual*. London: Schools Council, 1979.

Mackay, David, Brian Thompson and Pamela Schaub. *The Wendy House*. London: Longman, 1970.

MacKenzie, John. *Propaganda and Empire: The Manipulation of British Public Opinion, 1880–1960*. Manchester: Manchester University Press, 1984.

Mackie, Lindsay. 'Tapping the Deep Roots of Britain's Blacks'. *Guardian*, 27 December 1980: 2.

Mahon, Leah. 'Cecil Rhodes Statue at Oxford College Should Go Says Independent Report as Bosses at Oxford Oriel College Reject Plans'. *The Voice*, 20 May 2021. Available online: Cecil Rhodes statue at Oxford college should go says independent report as bosses at Oxford Oriel College reject plans – Voice Online (voice-online.co.uk) (accessed 1 June 2021).

Mahood, Kenneth. 'Tintin's Odyssey'. *Punch* 6469 (9 November 1983): 18–19.

Mallen, David. 'The ILEA Legacy'. In *Education in the Capital*, edited by Michael Barber, 61–73. London: Cassell, 1992.

Mann, Andrew. 'The Other Award'. *Signal* 18 (1975): 142–5.

Marshall, Margaret. *Libraries and Literature for Teenagers*. London: Andre Deutsch, 1975.

Marson, Una. 'Little Brown Girl'. In *Towards the Stars*, edited by Una Marson, 52–6. London: University of London Press, 1945.

Marson, Una. 'The Story of Jamaica'. *The Listener*, 27 July 1939: 166–7.

Matthew 2.13 (The Flight into Egypt). *KJV*.

Matthews, David. *Voices of the Windrush Generation: The Real Story Told By the People Themselves*. 2018. London: 535 Press, 2020.

McLean, Max, Rachel Sloper and Enda Mullen. 'Muslim Hiking Group Set Up by Coventry Man Faces Racist Abuse after Christmas Day Walk." *Coventry Telegraph Online,* 5 January 2022. Muslim hiking group set up by Coventry man faces racist abuse after Christmas Day walk – CoventryLive (coventrytelegraph.net) (accessed 24 February 2022).

McGilchrist, Paul (ed). *Black Voices: An Anthology of ACER's Black Young Writers Competition*. London: ACER, 1987.

McGillis, Roderick. ' "And the Celt Knew the Indian": Knowingness, Postcolonialism, Children's Literature'. In *Voices of the Other: Children's Literature and the Postcolonial Context*, edited by Roderick McGillis, 223–35. New York: Garland, 1999.

McGraw, Jason. 'Sonic Settlements: Jamaican Music, Dancing and Black Migrant Communities in Postwar Britain'. *Journal of Social History* 52, no. 2 (2018): 353–82.

McQuinn, Anna. *Zeki Gets a Check Up*. London: AlannaMax, 2018.

Mead, Stella. *The Adventures of Peter and Tess through the British Commonwealth*. London: Amex, 1944.

Mead, Stella. *Bim: A Boy in British Guiana*. London: Orion, 1947.

Mead, Stella. *Great Stories from Many Lands*. London: James Nisbet, 1936.

Mead, Stella. 'Khyber Pass'. *Daily Mail*, 18 August 1933: 10.

Mead, Stella. *The Land Where Tales Are Told*. London: James Nisbet, 1931.

Mead, Stella. *Travellers Joy*. London: University of London Press, 1952.

Mickenberg, Julia L. *Learning from the Left: Children's Literature, the Cold War, and Radical Politics in the United States*. Oxford: Oxford University Press, 2006.

Midgley, Claire. *Women Against Slavery: The British Campaigns, 1780–1870*. London: Routledge, 1992.

Miles, Robert. *Between Two Cultures? The Case of Rastafarianism*. Working papers on Ethnic Relations no. 10. London: SSRC, 1978.

Milne-Home, Mary Pamela. *Mamma's Black Nurse Stories*. Edinburgh: Blackwood, 1890.

'Mission Statement'. *The Black Curriculum*. 2020. Available online: The Black Curriculum (accessed 29 May 2021).

Mitchell, Rob and Shawn Sobers. 'Re:Interpretation: The Representation of Perspectives on Slave Trade History Using Creative Media'. In *Slavery and the British Country House*, edited by Madge Dresser and Andrew Hann, 142–52. Swindon: English Heritage, 2013.
More, Hannah. 'Babay: The True Story of a Good Negro Woman'. *Cheap Repository Tracts, Volume I*, 337–41. London: J. Marshall, 1797a.
More, Hannah. 'A True Account of a Pious Negro'. *Cheap Repository Tracts, Volume I*, 343–8. London: J. Marshall, 1797b.
More, Hannah. 'The Sorrows of Yamba; or, The Negro Woman's Lamentation'. *Cheap Repository Tracts, Volume I*, 681–92. London: J. Marshall, 1797c.
Moskalenko, Sophia and Clark McCauley. 'Measuring Political Mobilization: The Distinction between Activism and Radicalism', *Terrorism and Political Violence* 21, no. 2 (2009): 239–60, DOI: 10.1080/09546550902765508
Mufti, Rashid. 'Review: Come to Mecca and Other Stories'. *Dragon's Teeth* 1, no. 2 (May 1979): 9.
Mukherjee, Koel. 'David Olusoga: Not the "Angry Black Guy on Television"'. *Bristol Cable*, 18 August 2017. Available online: David Olusoga: Not the 'angry black guy on television' - The Bristol Cable (accessed 28 May 2021).
Mulvaney, Mike. 'The Impact of an Anti-Racist Policy in the School Community.' In *Education for a Multicultural Society: Case Studies in ILEA Schools*, edited by M. Martin Straker-Welds, 27–33. London: Bell & Hyman, 1984.
Naidoo, Beverley. *Censoring Reality: An Examination of Books on South Africa*. London: ILEA Centre for Anti-Racist Education and the British Defence and Aid Fund for Southern Africa, 1984.
Naidoo, Beverley. *Journey to Jo'Burg*. London: Pearson Educational, 1995.
Naidoo, Beverley. *The Other Side of Truth*. London: HarperCollins, 2000.
Naidoo, Beverley. 'The Story Behind *Journey to Jo'Burg*'. *School Library Journal* May 1987: 43.
Naidoo, Beverley. Unpublished description of cover photograph for *Journey to Jo'Burg*. Seven Stories Collections.
Naidoo, Beverley. Unpublished email to Karen Sands-O'Connor, dated 8 December 2021.
Naidoo, Beverley. Unpublished letter to 'Rachel', dated 14 October 1983. Seven Stories Collections.
Naidoo, Beverley. 'The Writer on Writing'. *Journey to Jo'Burg*. 1985. London: Pearson E Educational, 1995, pp. iv–xi.
'National Trust Seeks New Chair'. *National Trust* press release, 25 May 2021. Available online: National Trust seeks new Chair | National Trust (accessed 31 May 2021).

NCRCB. *Their Contribution Ignored*. London: NCRCB, 1988.

Nesbit, E. *Five Children and It, The Phoenix and the Carpet, and The Story of the Amulet*. 1904. London: Octopus, 1979.

Nesbit, E. *Wings and the Child*. London: Hodder and Stoughton, 1913.

'Newsround Talks to David Olusoga About His New Book on Black British History'. *CBBC*, 9 October 2020. Available online: Newsround talks to David Olusoga about his new book on black history - CBBC Newsround (accessed 28 May 2021).

Nichols, Grace. 'Babyfish'. *Folk Tales Around the World*. Loughborough: Ladybird, 1983.

Nichols, Grace. *Babyfish and Other Stories from Village to Rainforest*. London: Islington Community Press, 1983.

Nightingale Society. 'To Baroness Amos, Baroness Benjamin and Baroness Scotland'. Undated letter [2016?]. Seacole Statue – The Nightingale Society. (accessed 17 October 2021).

Nivedita, Sister (Margaret E. Noble). 'The Birth of Krishna'. *Cradle Tales of Hinduism*. 1907. 141–8. Calcutta: Swami Ananyananda, 1988.

Nivedita, Sister (Margaret E. Noble). *Cradle Tales of Hinduism*. 1907. Calcutta: Advaita Ashrama, 1988.

Nixon, Ron. *Selling Apartheid: South Africa's Global Propaganda War*. London: Pluto, 2016.

Norman, Alison. *Race, Gender and Colonialism: Public Life among the Six Nations of Grand River 1899–1939*. Toronto: University of Toronto Press, 2010.

'Notices'. *Library Association Record* 57 (1955): 322.

'Obituary: Stella Mead'. *The Times*, 14 April 1981: 16.

Oldfield, John R. 'Anti-Slavery Sentiment in Children's Literature, 1750–1850'. *Slavery and Abolition* 10, no. 1 (1989): 44–59.

Olowe, Sarah and Rehana Minhas. 'Introduction'. In *Against the Tide: Black Experience in the ILEA*, edited by Sarah Olowe, 11–18. London: Hansib, 1990.

Olusoga, David. *Black and British: A Forgotten History*. London: Pan, 2016.

Olusoga, David. *Black and British: A Short, Essential History*. London: Macmillan, 2020.

Opie, Amelia. *The Black Man's Lament*. London: Harvey and Darton, 1826.

Opie, Amelia. 'The Black Man's Lament, or, How to Make Sugar'. 1825. *Flowers of Delight: An Agreeable Garland of Prose and Poetry, 1765–1830*, edited by Leonard de Vries, 174–77. New York: Pantheon.

Osborne, Simon. 'National Trust In New Woke Row'. *Daily Express Online*, 6 April 2021. Available online: National Trust in new woke row: Accused of asking children to 'condemn Britain | UK | News | Express.co.uk (accessed 28 May 2021).

'Other Award Exhibition Catalogue'. London: Children's Rights Workshop, 1985.
'Our Jamaican Problem'. *British Pathé* (film), 1955.
Palmer, Amy. 'Nursery Schools for the Few or for the Many? Childhood, Education and the State in Mid-Twentieth-Century England'. *Paedogogica Historica* 47, nos. 1–2 (2011): 139–54.
Panaou, Petros and Janelle Mathis. 'Negotiating Agency, Voice and Identity through Literature'. *Bookbird* 57, no. 1 (2019): ii–iv.
Pateman, John. 'Library Dispersals'. *Times Literary Supplement*, 3 January 1992: 13.
Pears, Elizabeth. 'The Man Who Quietly Handled Business'. *The Voice Online*, 16 February 2013. https://archive.voice-online.co.uk/article/man-who-quietly-handled-business.
Pearson, Lucy. *The Making of Modern Children's Literature in Britain: Publishing and Criticism in the 1960s and 1970s*. London: Ashgate, 2013.
Pearson, Lucy, Karen Sands-O'Connor and Aishwarya Subramanian. 'Prize Culture and Diversity in British Children's Literature'. *International Research in Children's Literature* 12, no. 1 (July 2019): 90–106.
Philpott, Trevor. 'The Truth About Teenagers'. *Picture Post* 74, no. 11 (18 March 1957): 10–13.
'A Poet of the Lotus'. *Saturday Review*, 27 December 1913: 815–16.
'Poetry for Children'. *Times Literary Supplement*, 3 November 1972: 1329.
'Population of England and Wales by Ethnicity Over Time'. *Gov.uk Website*. 2020. Available online: Population of England and Wales - GOV.UK Ethnicity facts and figures (ethnicity-facts-figures.service.gov.uk) (accessed 31 May 2021).
Powling, Chris. 'Authorgraph 84: Geoffrey Trease'. *Books for Keeps*, 84. (January 1994). Available online: Children's Books – Articles – Authorgraph No.84: Geoffrey Trease | BfK No. 84 (booksforkeeps.co.uk) (accessed 28 May 2021).
Price, Susan. *Twopence a Tub*. London: Faber and Faber, 1975.
Price, Susan. *The Ghost Drum*. London: Faber, 1987.
Procter, James. 'Una Marson at the BBC'. *Small Axe* 19, no. 3 (2015): 1–28.
Purvis, Andrew. 'Book Boat'. *Punch*, 15 October 1986: 62.
Ramdarshan Bold, Melanie. 'The Eight Percent Problem: Authors of Colour in the British Young Adult Market (2006–16)'. *Publishing Research Quarterly* 34 (2018): 385–406.
Ramdarshan Bold, Melanie. *Representation of People of Colour among Children's Book Creators in the UK*. London: Booktrust, 2019.
Ramdarshan Bold, Melanie. *Representation of People of Colour Among Children's Book Creators in the UK*. London: Booktrust, 2020.
Rampton, Anthony. *West Indian Children in our Schools*. London: HMSO, 1981.

Randhawa, Ravinder. Author's Personal Website. 2022. Available online: https://www.ravinderrandhawa.com/about/ (accessed 8 April 2020).

Rawlinson, Kevin. 'National Trust Chairman Tim Parker to Step Down'. *Guardian*, 26 May 2021. Available online: National Trust chairman Tim Parker to step down | The National Trust | The Guardian (accessed 28 May 2021).

Ray, Colin and Sheila Ray. *Attitudes and Adventures*. 1965. Birmingham: Library Association, 1973.

Ray, Sheila G. *Children's Fiction: A Handbook for Librarians*, 1970. London: Brockhampton, 1972.

'Reception'. *The Daily Telegraph*, 31 July 1936: 15.

Reece, Andrea. 'Authorgraph: Catherine Johnson'. *Books for Keeps* 241 (2020): 8–9.

Reynolds, Kimberley. *Left Out: The Forgotten Tradition of Radical Publishing for Children in Britain 1910–1949*. Oxford: Oxford University Press, 2016.

Reynolds, Kimberley. *Radical Children's Literature: Future Visions and Aesthetic Transformations in Juvenile Fiction*. Basingstoke: Palgrave Macmillan, 2007.

'Roots in Britain'. *ITV News Production*, August 1981. Available online: Centuries of Black and Asian British History in Photographs on Vimeo (accessed 23 May 2021).

Rose, E. J. B. *Colour and Citizenship: A Report on British Race Relations*. Oxford: IRR, 1969.

Rosen, Connie and Harold. *The Language of Primary School Children*. Harmondsworth: Penguin, 1973.

Rosen, Michael and Susannah Steele. *Inky Pinky Ponky*. 1982. London: Collins, 1990.

Rowan, Ivan. 'Hatred in Red Lion Square'. *Sunday Telegraph*, 8 September 1974: 7.

Said, Edward. *Orientalism*. New York: Vintage, 1979.

Sandhu, Sukhdev. *London Calling: How Black and Asian Writers Imagined a City*. London: HarperCollins, 2004.

Sands-O'Connor, Karen. *Children's Publishing and Black Britain, 1965–2015*. Palgrave Macmillan, 2017.

Sands-O'Connor, Karen. 'Power Primers: Black Community Self-Narration, and Black Power for Children in the US and UK'. *Research on Diversity in Youth Literature* 3.1 (2021). Article 7. Available online at: https://sophia.stkate.edu/rdyl/vol3/iss1/7 (accessed on 24 February 2022).

Sands-O'Connor, Karen. 'Primitive Minds: Anthropology, Children, and Savages in Andrew Lang and Rudyard Kipling'. In *Childhood in Edwardian Fiction: Worlds Enough and Time*, edited by Adrienne E. Gavin and Andrew F. Humphries, 177–90. London: Palgrave Macmillan, 2009.

Sands-O'Connor, Karen. 'Punk Primers and Reggae Readers: Music and Politics in British Children's Literature'. *Global Studies of Childhood* 8, no. 3 (August 2018): 1–12.

Sands-O'Connor, Karen. *Soon Come Home to This Island: West Indians in British Children's Literature*. London: Routledge, 2008.

Sanyal, Sukla. 'Legitimizing Violence: Seditious Propaganda and Revolutionary Pamphlets in Bengal 1908–1918'. *Journal of Asian Studies* 67, no. 3 (August 2008): 759–87.

Sarup, Madan. *Education and the Ideologies of Racism*. Stoke-on-Trent: Trentham, 1991.

Sauvain, Philip. *Modern Times: History of Britain Book 4*. London: Macmillan, 1982.

Searle, Chris. *All Our Words*. London: Young World, 1986.

Searle, Chris. *Beyond the Skin: How Mozambique Is Defeating Racism*. London: Liberation, 1979.

Searle, Chris. *Classrooms of Resistance*. London: Writers and Readers, 1975.

Searle, Chris. *Fire Words*. London: Jonathan Cape, 1972.

Searle, Chris. *None But Our Words: Critical Literacy in Classroom and Community*. Buckingham: Open UP, 1998.

Searle, Chris. *One for Blair*. London: Young World, 1989.

Searle, Chris. *Our City*. London: Young World, 1984.

Searle, Chris (ed). *Stepney Words*. 1971. London: Centerprise, 1973b.

Searle, Chris. *Tales of Mozambique*. London: Young World, 1980.

Searle, Chris. 'The Story of *Stepney Words*'. *Race and Class* 58, no. 4 (2017): 57–75.

Searle, Chris. *This New Season: Our Class, Our Schools, Our World*. London: Calder and Boyars, 1973a.

Serroukh, Farrah. *Reflecting Realities: Survey of Ethnic Representation within UK Children's Literature 2017*. London: CLPE, 2018.

Serroukh, Farrah. *Reflecting Realities: Survey of Ethnic Representation within UK Children's Literature 2018*. London: CLPE, 2019.

Serroukh, Farrah. *Reflecting Realities: Survey of Ethnic Representation within UK Children's Literature 2019*. London: CLPE, 2020.

Seth, Sanjay. *Subject Lessons: The Western Education of Colonial India*. Durham, NC: Duke University Press, 2007.

Sethi, Anita. *I Belong Here: A Journey Along the Backbone of Britain*. London: Bloomsbury Nature, 2021.

Shaw, Clare MacDonald. 'Introduction'. In *Tales for the Common People and Other Cheap Repository Tracts*, edited by Hannah More, vii–xxxii. Nottingham: Trent, 2002.

Shaw, George Bernard. *Fabianism and the Empire*. London: G. Richards, 1900.
Sheley, Erin. 'Reciprocal Colonization in the Irish Fairy Tales of Lord Dunsany'. *Mythlore: A Journal of J. R. R. Tolkien, C. S. Lewis, Charles Williams and Mythopoeic Literature* 31, no. 1 (2012): 107–20.
Short, Edward. *Education and the Immigrants*. London: Educare, 1969.
Shukla, Nikesh, Hanif Kureishi, Kamila Shamsie, Margaret Busby, Danuta Kean, Simon Prosser, Daljit Nagra, Sarfraz Manzoor, Jackie Kay, Neil Morrison, Bernardine Evaristo, Nick Barley, Juliet Mabey, Ellah Alfrey, Andrew Franklin, Aminatta Forna, Isobel Dixon, Stephen Page and Akhil Sharma. 'How Do We Stop UK Publishing Being So Posh and White?'. *Guardian*, 11 December 2015. Available online: How do we stop UK publishing being so posh and white? | Publishing | The Guardian (accessed 31 May 2021).
Shuter, Paul and John Child. *The Changing Face of Britain*. London: Heinemann, 1989.
Simple, Peter. 'Classroom Comrades'. *Daily Telegraph*, 16 October 1975: 14.
Sivanandan, A. 'Challenging Racism: Strategies for the '80s'. *Race and Class* 25, no. 2 (1983): 1–11.
Sivanandan, A. *The Fight Against Racism: A Pictorial History of Asians and Afro-Caribbeans in Britain*. London: IRR, 1986.
Sivanandan, A. *How Racism Came to Britain*. London: IRR, 1985
Sivanandan, A. *Patterns of Racism*. London: IRR, 1982a.
Sivanandan, A. *Race and Resistance: The IRR Story*. London: Race Today, 1974.
Sivanandan, A. *Race, Class and the State: The Black Experience in Britain*. London: IRR, 1976.
Sivanandan, A. *Roots of Racism*. London: IRR, 1982b.
Smith, Evan. *British Communism and the Politics of Race*. Leiden: Brill, 2018.
Snaith, Anna. *Modernist Voyages: Colonial Women Writers in London, 1890–1945*. Cambridge: Cambridge University Press, 2014.
Solomos, John. *Black Youth, Racism and the State: The Politics of Ideology and Policy*. Cambridge: Cambridge University Press, 1988.
Srimad Bhagavatam. Available online: Srimad Bhagavatam (Bhagavata Purana): The Story of the Fortunate One (accessed 28 May 2021).
'Statement on Windrush Lessons Learned Review'. *UK Parliament*, 21 July 2020. Available online: https://www.parliament.uk/business/news/2020/july/statement-windrush (accesses on 24 February 2022).
Stephens, John. *Language and Ideology in Children's Fiction*. New York: Longman, 1992.
Stevenson, Robert Louis. *A Child's Garden of Verses*. 1885. New York: Henry Altemus, 1921.

Stone, Maureen. *The Education of the Black Child in Britain: The Myth of Multiracial Education*. London: Fontana, 1981.

Stones, Rosemary. 'A Black Children's Book Illustrator at Work: Errol Lloyd Talks to Rosemary Stones'. *Children's Book Bulletin* 1 (June 1979b): 3–4.

Stones, Rosemary. 'Books Without Bias: Where to Find Them'. *Where* 146 (March 1979a): 83–5.

Stones, Rosemary. *Gangs and Bullies*. London: Evans, 1998.

Stones, Rosemary. *Loving Encounters: A Book for Teenagers about Sex*. London: Piccadilly, 1988a.

Stones, Rosemary. *More to Life than Mr Right: Stories for Young Feminists*. London: Piccadilly, 1985.

Stones, Rosemary. *'Pour Out The Cocoa, Janet': Sexism in Children's Books*. London: Schools Council, 1983.

Stones, Rosemary. 'Radically Revised Reading Schemes?'. *Children's Book Bulletin* 6 (Summer 1981): 2–6.

Stones, Rosemary. "Review: *Come to Mecca*." *Children's Book Bulletin* 1 (June 1979c): 23.

Stones, Rosemary. *Someday My Prince Won't Come: More Stories for Young Feminists*. London: Piccadilly, 1988c.

Stones, Rosemary. '13 Other Years'. *Books for Keeps*, 3 (November 1988b): 53.

Stones, Rosemary. *Too Close Encounters and What to Do About Them*. London: Magnet, 1987.

Stones, Rosemary and Andrew Mann. 'Are Children's Books Still Racist?'. *Children's Book Bulletin* 2 (Autumn 1979): 3.

Stones, Rosemary and Andrew Mann. 'Censorship or Selection?'. *Children's Book Bulletin* 3 (Spring 1980): 3.

Stones, Rosemary and Andrew Mann. *Mother Goose Comes to Cable Street*. Harmondsworth: Puffin, 1977.

'Summer of Heat: 1976'. *BBC Television*, produced by Paul Burgess, 3 June 2006.

Swann, Michael. *Education for All*. London: HMSO, 1985.

Tagore, Rabindranath. *The Crescent Moon: Poems and Stories*. 1913b. New Delhi: Talking Cub, 2017.

Tagore, Rabindranath. *Gitanjali (Song Offerings)*. London: Macmillan, 1913a.

Tagore, Rabindranath. 'Introduction'. *The Web of Indian Life by Sister Nivedita*. 1904. London: Longmans, 1917.

Tagore, Rabindranath. 'My School'. *The Fresh Reads* website, 1933. Available online: My School by Rabindranath Tagore (thefreshreads.com) (accessed 28 May 2021).

Taipale, Ilkka. 'Remembering the Biafran Humanitarian Crisis'. *Medicine, Conflict and Survival* 3, no. 3 (2017): 207–11.

Talking Blues. London: Centerprise, 1976.

Taylor, S. A. G. *Capture of Jamaica*. Kingston: Pioneer, 1951.

'The First of the Second Generation'. *Daily Mail*, 23 October 1972: 6.

Theo. 'The Horse'. *Colonial Countryside Project* website, 2018. Available online: CharlecoteParkReinterpreted.PoemsbyColmorePrimary.pdf (accessed 28 May 2021).

Thomas, Odette. *Rain Falling, Sun Shining*. London: Bogle L'Ouverture, 1975.

Thomlinson, Natalie. *Race, Ethnicity and the Women's Movement in England, 1968–1993*. London: Palgrave, 2016.

Thompson, Ann. 'Errol Lloyd: Committed Artist'. *Dragon's Teeth* 2, no. 2 (June 1980): 5–8.

Thompson, Neil. 'Storm Over School Books That Inspired Kinnock'. *Daily Mail*, 26 March 1988: 3.

Thorpe, Vanessa. 'Subversive Rhymes Are Child's Play'. *Observer*, 16 December 2007. Available online: Subversive rhymes are child's play | UK news | The Guardian (accessed 29 May 2021).

Tomlinson, Sally. *Race and Education: Policy and Politics in Britain*. Buckingham: Open University Press, 2008.

Trease, Geoffrey. *Bows Against the Barons*. London: Martin Lawrence, 1934.

Trease, Geoffrey. *The Young Traveller in India and Pakistan*. London: Phoenix House, 1949.

Trease, Geoffrey. *The Young Traveller in England and Wales*. London: Phoenix House, 1953.

Troyna, Barry. 'Can You See the Join? An Historical Analysis of Multicultural and Antiracist Education Policies'. In *Racism and Education: Structures and Strategies*, edited by Dawn Gill, Barbara Mayor and Maud Blair, 63–91. London: Sage, 1992.

Turley, David. 'Complicating the Story: Religion and Gender in Historical Writing on British and American Slavery'. In *Women, Dissent, and Anti-Slavery in Britain and America, 1790–1865*, edited by Elizabeth J. Clapp and Julie Roy Jeffrey, 20–44. Oxford: Oxford University Press, 2011.

Umoren, Imaobong D. *Race Women Internationalists: Activist-Intellectuals and Global Freedom Struggles*. Berkeley: University of California Press, 2018.

United Nations General Assembly. *Declaration of the Rights of the Child*. G.A. res. 1386 (XIV), 14 U.N. GAOR Supp. (No. 16) at 19, U.N. Doc. A/4354, 1959.

Vernon, Patrick and Angelina Osborne. *100 Great Black Britons*. London: Robinson, 2020.

Vigne, Randolph and James Currey. 'The New African 1962–1969: South Africa in Particular and Africa in General'. *English in Africa* 41, no. 1 (May 2014): 55–73.

Vincent, John. *An Introduction to Community Librarianship*. Sheffield: Association of Assistant Librarians, 1986.

Visram, Rosina. *Asians in Britain: 400 Years of History*. London: Pluto, 2002.

Waddington, Mark, 'Leroy Cooper: The Toxteth Riots Were a Wake-Up Call and Did Some Good'. *Liverpool Echo Online*, 4 July 2011. Available online: Leroy Cooper: The Toxteth Riots were a wake-up call and did some good - Liverpool Echo (accessed 13 December 2019).

Walker, Martin. 'Future Is Out on Loan …'. *Guardian*, 4 January 1982: 11.

Walmsley, Anne. *The Caribbean Artists Movement 1966–1972*. London: New Beacon, 1992.

Ward, Lucy. 'A World of Frogs, Wolves and Knickers'. *Guardian*, 8 May 2007. Available online: A world of frogs, wolves and knickers | Schools | The Guardian (accessed 29 May 2021).

Warner, Arabella. 'How the Young Are Bullied – Even to Death'. *The Independent*, 5 October 1989: 4.

Waterhouse, Keith. 'Volume Control'. *Daily Mail*, 20 November 1986: 8.

Waters, Rob. *Thinking Black: Britain, 1964–1985*. Berkeley: University of California Press, 2019.

Waymark, Peter. 'Eeny, Meeny, Miny, Mo …'. *The Times*, 15 May 1997: 46.

Wedderburn, Robert. *The Horrors of Slavery*. London: Wedderburn, 1824.

West, W. J. 'If In Doubt, Chuck It Out'. *Times Literary Supplement*, 29 November 1991: 17.

Wheatle, Alex. *Brixton Rock*. London: BlackAmber, 1999.

Wheatle, Alex. *Cane Warriors*. London: Andersen, 2020.

Wheatle, Alex. *Uprising*. London: Diffusion, 2017.

Whitcombe, Bobbie. 'East–West: The Divided Worlds of Farrukh Dhondy'. *Children's Literature in Education* 14, no. 1 (1983): 35–43.

'Why Have Black and South Asian People Been Hit Hardest by COVID-19?'. London: Office of National Statistics, 14 December 2020. Available online: Why have Black and South Asian people been hit hardest by COVID-19? – Office for National Statistics (ons.gov.uk) (accessed 31 May 2021).

'William Blake'. *Tate Britain Exhibition*. Curators Martin Myrone and Amy Concannon. 11 September 2019–2 February 2020.

Williams, Elizabeth. 'Anti-Apartheid: The Black British Response'. *South African Historical Journal* 64, no. 3 (2012): 685–706.

Williams, Hazelann. 'Reliving the British Black Panther Movement'. *The Voice Online*, 9 January 2012. Available online: Reliving the British Black Panther movement | The Voice Online (voice-online.co.uk) (accessed 7 October 2019).

Williams, Nicola. 'A Black British Childhood'. In *Black Voices: An Anthology of ACER's Black Young Writers Competition*, edited by Paul McGilchrist, 235–6. London: ACER, 1985b.

Williams, Nicola. 'Black Achievement in Sport Is Not Enough Because …'. In *Black Voices: An Anthology of ACER's Black Young Writers Competition*, edited by Paul McGilchrist, 272–3. London: ACER, 1985a.

'Willingly to School'. *The Guardian*, 9 January 1982: 11.

Winter, Aaron. 'Race, Multiculturalism, and the "Progressive" Politics of London 2012: Passing the "Boyle Test"'. *Sociological Research Online* 18, no. 2 (2013). Availble online: https://www.socresonline.org.uk/18/2/18/18.pdf (accessed on 24 February 2022).

Wong, Ansel. 'Len Garrison – A Biography'. In *Beyond Babylon*, edited by Len Garrison, 4–5. London: Black Star, 1985.

'Words Words Words'. *The New African* 3, no. 5 (June 1964): 116.

Wordsworth, William. 'To Toussaint L'Ouverture'. In *Amazing Grace: An Anthology of Poems About Slavery 1660–1810*, 1802, edited by James G. Basker, 583–4. New Haven, Connecticut: Yale University Press, 2002.

Worpole, Ken. *Local Publishing and Local Culture: An Account of the Work of the Centerprise Publishing Project 1972–1977*. London: Centerprise, 1977.

Worsthorne, Peregrine. 'Get Class out of the Classroom'. *Sunday Telegraph*, 19 October 1975: 18.

Yeats, William Butler. 'Introduction'. *Gitanjali (Song Offerings) by Rabindranath Tagore*. London: Macmillan, 1913, vii–xxii.

Yeo, Sophie. 'Interview with Corinne Fowler'. *Inkcap*, 10 March 2021. Available online: "There is no doubt that colonial ideologies of race have left their legacy." – InkcapCommentShareCommentShare (inkcapjournal.co.uk) (accessed 28 May 2021).

Zephaniah, Benjamin. 'I Am Not De Problem'. *Newsnight*, 8 December 2015.

Zephaniah, Benjamin. '"Me?" I thought. "OBE? Me?"' *Guardian Online*, 27 November 2003. Available online: 'Me? I thought, OBE me? Up yours, I thought' | Books | The Guardian (accessed 28 May 2021).

Zephaniah, Benjamin. *Windrush Child*. London: Scholastic, 2020.

Index

abolition
   of the ILEA 64–5, 108, 115–18, 139
   of slavery 3–4, 11–12, 18–26, 140–1, 160, 163–4, 173
Africa (*see also* individual countries) 17, 44–7, 62–3, 100, 140–8
   aid to 138, 140–1, 148
   and Christianity 24
Afro-Caribbean Education Resource center (ACER) 118, 130–9
Alexander, Ziggi 92, 105–8, 119
All-London Teachers Against Racism and Fascism (ALTARF) 11, 114–15
Amnesty International 54, 66, 166
Anti-Apartheid Movement (AAM) 75, 140–5
anti-colonial 3–4, 12, 19, 26–51, 91, 156
Anti-Nazi League (ANL) 113, 119
anti-racism 6, 8, 18, 51, 62–3, 65–76, 81, 108–19
apartheid 45–8, 61, 76, 122, 139–45, 148, 173
assimilation 110, 119, 121, 128

Babylon 130, 138–9
   Siege of Babylon (Dhondy) 128–30
Baker, Kenneth 114–16
Barbauld, Anna Laetitia 18
Beauchamp, Kay 61–4
Beckles, Michael 137
Bennett, Louise 29, 42–3
Berg, Leila 6, 10, 57–9, 63
Biafra 139–41, 145
Black Cultural Archives 4, 137
Black Curriculum 160–1
Black Liberation Front 11
Black Lives Matter 153, 155
Black Panthers 13, 125–6
   British Black Panthers 13, 126, 129
Black Parents' Movement 11, 123

Black People's Day of Action 11, 123
Black Power 3–4, 6, 11, 13, 67, 122–6, 167
Black Youth Penmanship Competition 136–9
Blake, William 23–6, 154
Boakye, Jeffrey 12, 13, 151, 159–63
Bogle L'Ouverture 6, 9, 123–4
Booktrust 7, 151, 170–2
Bourne, Jenny 113, 118
Breinburg, Petronella 71, 94–5
British Communist Party 11, 64
Bullock Report (1975) 110, 133
bullying 76–8, 83, 85

Campaign Against Racial Discrimination (CARD) 92
Carby, Hazel 75
Caribbean Artists Movement (CAM) 91, 93, 99
Carnegie Medal 6, 56, 72, 98, 101
Carnival 91, 96–101, 133, 161
Centerprise 60, 69, 73, 80, 135
Centre for Literacy in Primary Education (CLPE) 6–8, 151, 153, 170–2
charity
   children's 39–40
   commission (UK) 158
   educational 160–1, 170–1
   public appeal for 141, 144, 146
Chartered Institute for Library and Information Professionals (CILIP) 6
Cheap Repository Tracts 18, 21
Chetty, Darren 6, 161, 172–3
Children's Rights Workshop 10–11, 69–72, 75, 79–80
Clapham Sect 20–2
class (socioeconomic) 5, 20, 55, 57, 59–65
   Black middle class 41
   criticism of white middle class 27, 54, 70, 127–30

intersection with race 9, 55, 79–88
working class readers 6, 10, 54, 80. 103
working class writers 59–61, 158
Coard, Bernard 124–5, 145
Colonial Countryside project 8, 153–9
Commonwealth 39, 41, 42, 50, 102, 109, 111, 118, 123, 140
  Commonwealth Immigration Act (1962) 92
communism 4, 11, 54, 79, 87
  Black communists 39, 59–61, 64, 124, 131
  white communists 59–61, 64, 113, 127
community librarianship 103–8
Cooperative Children's Book Council (CCBC) 171
Council on Interracial Books for Children (CIBC) 69–70
Cox, Caroline (Baroness) 104, 115

Delius, Anthony 4, 17, 44–7, 48–9, 145
Dewjee, Audrey 105–6
Dhondy, Farrukh 4, 5, 71, 72, 126–30, 145, 148, 173
dreadlocks 68, 74, 138

Edgeworth, Maria 18–19
education 10, 51, 53–5, 62, 65, 122, 125, 128, 139
  Acts (UK) 54–5, 116–18, 132, 134
  anti-racist 108, 111–19, 148
  apartheid and 141
  Black Panthers 126
  colonial education 30, 36–8, 42, 44, 46
  disadvantage 8, 11, 96, 135, 147
  Educationally Sub Normal (ESN) 18, 91, 94, 124
  educational publishing 42
  girls 69
  'immigrant' 133
  imperial 26, 30, 162, 166
  London, *see* Inner London Education Authority
  multiracial 110–11, 113, 134
  progressive 57
  Rastafarians 131
  reform 20, 27–8, 31, 58, 69
  Rousseauian 36
  supplementary, *see* supplementary schools
Emecheta, Buchi 140–1, 145–8, 173
enslavement 4, 18, 114–15, 117, 124, 140, 153, 155–8, 166
  African 11, 81, 85
  in Britain, 85–6, 153, 155–8, 160–1
  in the Caribbean 18–26, 83, 163, 166–7
  depictions in children's literature 18–26, 70, 81–3, 85–6, 114–15
Equiano, Olaudah 1, 20, 160, 164
Evangelicalism 20–4

Fabian Society 5, 12, 19, 27–8
famine 138, 141, 144
fantasy 27–8, 51, 54, 80, 83–6, 170
feminism 9, 70–8
Floyd, George 8, 151, 153, 169
Fowler, Corinne 151, 153, 154–9

Garrison, Len 10, 13, 108, 130–9
Garvey, Marcus 19, 139
Gilroy, Paul 67–8, 78, 94, 113
Grange Hill series 86–7
Greater London Council (GLC) 62–3, 111, 118, 137

Habib, Sadia 2, 121
Haiti 20, 23, 167
Hall, Stuart 64, 78, 125, 138
Henty, G. A. 4, 81, 166
Hill, Janet 47, 102–4, 106
Hinduism 30, 32–4, 38, 48–9, 51, 111
historical fiction 80–3, 86, 151, 163–9
Hostile Environment Policy 12, 151–4, 160
Huntley, Jessica and Eric 6, 93, 123–5, 130–1, 148, 169

Ibekwe, Stella 73–4
'I Have a Dream' speech (Martin Luther King, Jr.) 136–9
Ikoli, Tunde 66
immigrants 94–5, 118, 162, 165
  African 145, 147
  books for 101–2
  education of 133
  illegal 85, 152
  or migrants 11–13

restrictive acts (UK) 92, 95
  treatment of 60, 85, 109–10, 127
  Windrush Scandal 123, 152, 165
  working class 54
India
  British rule 30–1, 37, 38, 49
  colonial education 30, 36–7
  folklore 30, 32–4
  immigration from 11, 60
  independence movements 30–2, 38
  partition 11, 49, 122
  pre-colonial 47–8
  religion 48–9
Inner London Education Authority (ILEA) 63–5, 113, 115, 130
  abolition of 64–5, 108, 115–18, 139
  anti-racism 111, 114–15, 134–5, 137
  as publisher 10, 132–6
Institute for Race Relations (IRR) 103, 108–19
intersectionality 9, 55, 58–65, 68–78
Ireland 27, 30–1, 34–6, 118
Iremonger, Lucille 50

Jackson, Sharna 170
Jamaica
  Anansi stories 29, 42
  history 166–7
  migrants from 5, 19, 38–40, 43, 50, 92–101, 130, 164–6
  music 162
  patois 29, 43
  publishing 42–3
  technology 41
Jekyll, Walter 29–30
Johnson, Catherine 1, 14, 151, 163–4, 166
Johnson, Linton Kwesi 65, 126, 162, 167
Jones, Dan 10, 54, 65–8, 88–9, 95

Kate Greenaway Medal 6, 72, 93–4, 101
Keats, Ezra Jack 14, 70
Kenlock, Neil 126
Kipling, Rudyard 2, 28, 102, 127
Knights Of publishing 169–70
Kuya, Dorothy 53, 64, 106, 113

Lang, Andrew 2, 29–30, 32
La Rose, John 5, 97, 123–5, 148
Lawrence, Patrice 14, 170

Lawrence, Stephen 77
League of Coloured People 19, 39–40
Leeson, Bob 5, 54–5, 57, 69, 79–89, 163
Liberation Press 61–2, 65
Little Rebels Award 163–4
Lloyd, Errol 10, 14, 91, 92–101, 119, 133
L'Ouverture, Toussaint 23

Mann, Andrew 10, 67–8, 71–3, 75, 79
Marley, Bob 22
Marson, Una 5, 38–43, 51, 169
May, Theresa 152, 153 n.1
Mead, Stella 40–2, 44, 51
Milne-Home, Mary Pamela 29–30, 50
Moody, Harold 19, 39
More, Hannah 18, 20–2, 169
Mozambique 62–3, 72
mugging 78, 94
multiculturalism 4, 62, 85, 103, 110–13, 116–19, 133–4, 152
murder (race-related) 8, 65, 77–8, 151, 153, 169
Museum of Childhood (Bethnal Green) 66–7
Muslims 48–9, 84, 154 n.2

Naidoo, Beverley 14, 45, 140–9, 173
National Curriculum 116, 118, 152, 159–60
National Trust 153, 155–9
Nesbit, E. 2, 27–8, 51
New Beacon 93, 97–8, 123–4
New Cross fire 11, 64, 91, 123, 167
Nichols, Grace 73–4
Nigeria 73, 111, 140–1, 145, 148
Nightingale, Florence 152, 156
Nivedita, Sister (Margaret Noble) 4–5, 30–4, 36, 38, 51
Nobel Prize 30–1, 34–5, 38 n.3

Olusoga, David 18, 151, 154, 159–61, 162, 163, 169
Olympics Opening Ceremony (2012) 151, 152, 166
Opio, Amelia 18, 20, 24–5, 165, 173
Other Award 63, 72–3, 79, 142, 148, 164

Pakistan 47–9, 60, 111, 123, 127, 147
Pan-Africanism 124–5
partition of India 11, 31, 122

Patel, Priti 153
patois 29, 43, 74
Peach, Blair 65, 129
Phototalk series (ILEA) 133–4
Pioneer Press 42–3
police
    civilian deaths and 8, 62, 65, 117, 143, 153
    condemnation of 61
    depiction in children's books 66–9, 96–7, 100, 114–15, 117–18, 129, 133, 135, 137, 143, 162, 165
    oppression 13, 59, 64, 66, 89, 114, 135, 148, 167
    sus powers 11, 17, 18 n.1
    tension with Black community 87, 92, 94–5, 96, 106, 110, 122–3, 126, 131
Powell, Enoch 18 n.1, 94, 96, 105

Quakers 20, 24–5

Race Relations Bill (1968) 91, 95
    (1976) 134
Ramdarshan Bold, Melanie 6, 7, 14, 171–2
Rampton Report 123
Rastafarianism 11, 13, 67–8, 124, 130–1, 136–9, 167
Reflecting Realities reports 6–7, 8, 13, 153, 169–72
reggae 99, 103, 136
riots, uprisings
    1919, Cardiff, Liverpool 19
    1947, India and Pakistan 49
    1958, Notting Hill 109
    1971, Mangrove Nine 91
    1981, Brixton, Handsworth, Toxteth 68, 97, 106, 111, 117, 123, 162, 167–9
    1985, Brixton, Handsworth, Bradford 114, 137–8
Rock Against Racism 6, 11
Rosen, Michael 65, 68

Salkey, Andrew 43, 124
school stories 54, 86–8
Seacole, Mary 106, 152, 156–7
Searle, Chris 10, 54, 57, 58–65, 68, 71–2, 80, 88–9, 101, 104, 107, 127, 131, 135, 138, 157–8, 169
Serroukh, Farrah 6, 7, 13, 14, 171–2

sex and sexuality 8, 9, 72–4, 128–30
Sherlock, Philip 42–3
Sikhs 19, 49
Sivanandan, A. 4, 10, 64, 92, 103, 108–19, 145, 148, 169
slavery, *see* enslavement
Solomos, John 78, 116, 121
Sons of Africa 20, 164
South Africa 44–5, 122, 139, 140–1, 148
    depictions in children's literature 17, 44–50, 61, 75–6, 138, 141–5, 148
statues
    Edward Colston 153, 156, 160
    Mary Seacole 152
Stevenson, Robert Louis 2, 36–8
Stones, Rosemary 5, 9, 10, 55, 63 n.2, 67, 68–79, 88–9, 93, 100, 104, 127, 130
supplementary schools 5, 130, 135, 161
sus law 11, 17, 18, 167

Tacky's War (1760) 166–8
Tagore, Rabindranath 5, 30–1, 34–8. 39, 51
television 86–7, 132, 162
Thatcher, Margaret 167
Thiong'o, Ngugi Wa 63
Trease, Geoffrey 43, 47–50, 81
Trinidad 39, 99–100, 170

Ugandan Asians 11, 123, 127
United Nations (UN) 53, 57, 138
United States 19, 32, 70, 125, 138, 151, 153, 171
Universal Negro Improvement Agency (UNIA) 19
Usherwood, Vivien 135

Vivekananda, Swami 30–2

Wedderburn, Robert 20, 22
Wheatle, Alex 151, 163, 165, 166–9
Wilkins, Verna 6, 169
Williams, Nicola 136–7
Windrush Generation 11, 17, 109, 112, 123, 125, 152, 164–5, 169
Windrush Scandal 8, 18, 152–3, 162, 164–6, 169
Wong, Ansel 135, 138
Wordsworth, William 23

X, Michael 110

Yeats, William Butler 30, 34–6
Young India movement 30, 31, 36
Young Travellers series 17, 43–51, 145

Young World Press 63–5, 72
Youth Libraries Group (YLG) 102, 107

Zephaniah, Benjamin 151, 163–6
Zong Trial (1783) 163–4

www.ingramcontent.com/pod-product-compliance
Lightning Source LLC
Chambersburg PA
CBHW061828300426
44115CB00013B/2286